Soldiering in the Army
of Northern Virginia

Civil War America

Gary W. Gallagher, editor

Soldiering in the Army of Northern Virginia

A Statistical Portrait of the Troops Who Served under Robert E. Lee

JOSEPH T. GLATTHAAR

The University of North Carolina Press

Chapel Hill

© 2011 The University of North Carolina Press

All rights reserved

Set in Whitman and Chaparral

Manufactured in the United States of America

The paper in this book meets the guidelines for permanence and durability
of the Committee on Production Guidelines for Book Longevity of the
Council on Library Resources.

The University of North Carolina Press has been a member
of the Green Press Initiative since 2003.

Library of Congress Cataloging-in-Publication Data

Glatthaar, Joseph T., 1956–

Soldiering in the Army of Northern Virginia : a statistical portrait
of the troops who served under Robert E. Lee / Joseph T. Glatthaar.

p. cm. — (Civil War America)

Includes bibliographical references and index.

ISBN 978-0-8078-3492-3 (cloth : alk. paper)

1. Confederate States of America. Army of Northern
Virginia—Statistics. 2. Soldiers—Confederate States of
America—Statistics. 3. Soldiers—Confederate States of
America—Social conditions. I. Title.

E470.2.G59 2011

973.7'42—dc22

2010053994

15 14 13 12 11   5 4 3 2 1

THIS BOOK WAS DIGITALLY PRINTED

For Vimy, who joined voluntarily,
and for Parks, who taught me some statistics
and made it fun in the process

CONTENTS

Preface ix

Acknowledgments xv

1 The Army 1

2 The Infantry 21

3 The Cavalry 33

4 The Artillery 44

5 Northern- and Foreign-Born Soldiers 57

6 Upper and Lower South 68

7 Officers and Enlisted Men 83

8 Year of Enlistment 97

9 Age 115

10 Marriage and Fatherhood 127

11 Economic Class 140

12 Slaveholding 154

Conclusion 166

Notes 179

Sources 201

Index 203

"Certainly there never was such an Army in ancient or modern times," an artilleryman in Robert E. Lee's famed Army of Northern Virginia boasted of his
comrades. Their success was almost legendary. For nearly four years, Lee's
army and its predecessor, the Army of the Potomac, endured staggering losses
and suffered dreadful hardships while holding a larger and better-equipped
Union field force at bay. When the Federals brought their most successful
general, Ulysses S. Grant, back East to oversee the campaign against Lee in
1864, another Rebel scoffed at the idea. "He will find a different set of men to
fight here than he ever fought in Tennessee," the soldier insisted. "He will fight
men who never heard of the[m] being whipped and more than that men who
love to obey and follow their leader." So powerful had the image of Lee and
his army become in the minds of Federals and Confederates alike that Union
secretary of war Edwin M. Stanton declared, "Peace can be had only when
Lee's army is beaten, captured, or dispersed." Even as late as mid-March 1865,
after William T. Sherman's Federals marched through South Carolina, leaving
wreckage in their wake, and into North Carolina, Emma LeConte of Columbia
consoled herself with the words: "Only to Gen. Lee and his poor half-starved
army can the people look — yet an army that has never suffered defeat, a contrast to the Western army." Stanton and LeConte were right. While Lee's army
survived, the viability of an independent Confederacy continued to exist.[1]

In my book, *General Lee's Army: From Victory to Collapse*, I studied Lee's Army
of Northern Virginia, its campaigns, its soldiers and their experiences, and
what the army meant to the Confederacy. *Soldiering in the Army of Northern
Virginia: A Statistical Portrait of the Troops Who Served under Robert E. Lee* has
emerged from that larger project. In gathering research materials for *General
Lee's Army*, I decided to develop a sample of 600 soldiers in the Army of Northern Virginia. The hope was that it would generate valid statistics on their prewar, wartime, and postwar worlds. I believe that the best scholarship on subjects such as this blends qualitative with quantitative evidence. When paired
with more traditional evidence from letters, diaries, government documents,
and the like, this statistical information would help readers gain a greater

understanding of Lee's troops and their experiences. Even in instances where data confirmed existing thought, at least we would have hard numbers to buttress our qualitative evidence. Once my longtime friend Dr. Michael S. Parks of the Department of Decision and Information Sciences, Bauer School of Business, University of Houston, began crunching the data, it became apparent that only a fraction of it could find its way into the pages of *General Lee's Army*. The volume of statistical tables alone — approximately 400 of them — would have pushed an already long book into a multivolume work and would have obliterated any narrative flow that the text presented. Yet these unused tables contained extraordinary data on the background and service of the troops in the Army of Northern Virginia. Much of the information was novel, and it would help provide a broader, fuller portrait of the men who served under General Robert E. Lee. Since then, with the help of Dr. Karl Eschbach, I have learned to use a computer software program called STATA, which has enabled me to crunch data myself. Statistics varied by chapter, but they ranged from over 30 pages of tables to over 100.

After consulting Gary Gallagher about the project, I decided to write a book about these statistics. To avoid the mind-numbing burden of wading through page after page of complicated tables, it made sense to employ simple bar charts as figures to make it more "reader friendly." I could offer little for those readers who were severely "mathematically challenged," but I could try to convert the information into forms that anyone who was comfortable with basic numbers could grasp. I would include text to explain the significance of figures and to give specific examples to clarify those points. It was my intention to provide some direct, comparative analysis and to develop linkages with other statistics, which would enable readers to gain a greater understanding of the Army of Northern Virginia and the men who composed it.

Dr. Kent Tedin, another friend and an expert on sampling, designed this one. If we had a list of the names of every soldier who ever served in the army, I would have created a pure random sample. Because none exists, Kent had to conceive a more complicated process. This sample consists of 600 soldiers who were chosen through several random selection steps. In technical terms, it is called a "stratified cluster sample." By design, 300 soldiers were selected from the infantry, 150 from the cavalry, and 150 from the artillery. This breakdown allowed us to examine them by branches of service. Data was then collected in 54 categories for each soldier, ranging from date and place of birth to dates and experiences of service to date, manner, and place of death. Sources for the data included military service and census records, pension files, newspapers, genealogical books and websites, county histories, regimental histories, tax records, city and town directories, and even burial records. The appendix in *General Lee's Army* provides detailed information on the formation of the sample and the calculation process. With no master list of Lee's army, it took me months of work just to generate the 600 names; I accumulated the data over the course of years.[2]

The random selection process happened to choose soldiers from each Confederate state, plus Kentucky, Maryland, and West Virginia. All of those states had units in the Army of Northern Virginia. The soldiers are not in strict proportion to the number who served in Lee's army, but the randomness of the sample factors out the possibility of disproportional data. According to the sample of 600, the number of soldiers who served in military organizations from the following states was:

Alabama	24	Mississippi	19
Arkansas	4	North Carolina	96
Florida	4	South Carolina	77
Georgia	86	Tennessee	16
Kentucky	4	Texas	4
Louisiana	17	Virginia	239
Maryland	10		

How good is the sample? It is very well designed, almost equal to a pure random sample. The confidence limits, which tell us how dependable these statistics are, vary from subject to subject, but in fundamental issues such as slave ownership or wealth for the entire army they are precise. In a category such as living in a slaveholding household, the margin for error is about 5%. That means if we used the same system to gather statistics like I did 100 times, in at least 95 of those times the statistics would be within a range of 5% less or 5% greater than my number. For example, 44.4% of soldiers lived in households with slave ownership. The margin for error would range from approximately 39% to 49%. In categories such as wealth, the confidence limits are closer to 4%. By social science standards, this is a very good sample.

When I present statistics and statistical charts, there will be two tests to demonstrate the accuracy of the data. In some figures there will be a vertical black line extending through the top of the bar. That line indicates the confidence limits. It means that if you created a sample with the same approach as mine, there would be at least a 95% chance (19 out of every 20 times) your statistic would be within my upper and lower confidence intervals (UCI and

LCI). Other times, the figures would be too crowded with confidence limits included, so I have placed the information in the endnotes. There is also a chi^2 test, which tells us the relationship between two subjects. For instance, if we tested the relationship between personal and family slave ownership and personal and family wealth, the chi^2 test would tell us P=.0000. That means if you were to create 10,000 samples like mine, there would be a correlation between family wealth and family slaveholding—the wealthier a family became after a certain point, the more likely it was to own slaves and the number of slaves was likely to rise with increased wealth. The level of 95% base is the standard of accuracy for social scientists, whereas the U.S. Census Bureau employs a 90% standard.

The first chapter gives basic information on Lee's army itself. Each succeeding chapter merely represents a different way of slicing the statistical pie. Sometimes the statistics provide firm conclusions. Other times, they only imply or hint at what was going on in the army or taking place in soldiers' minds. Because I am slicing the database in ways that are different from the original intention, some calculations are not statistically valid. That does not mean they are wrong; it merely means we should not rely on them as fact. I calculated and included those statistics because they contribute interesting pieces of information and may suggest future courses of study by other scholars.

Among all the statistics in the census of 1860, wealth is by far the most complicated. The U.S. government did not measure income; rather, it tallied the value of real estate and the value of personal property. The U.S. government issued census takers the following guidelines:

12. *Value of Real Estate.* — Under heading 8, insert the value of real estate owned by each individual enumerated. You are to obtain this information by personal inquiry of each head of a family, and are to insert the amount in dollars, be the estate located where it may. You are not to consider any question of lien or encumbrance[;] it is simply your duty to enter the value as given by the respondent.

13. *Value of Personal Estate.* — Under heading 9, insert (in dollars) the value of personal property or estate. Here you are to include the value of all the property, possessions, or wealth of each individual which is not embraced in the column previous, consist of what it may; the value of bonds, mortgages, notes, slaves, live stock, plate, jewels, or furniture; in fine, the value of whatever constitutes the personal wealth of individuals. Exact accu-

racy may not be arrived at, but all persons should be encouraged to give a near and prompt estimate for your information. Should any respondent manifest hesitation or unwillingness to make a free reply on this or any other subject, you will direct attention to Nos. 6 and 13 of your general instructions and the 15th section of the law [warning them that providing false information was a federal crime punishable by a $30 fine].[3]

Thus, young, talented, or well-educated persons probably had their wealth underestimated. They may have had great earning potential but had not yet accumulated much in the way of real or personal property. Many older persons or adult children who still lived with older family members would often have had their wealth overestimated. Their parents had accumulated wealth over decades but had passed the peak of earning potential. With regard to Civil War soldiers, this was more likely to be the case when the young men and women moved away, thereby diminishing the labor force on farms and elsewhere. Also, in years of low income due to sickness, economic hardship, or other factors, the method of assessing wealth was probably more accurate than the method of assessing income. In the end, I had to use the means at my disposal, for better or worse, and the method of calculation was reasonably accurate.

This is not the sort of book someone is likely to absorb in an afternoon or two. Admittedly, the reading is slow. No matter how polished one's sentence structure, it is difficult to gussie up statistics. For this I am sorry, but I see no way around it.

For readers who are interested in more information about the Army of Northern Virginia, I refer you to my larger volume *General Lee's Army*. In some instances, statistics vary slightly between this book and that one. Since the publication of *General Lee's Army*, I have come to realize that a few soldiers in the census were not the soldiers I was seeking, despite their having the right name and age. As a result, minor changes appear in this volume.

It is my hope that these statistics will offer fresh insights into Lee's famed Army of Northern Virginia and paint a fuller portrait of the officers and enlisted men who served in that command. I believe that to a great extent Civil War scholarship that focuses on soldiers is stuck. In the case of Civil War soldiers, we have gotten caught in a game of "he said, he said." We pluck something from a soldier's letter, diary, or memoir and make claims that this opinion represents most or even a substantial portion of those soldiers. If a scholar searches long enough, he or she will find evidence to justify virtually any contemporary attitude and buttress virtually any argument the scholar may pose, regardless of its representativeness. For that reason, valid statistics may break that scholarly logjam. Evidence presented in this book will challenge some existing arguments about Lee's army and the Confederacy, confirm other assertions, and offer intriguing ideas for future studies of other armies and the Confederacy as a whole.

ACKNOWLEDGMENTS

As in any book project, there are numerous individuals who deserve thanks. Dr. Kent Tedin, professor of political science at the University of Houston, expertly designed my sampling method. Dr. Michael S. Parks, associate professor of decision and information sciences at the Bauer School of Business, University of Houston, taught me about the software program ACCESS. After I gathered and loaded the data in ACCESS, he made the first pass at calculating the numbers. Once Parks computed hundreds of tables of data, it became apparent to me that only a small portion of the statistical evidence could go into *General Lee's Army*. This spawned the idea of a separate book for the statistics presented here.

Later, Dr. Karl Eschbach, then state demographer of Texas and now professor of geriatrics at the University of Texas Medical Branch at Galveston, introduced me to the world of STATA and IPUMS. Karl converted my database from ACCESS to STATA and taught me some basics in STATA. Over the months, he answered countless questions about STATA, and after I crunched my own numbers he verified the accuracy of my work.

For the data, individuals at the National Archives have always been so helpful. I would like to thank Connie Potter in particular. Whenever I come to the Archives Connie and I joke about how we have outlasted nearly everyone, and we still have a ways to go. Most of my census work was done at the Clayton Genealogical Library, part of the Houston Public Library. It is a gem of a research facility, and over the years the staff has been just great. I also traveled throughout the South, looking at pension files in various state archives. Once again, staffs were pleasant and helpful. Selected individuals responded to my queries on Ancestry.com. For their help I thank them as well.

Long ago, when Michael Parks first crunched some numbers, Dr. James M. McPherson, George Henry Davis 1886 professor of American history emeritus at Princeton University, sat with me in an airport lounge and went over that initial data. Over the years, Jim advised me on boundaries for economic class and warned me about pitfalls of wealth versus income, especially in relation to age. When I first calculated IPUMS statistics, he and I had a lengthy phone conversation about that data. He and his wonderful wife Pat have been great friends to me, and I thank them for their support and aid.

Like Jim, Gary Gallagher, another great and longtime friend and the John L. Nau III Professor of the American Civil War at the University of Virginia, was intrigued by the possibility of using accurate statistics to weigh in on some of the important debates and issues in Civil War scholarship. Over the years Gary discussed numerous findings and even attempted to help me explain various statistical tendencies. The idea of publishing in his series was a natural. I had long wanted to work again with Gary, and I thank him for embracing the idea of a statistics book enthusiastically.

I would like to thank my colleagues and staff at the University of North Carolina at Chapel Hill, especially those in the History Department. Their professionalism, collegiality, and fundamental decency have established an atmosphere that is conducive to research, teaching, and service at the highest level.

At the University of North Carolina Press, my friend David Perry has been enthusiastic and patient. I also want to thank Heidi Perov for converting my figures into book-quality products and Ron Maner for shepherding my manuscript along.

My wife, Jackie Hagan, enjoyed countless nights reading while I worked on Ancestry.com, crunched my numbers, and explored new ways of looking at the data. I thank her for her patience, which, some who know her well might say, is out of character.

I have dedicated this book to my son-in-law, Vimy Ha. He married my pride and joy, Danielle, and has become a wonderful addition to our lives. I could not imagine a better son-in-law. I have also dedicated it to my friend Michael S. Parks, whose enthusiasm for numbers helped to inspire what I have done here.

Chapel Hill, North Carolina
December 2010

Soldiering in the Army
of Northern Virginia

CHAPTER ONE

The Army

The name, Army of Northern Virginia, took some time to gain credence. Generals Joseph E. Johnston and P. G. T. Beauregard had called the principal field command in Virginia the Army of the Potomac, but over time various individuals had occasionally referred to it as the Army of Northern Virginia. When Lee replaced the badly wounded Johnston in June 1862, he referred to it as the Army of Northern Virginia. Lee's headquarters continued to issue directives from the Department of Northern Virginia, and over the course of weeks, the name Army of Northern Virginia became firmly fixed in the minds of soldiers, government officials, and the Confederate public.[1]

Over the entire war approximately 200,000 men served in that command, somewhere between 20% and 25% of all Confederate soldiers. So skillful were they that the Army of Northern Virginia inflicted about 45% of all combat fatalities and injuries that the Union suffered in the war. The Rebels' battlefield prowess reached such proportions that they came to symbolize Confederate independence and resistance among Northerners and Southerners.

Many credited Southern society for that combat prowess. Confederate soldiers simply assumed that their culture produced a society of extraordinary white men, men who possessed unusual leadership abilities, great courage, intelligence, and effective decision making. All of this translated into excellence on the battlefield. Captain Charles W. Dabney accorded early Confederate combat achievements to "the superior class of men in our army as to anything else." So, too, did Lieutenant James Langhorne, who thought "There is not a man in the Southern Army, who does not in his heart believe that he can whip three Yankees." Langhorne went so far as to doubt that the entire world could defeat the Confederacy in ten years.[2]

Joseph E. Johnston, the commander of the Army of the Potomac, did not accept the notion of Southern superiority of character as the distinguishing quality in combat. Rather, he thought Confederates outfought Union troops, at least early in the war, because of their motivation. After the Battle of First Manassas in July 1861, Johnston claimed, "The most gratifying fact connected with the recent action is the evidence it furnishes of the superiority of our troops over those of our Northern enemy, a superiority due solely to the spirit with which they fight, a spirit excited by patriotism—& consciousness of the magnitude of the stake. This superiority is the difference between men fighting for independence—to drive back invasion—& those who will hire for eleven dollars a month," as he believed the Federals did.[3]

John T. Thornton, recently promoted from captain to lieutenant colonel in the regimental reorganization of April 1862, explained the Confederate perspective well to his wife when he predicted what a history book of the past year would record:

> It will tell of a government created by wise patriots overthrown by mad ambition, sectional hate and unreasoning fanaticism. It will tell of a peaceful people summoned to arms to resist invasion and subjugation. The nations of the Earth have looked with complacency upon the spectacle of a fierce and strong democracy, in a spirit of direct hate and meanest vengeance, striving in Every way to crush and subjugate a feeble people who only ask to be let alone.

At the Battle of Antietam in September 1862, Thornton gave his life for the Confederate cause. South Carolinian James D. Nance justified the sacrifice of Thornton and tens of thousands of others by arguing that "martyrs and survivors" fought for posterity. "Death, to slavery and degradation, is their sublime preference; and they have not lived in vain, though they live not to see the full fruit of their labors and sacrifices," Nance wrote a woman back home. Others translated the disastrous loss of life into hatred. "I certainly love to live to hate the base usurping vandals," a Georgia private wrote his father in 1863. "If it is a sin to hate them; then I am guilty of the unpardonable one."[4]

Lee suggested that it was a combination of culture and commitment. In his justification for building works around Richmond to enhance defensive power and shield soldiers from enemy projectiles, Lee explained their merits: "Combined with valor fortitude & boldness, of which we have no fair proportion, it should lead us to success." Three months later Lee elaborated on the quality of his army: "I need not say to you that the material of which it is composed is the best in the world, and, if properly disciplined and instructed, would be able successfully to resist any force that could be brought against it." He insisted that "nothing can surpass the gallantry and intelligence of the main body," but a failure of discipline impaired its combat prowess. Southern culture had produced men of genuine character who exhibited greater courage, aggressiveness, and martial prowess than their opponents. Lee also believed that Confederate motivations—individuals fighting for independence and in defense of hearth, home, and the threatened institution of slavery—instilled in them a capacity to endure hardships and a spirit of resolve to see the war through to a successful conclusion, regardless of the costs.[5]

So who were these men whom Lee praised for their unsurpassed "gallantry and intelligence?" The oldest soldier in the sample was John Allen, a private in the Bryan Artillery. Allen was a 71-year-old planter with 22 slaves and a total wealth of $40,000 in 1860. Unfortunately for Allen, his enthusiasm to carry the war to the Federals proved much more than his body could give. After a brief service, officials deemed him "too old to go through the fatigue of camp duty" and gave him a discharge from the army. At the other end of the sample's age spectrum were two young men who were born in 1848. One of them, New York–born John C. Bishop, enlisted in January 1863 in the 20th South Carolina Infantry. In a strange twist of fate, authorities discovered his true age and out of concern for his youth transferred him to the 4th Battalion South Carolina Reserves. Bishop then contracted a disease and died in October 1864.

The old and young soldiers proved burdensome for Lee. Too many times they could not stand the hardships, and either the older men themselves or the parents of soldiers petitioned for their release from service. At age 48 Hiram J. Mitchel of the 50th North Carolina Infantry rose from sergeant to second lieutenant, but the strain of military duty proved too much for him. Rheumatism in his back and the burden of six children at home prompted his request to leave the service. T. W. Anderson, a 16-year-old, enlisted without his father's consent. The adolescent was "full of spirit" and suffered two wounds before his father sought the young man's release. In fact, so many underage soldiers or their families petitioned for release from military duties that Lee cracked down on their recruitment and release. In accordance with the law, he punished recruiting officers by assessing them any amount of bounty money that the government paid to underage soldiers who left the service. Lee also complained to the Confederate War Department that parents and underage troops waited long periods before seeking release from military obligations. The War Department ruled that there would be a six-month time limit for them to file a protest for a minor's release, unless the minor became ill or incapable of performing his duties.[6]

For the entire army, the median year of birth (that is, of the person who was in the absolute middle of all soldiers) was 1838. This means that half of all soldiers were born in 1838 or before and half were born in 1838 or afterward. The average year of birth was 1835.7. The single largest bloc of soldiers, nearly a third (32.5%) of the entire army, ranged in birth years from 1836 to 1840.

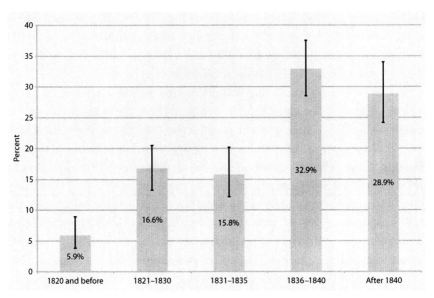

FIGURE 1.1. Year of birth

Troops in the second largest group, nearly 3 in every 10 (28.8%), were born after 1840. It was definitely a younger man's fight, with slightly more than 1 in 20 soldiers who were older than 41 when the war began. By contrast, more than 1 in every 10 was 16 or younger when Abraham Lincoln was elected president.[7]

Figure 1.1 tracks the year of birth of soldiers in the Army of Northern Virginia.

Just under half (46.7%) of all soldiers in Lee's army were born in Virginia or North Carolina. With South Carolina and Georgia added, 3 of every 4 (75.1%) troops came from those Southern coastal states. One in every 13 (7.8%) was born in the North (a state that remained in the Union) or in a foreign country. Those numbers included young Private Bishop, the son of a fisherman, who originally hailed from New York and moved with his family to South Carolina.

According to the sample, more than one-quarter (25.8%) of all soldiers who served in Lee's army resided in Virginia at the time of the war. Slightly more than 1 in 5 (21.4%) lived in North Carolina, with 1 in 6 (17.0%) from Georgia and 1 in 9 (11.2%) from South Carolina. Five of every 9 (55.0%) men lived in the Upper South and 4 of every 9 (45.0%) in the Lower South. Almost 3 of every 4 (73.9%) soldiers resided in the same state in which they were born. When we factor out those of foreign birth, close to 4 of every 5 (76.8%) soldiers still lived in their birth state. Not surprisingly, migration patterns for the other one-sixth flowed predominantly from east to west. The war offered most troops an opportunity to fulfill their spirit of adventure through travel to new states and sometimes to new regions.[8]

About 1 in every 44 (2.3%) soldiers enlisted in a state other than their 1860 residence. Boundaries were artificial barriers that frequently separated families and friends from one another. In most cases in which soldiers enlisted in a state other than their own, they crossed boundaries to serve with nearby relatives or friends who happened to reside in another state. Elbert C. Leech lived in Lowndes County, Mississippi, which bordered Alabama. He served in the 3rd Battalion Alabama Infantry and then as captain in the 26th Alabama. Some men who had migrated elsewhere returned to their old home community, where they had an extensive friendship network, before enlisting. Miles Lamb grew up in Sumter County, Georgia. When the war broke out, he was working as an overseer in Kentucky but went back home to join the Sumter Artillery.[9]

Like the Confederacy as a whole, these men came predominantly from farming communities. Only about 5.7% of all soldiers in Lee's army resided in communities with populations over 9,500 (the top 100 cities in the United States in 1860), which meant that 16 of every 17 troops lived in rural areas. Many of those in rural communities or on farms viewed the war as a chance to get away, to see new places.[10]

This rural dominance affected the kinds of jobs that many soldiers held before the war. Not surprisingly, nearly 5 of every 9 (52.9%) soldiers were farmers or farmhands. Some labored as farmhands on their family's land, while 1 in every 10 (10.6%) who tilled the soil lived in the household of a nonfamily member. Only 1 in every 20 (4.8%) soldiers in the sample was both the head of household and a tenant farmer, that is, the person owned no land and instead rented it for cultivation. Close to 1 in every 7 (13.8%) was a student of some kind, and 1 in 8 (12.9%) was unskilled. Professional (5.8%) and white-collar (4.7%) positions, usually clerks, combined to make up 1 in 10, while only 1 in 10 (10.0%) was a skilled worker. Because the army had so few residents from urban areas and skilled workers clustered in cities, the low number of skilled workers is not surprising. The same was true for professionals and white-collar workers.

Figure 1.2 highlights the occupations of soldiers before the war.

Soldiers were more likely to come from heavier slaveholding counties than the recruiting states as a whole. The sample consisted of men in Lee's army who resided before the war in all 11 Confederate states (Alabama, Arkansas, Florida, Georgia, Louisiana, Mississippi, North Carolina, South Carolina, Tennessee, Texas, and Virginia), plus the slaveholding states of Kentucky and

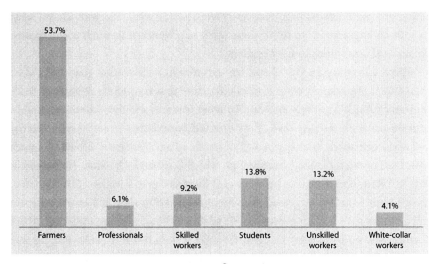

FIGURE 1.2. Occupation

Maryland. Their home counties on average had 16.6% more slaves to whites than the average of all the counties in those states. From the perspective of the white population, slavery was a personal, family, and community institution. As slaveholders well knew, everyone in the community needed to take an interest in slavery, to enforce discipline and to prevent its breakdown. Any weak link in the community chain could lead to the erosion or collapse of bondage. If a white family failed to challenge slaves away from their plantation, for example, runaways could escape. Thus, mere residency among heavy slaveholding communities may indicate a stronger bond to the institution of slavery than in other areas of the Confederacy.

Figure 1.3 gives slave-to-white ratios in the counties in which Lee's soldiers resided.

Single men—those with the fewest ties to keep them at home—rushed off to war, and, except for a shift in 1862, unwedded men dominated the army. In 1860, 3 in 8 (37.5%) were married—a percentage that most assuredly increased a bit before soldiers entered the army—and only a fraction more (38.0%) were heads of their own household. Nearly half (48.5%) of all soldiers lived with their parents or siblings in 1860, and 7 of 11 (62.0%) troops depended on someone else as their principal breadwinner. In the sample, the largest family consisted of a father, mother, and 11 children. Among the married men, just less than 1 in 5 (17.8%) had no children in 1860. Half of all married men had between 1 and 3 children. The average was a bit higher than 2.5

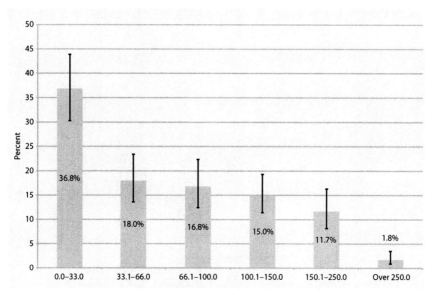

FIGURE 1.3. Slave-to-white ratio in home county

children per soldier-parent, with a median of 3. Only 1% of all single soldiers had children.[11]

Personal wealth reflected age and marital status. Based on research and consultation with other scholars, the poorer economic class ranged from $0 to $799 in real and personal property, the middle from $800 to $3,999, and the wealthy people from $4,000 and above. Nearly 3 of every 4 (74.1%) soldiers had a total personal wealth—a combination of the value of real and personal property—of $400 or less, and 4 of every 5 (79.2%) had accumulated personal wealth of less than $800. Only 1 in 10 (10.5%) was in the middle bracket of wealth, and another 1 in 10 (10.3%) was rich. The median wealth was $0, and the average was $1,728.

Figure 1.4 shows personal wealth, a combination of personal and real property.

While these financial statistics may seem surprising, they are misleading. Nearly half of all soldiers still lived with their parents or older siblings and 7 of 11 resided in someone else's household. With half of all soldiers born in 1838 or later, most were just beginning their careers and had little time to accumulate personal riches. Howlit Irvin, for example, was a prewar student who owned nothing in 1860, according to the census taker. But he was also the son of the former lieutenant governor of Georgia. His father possessed nearly

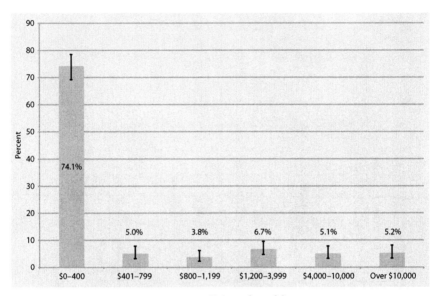

FIGURE 1.4. Personal wealth

$170,000 in wealth, including an estate with 117 slaves. After the census taker had passed through the community, his father died in an explosion. Howlit and his brother took over the family plantation. Without incorporating his father's wealth into the equation, the statistics would have missed his social and economic position. Almost half of all soldiers still enjoyed the benefits that their parents or siblings provided. A much more accurate means of discerning their background, then, is to include the wealth of family members if they resided with them. By combining personal and family wealth, a clearer portrait of these soldiers emerges. More than 2 of every 5 (41.7%) remained in the poorer category, but the middle economic class more than doubled (22.8%), and over a third (35.5%) belonged to the wealthy class. One in every 5 (20.5%) came from families worth more than $10,000. The median wealth soared from $0 to $1,295, which placed the intermediate soldier solidly in the middle economic class. The average wealth leaped to $8,544, reflecting the skewing power of troops from truly opulent backgrounds.

Figure 1.5 tracks personal and family wealth if the soldier lived with his family.

An examination of households indicates even greater wealth. The percentage of soldiers who came from households in the poorer category, less than $800 of total wealth, fell to a third (33.0%). Essentially as many (26.2%) soldiers came from households worth over $10,000 as came from households

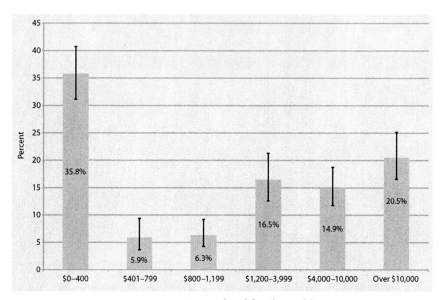

FIGURE 1.5. Personal and family wealth

valued at $400 or less (26.8%). Men from the middle economic class grew to just fewer than 1 in 4 (23.3%), but the upper class, households with $4,000 or more in total wealth, jumped to almost 4 in every 9 (43.7%) soldiers. The median household wealth reached $2,500, and the average climbed to $11,644. Seventeen-year-old Robert F. Small was employed as a clerk and lived in the household of merchant E. J. Bonney. Even though Small possessed little wealth himself, he benefited from the lifestyle of Bonney, who owned nine slaves and was worth nearly $90,000.

Figure 1.6 surveys household wealth.

Slave ownership reflected the polarized wealth among soldiers in Lee's army. According to the 1860 census, 1 in every 20 (4.9%) adults owned slaves and 1 in every 4 (24.9%) households had slaves. In Lee's army, more than 1 in every 8 (13.0%) soldiers owned slaves, and for those who lived with family members, approximately 3 in every 8 (37.2%) had slaves. Four of every 9 (44.4%) troops resided in a slaveholding household, some 78.0% greater than the South as a whole. Not surprisingly, wealth was tied to slave ownership. Approximately 92% of all soldiers' households with a minimum total wealth of $4,000 possessed slaves. More than 1 in every 15 soldiers or his family (6.9%) achieved planter status—owning 20 or more slaves—and 1 in 11 soldiers (9.3%) resided in planter households. By contrast, 1 in 32 (3.2%) households in the South qualified as a planter. This was not, therefore, a rich man's war

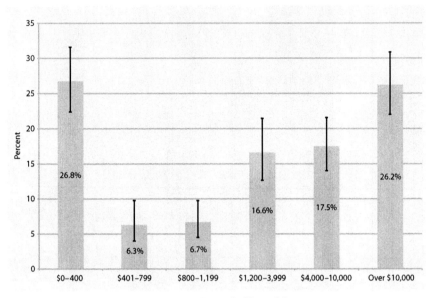

FIGURE 1.6. Household wealth

and a poor man's fight. Slaveholders, who also happened to be rich, served in disproportionately high numbers in Lee's army. It was a rich, moderate, and poor man's fight.[12]

Figure 1.7 compares personal, combined personal and family, and household slaveholding.

In the sample, roughly 5 of every 9 (56.1%) men enlisted in one of the two great waves of 1861. An additional 3 in 10 (29.9%) entered the service the following year. In the winter and spring of 1862, the Confederate Congress debated and passed a conscription law. While it certainly compelled some men to volunteer, it is difficult to determine just what impact it had. Half of all 1862 enlistees joined the army before passage of the act, and well over 3 of 4 (77.3%) entered the service by the end of May, long before the Confederate government began enforcing the law. Less than 1 in every 7 (14.0%) soldiers entered the army in 1863 or 1864, reflecting the dearth of manpower at home.

Figure 1.8 indicates year of enlistment.

According to records on Camp Lee, the rendezvous and training center for men designated for service in the Army of Northern Virginia, 14,885 conscripts were assigned through December 1864. Information on individual conscription and substitution is scarce. Only North Carolina regularly recorded conscription data on muster rolls, so the Compiled Service Records (CSRs) in the National Archives fail to reflect the actual number. The sample includes

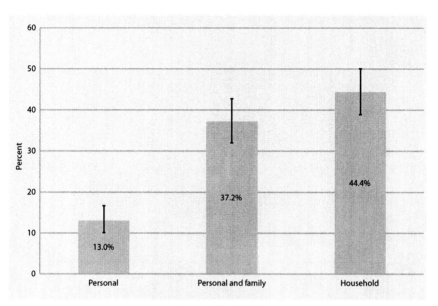

FIGURE 1.7. Slaveholding

3% who were conscripted; most likely, between 6% and 8% of the men in Lee's army were conscripts. Nearly 2 of every 3 (65.3%) conscripts were married, and every one of those soldiers had children, a responsibility that would certainly discourage enlistment. Three of every 5 (59.0%) conscripts were farmers, while the army included slightly more than half (52.9%) farmers. Wealth was also a concern. More than half of all conscripts or their families (52.9%) possessed total property worth $400 or less, compared to 4 of 11 (35.8%) for the entire army. Men of modest means had to produce for their families to live adequately. Small independent farmers relied on their own labor to put food on the table, which would discourage them from enlisting.[13]

While a larger percentage of conscripts were in the poorest category, the percentage of conscripts who were very wealthy, with property valued at over $10,000, was well below that of the entire army, 12.1% compared to 20.5%. As a whole, soldiers in Lee's army and their families with whom they resided were more than 1.6 times (37.2%) as likely as conscripts (23.3%) to own slaves. Conscripts, however, came from almost the same percentage of slaveholding households (23.7%) as the general Southern population (24.9%). Thus, conscripts from slaveholding households were not underrepresented in the army; volunteers from slaveholding households were overrepresented.

Although all states maintained information on muster rolls on substitution, less than 1% of all soldiers in Lee's army were involved in hiring or being hired

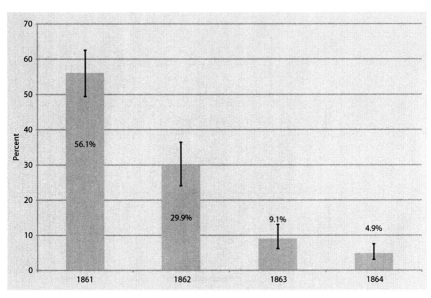

FIGURE 1.8. Year of enlistment

as a substitute. Quite a number of soldiers, like Private Christian Hege of the 48th North Carolina Infantry, wanted to find substitutes but never acted on it. Less than ten days after he was mustered into the regiment, Hege wrote his father: "I want you to try to hire a substitute for me if you possibly can. I would rather be at home and work like a negro than be here in camp." Three months later, Hege settled into army routine. "I like the army life a great deal better than I did when I first came out, but I can tell you that it is a hard life any way that you take it."[14]

In the sample, 44 men held commissions as officers. The highest ranking officer in the sample was Colonel John L. Miller of the 12th South Carolina Infantry. He was killed in action at the Wilderness in May 1864. The remaining 556 men were privates, corporals, and sergeants. The ratio of officers to enlisted men is a reasonable approximation of Lee's army as a whole.

The army distinguished absent without leave (AWOL) from desertion by what officials perceived as the soldier's motive. If officers and the court believed that the soldier intended to return, he was charged with AWOL; if they concluded that the soldier had no intention of returning, he was prosecuted for desertion. Desertion was an offense tried by general court-martial and sometimes resulted in a death sentence. Absence without leave, also tried by general court-martial in most instances, warranted much milder punishments.

Based on the CSRs, 1 in 12 (8.3%) soldiers went AWOL. Most were from units raised in Virginia or North Carolina until the last quarter of 1863, when Lieutenant General James Longstreet led two divisions to Georgia and Tennessee. With troops from the Lower South suddenly close to home, some took advantage of that proximity and absented themselves from their commands temporarily. The average length of absence was just shy of three and a half months (3.4).[15]

According to the sample, some 15.5% of all soldiers in Lee's army deserted at least once. Over the final seven months of the war, particularly during 1865, many muster rolls did not survive. As a result, the statistics on desertion in Lee's army are inaccurate. By Lee's own admission, in February and March 1865 his army lost approximately 120 men per day to desertion, yet, with rare exceptions, only soldiers who deserted to Federal lines appear in the CSRs. On a few occasions throughout the war the Confederate government offered amnesty, and 1 in every 6 (16.4%) deserters in the sample returned to the army.[16]

Desertion reflected the compounding hardships and fatalities and the declining morale of the Confederate population. Only 9% of all soldiers who deserted did so during 1861. Caught up in the rush to arms, thrilled by the victory at First Manassas in July 1861, and intrigued with the novelty of military life, soldiers maintained high morale throughout most of that first year. By 1862, as fighting picked up and hardships abounded, enthusiasm for war began to sag in some men. The Conscription Act of 1862 forced all soldiers to remain in the army an additional two years, and it compelled others to enlist or to enter military service against their preferences. In the following year, 1863, desertions almost doubled those of the previous year. Yet it was more than just the tough campaigning at Chancellorsville and Gettysburg. Deserters' records indicate that opportunity was a large factor. Soldiers from the Lower South tended not to desert until Longstreet took the two divisions to Georgia and Tennessee. Before then, those soldiers had no reasonable hope of making it home. Once the Confederate government transported them to the area, successful desertion became a viable option. The percentage of deserters soared — over half (52%) of all deserters that year left from September to December — and the bulk of them came from the Deep South or west of the Appalachian Mountains. This trend continued in the first four months of 1864, when nearly all the deserters in the sample came from the Deep South. In 1864 the desertion rate continued to rise, with 40% of all deserters in the war taking off during that year. Fighting in 1864 was especially savage, and hardships abounded for Lee's men. Almost 4 of every 9 soldiers who deserted the army in 1864 did so when the cause began to look hopeless. They hung on until November, when Union major general William T. Sherman launched his march through the heart of Georgia and Lincoln won reelection to a second four-year term. By then, the future of the Confederacy appeared bleak, and soldiers began losing heart and fleeing the army in droves. Despite the dearth of individual records, it is evident that Confederates in 1865 continued to desert in enormous numbers.

Figure 1.9 traces the annual rate of desertion from Lee's army.

Figure 1.10 breaks down desertion by quarters throughout the war. Because of the few numbers in any given month, the figure is unweighted.

Among occupations, farmers were the most likely to desert and the most likely to remain in the army. Just less than 5 in every 9 (52.9%) who remained in the service were farmers, and just less than 5 of every 9 (53.8%) deserters tilled the soil for a living. Of all soldiers who held fast in the ranks, 1 in 18 (5.5%) were professionals, while 1 in 12 (8.6%) who abandoned their comrades had held professional positions before the war. Skilled workers composed slightly less than 1 in every 6 deserters, but they comprised only 1 in 12 (8.8%) of the men who refused to flee military service. Unskilled workers, too, deserted in disproportionately high ratios, with 1 in 8 (12.6%) remaining in the army and just less than 1 in 6 (15.8%) deserting. White-collar workers made up 1 in every 20 (5.1%) of the nondeserters in the sample, yet none in the sample fled the army. Students, too, tended to remain with the army. Students constituted less than 1 in 6 (15.2%) soldiers who continued to rally around the flag and less than 1 in 17 (5.7%) who deserted.

Not surprisingly, deserters tended to be poorer than other soldiers. The median personal and family wealth for deserters was $713, less than one-half the median for nondeserters. Soldiers who remained with the army were 81% more likely to come from slaveholding households and 85% more likely to own slaves (personally or their families) than deserters. Poorer troops may have possessed a weaker sense of commitment to maintaining the standard social order and protecting the community. The defense and preservation of slavery may not have been as critical in their lives as it was to those who owned bondsmen and bondswomen. Soldiers from the lower class also had a more limited margin for error. Their families could not always rely on the labor of others to provide food for the family, nor did they have a filled larder or a hefty bank account to tap as necessities ran low. Loved ones in poorer homes suffered shortages of essentials more quickly, and troops felt greater pressure to leave the army to care for them.[17]

Wealth may have been the reason so comparatively few students and white-collar workers abandoned the Confederate flag. Students were young men

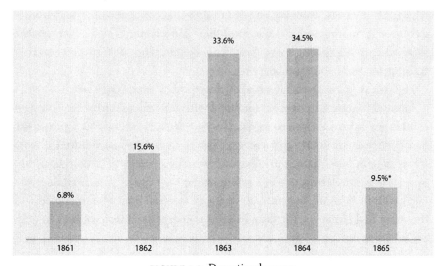

FIGURE 1.9. Desertion by year

*Desertion statistics for 1865 exist almost exclusively for those who fled to Union lines.

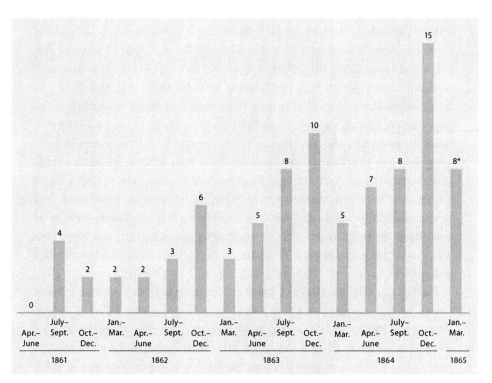

FIGURE 1.10. Desertion by month (unweighted)

*Desertion statistics for 1865 exist almost exclusively for those who fled to Union lines.

who generally came from well-to-do families that could afford to pay for more advanced schooling and did not need their son's labor. White-collar workers were also usually young men, fresh from school, and most of them were in training for good commercial jobs.

Figure 1.11 gives a breakdown of all deserters by economic class.

Limited financial resources combined with fatherhood proved to be a powerful factor in the decision to desert. Nearly 3 in every 10 (29.2%) nondeserters had children, but nearly 4 in every 9 (43.2%) deserters had children. Among all soldiers in Lee's army, 1 in 5 (20.0%) were deserters with children, while 1 in 9 (11.9%) nondeserters was a father. Almost all (98.2%) married deserters had children at home; by contrast, 72.6% of married men who remained with the army had children. Wartime hardships compelled these soldiers to grapple with the critical dilemma: whether their primary loyalty rested with their family or their fledgling nation. Because so many others depended heavily on them for their immediate welfare, fathers in Lee's army confronted these issues at an earlier stage in the war than most others. Many of them ultimately chose their family.

The age of soldiers, too, influenced their desertion rates. Although men who were older than 40 were well established financially, the demands of war took a toll on them; thus they were more likely to die of disease or become disabled due to sickness. Nonetheless, close to 1 in 5 (17.9%) of them deserted. A slightly lower percentage, 17.0%, were born between 1821 and 1830, and 16.3% of the year groups 1831 to 1835 fled the service. Despite a decline in the percentages, a notable spike in actual desertions occurred among soldiers who were born between 1835 and 1840. One-third (33.2%) of all deserters in Lee's army fell into this bracket, but because these men constituted such a large proportion of the army, the rate of desertion actually declined to 13.5%. These young men were just becoming established. A fair proportion of them had young children at home, an issue that helps to explain the sizable number of desertions. Among soldiers who were minority ages when the war broke out, 1 in every 8 (12.3%) deserted. That was the group least likely to have children at home.

During the war, the Army of Northern Virginia suffered extremely heavy losses. In the sample, nearly 1 in every 8 (12.3%) men was killed in action. Almost the same number (11.6%) died from disease. Along with those who were killed in accidents, executions, or other noncombat violence, nearly 1 in every 4 (24.5%) men died while in military service. Approximately 1 in every 4 (25.0%) soldiers who was not killed in action was wounded at least once. Some in the sample, such as Foxhall Daingerfield, endured multiple injuries:

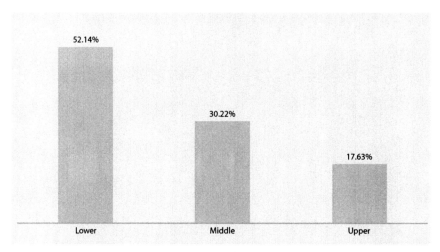

FIGURE 1.11. Desertion by economic class

Daingerfield was wounded five times. Another 1 in 7 (14.3%) men who did not experience a violent or tragic fate was captured before the final surrender. In total, nearly half (49.4%) of all soldiers were killed, wounded, or died of disease, and nearly 2 of every 3 (63.7%) were killed, wounded, captured, or died of disease. With discharges for disabilities and diseases, 7 of every 10 (70.1%) soldiers who ever served in Lee's army were victims. By factoring out those who deserted for the rest of the war, 3 of every 4 were killed, wounded, captured, died of disease, or discharged for disability. Only 1 in every 13 men surrendered at Appomattox.[18]

Figure 1.12 categorizes the total losses in Lee's army.

Figure 1.12 only reflects losses for each soldier. Thus, a soldier who sustained wounds in two battles is counted in the "Wounded" column once. A cavalryman who was wounded once and later killed in action is counted in the "Killed" (not "Wounded") column. The categories of losses—from most to least severe—are (1) killed in action, (2) died of disease, (3) died accidentally (not in combat), (4) wounded in action, (5) captured by the enemy, and (6) discharged for some disability.

A comparison between death by disease and death by combat indicates that age was a powerful factor. Older soldiers tended to die more frequently from disease but seldom fell in battle. The gap closed quickly as men in their thirties died in roughly equal percentages from combat and illness. A new trend developed for those who were born in the late 1830s and more recently. They died of disease far more infrequently, whereas combat claimed their lives in ever-increasing numbers. The transition point between death by battle and death

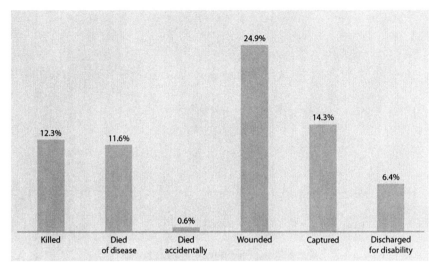

FIGURE 1.12. Total losses

by disease was 26 years of age. Most likely, the immense hardships of military life broke down older soldiers, reducing their resistance to disease. Although younger men did not care for themselves as well and probably had less exposure to killing illnesses in their youthful lives, they generally had stronger constitutions and could fight off sickness better than their older comrades-in-arms. Younger men, feeling that spirit of youthful masculine invincibility, most likely took greater risks and were therefore struck down in battle more often. Death may have been around them, but few younger soldiers contemplated their own mortality. Death was something that happened to others. As the war dragged on, many of them learned the concept the hard way, as relatives and friends lost their lives. By contrast, older soldiers better understood the fleeting nature of life. They had confronted death in real and intellectual terms and were less likely to think of themselves as invincible. This mind-set did not necessarily make them cautious soldiers; it simply convinced them to avoid unnecessary risks and to be constantly wary.

The median length of service prior to death from disease was 12 months. In the second year, fatalities from illness declined 60%, and in the third year, they fell off 256% from that first year. Of course, the longer soldiers served, the more likely they would be killed in battle or discharged because of their wounds. Some of those men certainly would have succumbed to illness had they not suffered calamities on the battlefield. Still, the decline was both precipitous and telling.

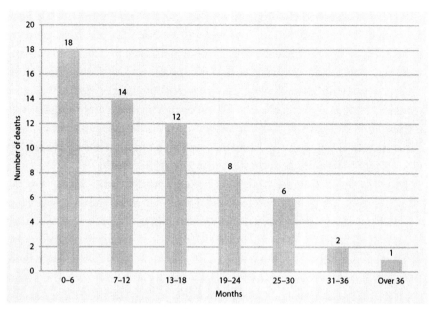

FIGURE 1.13. Deaths from disease by months of service

Figure 1.13 breaks down death due to disease by the number of months a soldier served.

Soldiers who died of disease were substantially poorer than those who did not. The median personal and family wealth of those who died of disease was $800, while those who did not were worth $1,421. Four of every 9 (45.3%) men who succumbed to illness had a total wealth of $400 or less, compared to fewer than 4 of every 11 (34.6%) who escaped death from disease. On the opposite end of the wealth scale, slightly more than 1 in 8 (14.3%) who died of sickness was worth more than $10,000, while more than 1 in 5 (21.3%) of those who managed to survive camp diseases topped $10,000 in total wealth. The extremes of ages—older men who had accumulated wealth and sons of rich parents—in the latter bracket help explain this incongruity. Slave ownership reflected these wealth distinctions. Among troops who died of disease, 3 of 10 (29.6%) of them or their families with whom they resided owned slaves, and 5 of 13 (36.1%) lived in slaveholding households. Those who were not felled by sickness had slightly stronger attachments to slavery, with 38.2% of soldiers or their families owning slaves and 45.5% residing in the homes of slaveowners.

Clearly, wealth increased the likelihood of survivability from sickness, especially early in the war. Soldiers with more wealth could supplement their meager diets through purchases and care packages from home. They could also buy much-needed clothing and blankets. As the war entered its third and fourth years, food and clothing were seldom available for purchase. By then, though, many veterans had developed some resistance to camp illnesses and were better able to survive despite dietary deficiencies and clothing shortages.

The relationship between length of service and fatalities in combat was more complex. Early in the war, soldiers did not campaign much and comparatively few lost their lives in battle. By the second year, the frequency and lethality of battle increased dramatically. The peaks for killed in action occurred from the 9th to the 16th month and from the 25th to the 36th month.

Wealthier and slaveholding soldiers not only turned out to serve, they endured more combat losses. Soldiers who were killed or wounded in battle had a higher median wealth ($1,430) than noncasualties ($1,150). Two of every 5 (40.9%) soldiers who were wounded or killed had a combined wealth of $4,000 or more, and more than 1 in every 4 (26.1%) were from families worth more than $10,000. Among soldiers who did not suffer combat injuries, less than a third (32.5%) possessed a personal and family wealth of $4,000 or greater, and 1 in 6 (17.0%) came from families worth more than $10,000. They or their parents also were more likely to have slaves. Four of every 9 (43.3%) either owned or their parents owned slaves, compared to 1 in 3 (33.4%) of those who were never killed or wounded. Obviously, the wealthy in general and slaveholders in particular had a strong stake in Confederate independence.

Lee commanded an army of upper, middle, and lower-class soldiers who shared a belief in the cause and endured tremendous hardships and sacrifices to fight in defense of their homes, their property, and rights they held sacred. At the outbreak of the war they were predominantly young and single and possessed strong ties to slavery. Four of 9 came from slaveholding households, and many others worked for slaveowners or had them as their principal clients. To gain Confederate independence, men in Lee's army incurred tremendous risks and suffered staggering losses.

CHAPTER TWO

The Infantry

In traditional military parlance, the infantry was designated the "queen of battle." That was absolutely true in the case of Lee's army. Throughout the war, it carried the fight to the Federals and bore the brunt of the Union onslaught. Time and again, infantrymen proportionately suffered the heaviest losses, and they inflicted the vast majority of enemy casualties.

The infantry composed almost 82% of the manpower strength in Lee's army. While data about the experiences of cavalrymen and artillerymen often varied from that of the army overall, infantrymen so dominated the makeup of the army that the statistics for their branch largely dictated the data for the entire army.

Only 1 in every 12 (8.7%) infantrymen in the sample was an officer. The highest ranking officer in the infantry as well as in the entire sample was Colonel John L. Miller of the 20th South Carolina Infantry. Miller, a prewar lawyer, rose from captain before he was killed in action at the Wilderness in May 1864. Of all the infantry officers, nearly 4 of every 9 (42.3%) had served as an enlisted man at one time. Henry H. Simmons of the 21st Mississippi advanced from private to sergeant, to first lieutenant, and finally to captain during the war. A prewar plantation overseer, Simmons sustained a severe leg wound at the Battle of Gettysburg in July 1863 and was discharged for his combat injury. He lived until 1923. Like Simmons, 8 of every 9 (88.0%) soldiers served at some time as a private, and 1 in every 6 (16.7%) at one time was a noncommissioned officer (corporal or sergeant). Seven of 9 (77.0%) only held the rank of private.

The oldest infantryman in the sample definitively was Private Samuel W. Compton of the 21st Georgia Infantry. Born in 1815, Compton enlisted in June 1861, only to contract a fever in November; he died of illness a year later. Private John C. Bishop, the New York–born soldier from South Carolina, was the youngest. At the age of 13, Bishop enlisted in the 20th South Carolina Infantry and upon discovery was transferred to a South Carolina Reserve unit, only to die of illness. Bishop was born in 1848, whereas the median birth year for

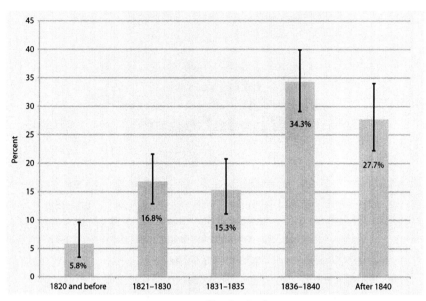

FIGURE 2.1. Year of birth of infantrymen

infantrymen was 1838 and the average year of birth was 1835.7. More than 3 of every 5 (62.1%) infantrymen were born in 1836 or later.[1]

Figure 2.1 tracks the year of birth of infantrymen.

Infantrymen were born overwhelmingly in the Atlantic coastal states from Virginia to Georgia. Over a quarter of all infantrymen in the sample were born in North Carolina (25.6%), followed by Virginia and Georgia (both 17.2%), then South Carolina (12.6%). One in 12 (8.4%) claimed Tennessee as his birth state, and 1 in 16 (6.7%) was originally an Alabamian. Northern- (2.5%) and foreign- (3.5%) born totaled 6.0%.

At the time of the secession crisis, more than 7 of every 10 (71.2%) soldiers resided in those same Atlantic coastal states. More than a quarter (25.6%) lived in North Carolina. Georgia (17.5%) and Virginia (17.5%) were next with approximately 1 in every 5, and South Carolina was home to 1 in 8 (12.4%). One in 14 (6.9%) came from Alabama. Infantrymen split with almost half from the upper (51.1%) and lower (48.9%) South. More than 1 in 5 (21.9%) infantrymen did not reside in their birth state, with Georgia, Alabama, and Mississippi making up almost 3 of every 5 (58.1%) of that total. When foreigners and Northerners by birth were factored out of the equation, just fewer than 1 in 5 (18.4%) lived in a state other than their birth state, a ratio 60% higher than the next branch of service.[2]

Like the army as a whole, the infantry was predominantly rural in compo-

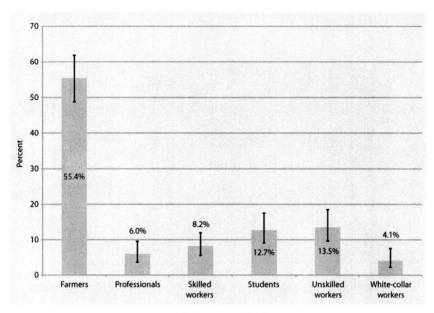

FIGURE 2.2. Occupation of infantrymen

sition. Only 1 in every 20 (5.1%) came from cities in the top 100 in population in 1860, defined as communities with 9,500 or more. Prewar occupations reflected that rural dominance. Five of every 9 (55.4%) infantrymen worked on farms. Unskilled laborers (13.5%) and students (12.7%) made up one-eighth each. One in every 10 was either a professional (6.0%) or a white-collar worker (4.1%); skilled workers composed 1 in 12 (8.2%) in infantry regiments.[3]

Figure 2.2 surveys the prewar occupations of infantrymen.

Infantrymen resided primarily in counties with high slave populations. For every 1,000 white people, there were on average 744 slaves in the home counties of infantrymen. By comparison, the counties of states from which the Confederacy drew soldiers averaged 526 slaves for every 1,000 whites. Thus, the community bond to the institution of slavery was strong.[4]

Just fewer than 2 in every 5 (39.3%) infantrymen were married. That was the highest percentage of married men in any branch of the service. Of those with spouses, 5 of every 6 (83.2%) had children in 1860. Among those soldiers with children, infantrymen averaged the highest number at almost three (2.7). Typical was Private Samuel Compton, a married father of three from Cassville, Georgia. Compton enlisted in the 21st Georgia Infantry in 1861 and died of illness the following year. Private John H. Allison of North Carolina

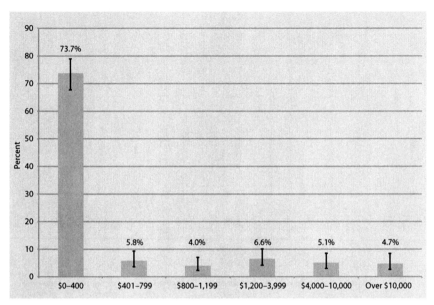

FIGURE 2.3. Personal wealth of infantrymen

boasted the largest infantryman's family in the sample at eleven children, followed by three homes with nine. Slightly more than a quarter (25.9) had only one child in 1860.[5]

Because infantrymen constituted such a high percentage of the total army, personal wealth among foot soldiers generally paralleled that of Lee's army. Almost 3 of every 4 (73.7%) infantrymen had a total personal wealth of $400 or less, and 4 of 5 (79.6%) were in the poor category with under $800. Less than 1 in 9 (10.6%) was in the middle bracket, and a slightly lower ratio, 1 in 10 (9.9%) achieved wealth.

Figure 2.3 depicts the personal wealth of infantrymen.

Although the infantry, among all three branches of the service, had the lowest percentage of soldiers who resided in someone else's home, greater than 3 of every 5 (61.3%) did so. And for most of those who lived with parents or other family members, the financial situation changed dramatically. Nineteen-year-old Thomas J. Chitwood of the 42nd Virginia had no wealth in 1860. Yet he still resided with his parents, who owned 11 slaves and property valued at nearly $11,000, and enjoyed a very different lifestyle than someone who had no appreciable personal wealth and lived alone. By factoring in the wealth of family members with whom they lived, the poorest component, those who owned $400 or less in real and personal property, declined by half to 35.8%, and the poorer segments, those who owned less than $800, fell from 4 in 5 to

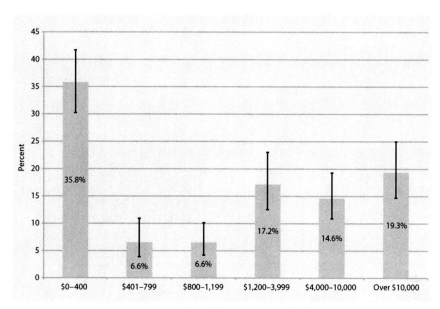

FIGURE 2.4. Personal and family wealth of infantrymen

fewer than 4 in 9 (42.3%). The middle category, between $800 and $3,999, jumped to nearly 1 in every 4 (23.7%), and the rich increased to 1 in every 3 (33.9%). The median wealth was $1,225, which placed it solidly in the middle bracket.[6]

Figure 2.4 indicates the combined personal and family wealth of infantry-men.

Household tabulations indicated even starker differences in personal wealth. Slightly more than one-third (34.3%) of the army's infantrymen were situated in the two poorest categories, while more than 2 of every 5 (41.2%) fit within the richest brackets. The middle categories witnessed fractional changes, up less than 1.0% to 24.5%. The median household wealth increased to $1,426. Henry H. Simmons, who rose from private to captain in the 21st Mississippi, worked as an overseer for S. M. Lanier. Lanier was worth more than $175,000 in property, including 64 slaves. Simmons lived in the big house and enjoyed the comforts of opulence and slave labor, even though he was worth only $800.[7]

Figure 2.5 shows the household wealth of infantrymen.

Slaveholding was weakest among infantrymen, yet compared to Confeder-ates as a whole they exhibited strong ties to the institution. One of every 8 (12.8%) men in infantry regiments owned slaves, and 4 of every 11 (36.1%) soldiers or family members with whom they lived were slaveholders. Although

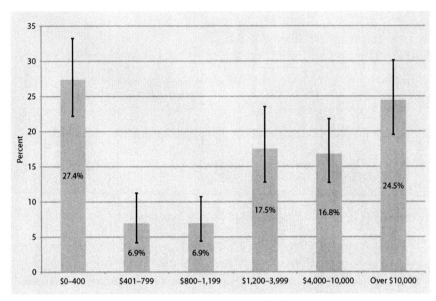

FIGURE 2.5. Household wealth of infantrymen

just fewer than 3 of every 7 (42.3%) infantrymen lived in households with slaves, by far the lowest of the three branches, men in the infantry were 70% more likely to live in slaveholding households than Southern whites in general.

Figure 2.6 categorizes slave ownership among infantrymen.

Infantrymen or their families owned a considerable number of bondsmen and bondswomen. The largest single block of slaveholders, 1 in every 8 (12.4%) infantrymen, possessed between three and ten slaves. Slightly less than 1 in every 16 (6.2%) infantrymen or the family head with whom he lived was a planter and more than 1 in every 12 (8.8%) came from a planter household.[8]

Figure 2.7 indicates the number of slaves owned by infantrymen and their families.

In the sample, 3 of every 5 (61.0%) infantrymen entered military service in 1861. Another 5 of every 18 (27.7%) joined the army the following year, which meant that 8 of every 9 (88.7%) infantrymen who served in Lee's army began fighting by 1862. As the manpower crunch hit the army, the home front could provide few additional soldiers. Those who entered the army as infantrymen in 1863 and 1864 tended toward more extremes in age: young males coming of age and adults in their thirties with families.[9]

Although the Confederate government was slow to acknowledge the pressing manpower needs of the infantry, it eventually adapted its policies and made a conscious effort to direct conscripts to that branch. From December

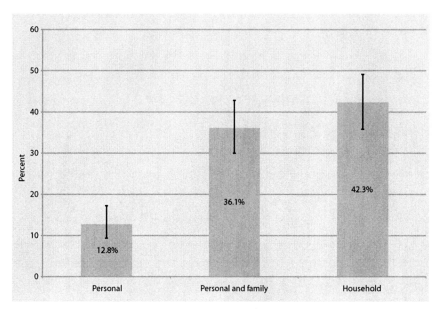

FIGURE 2.6. Slaveholding of infantrymen

1862 through January 1864, the government assigned 4,935 men from Camp Lee, the principal replacement depot and training center for conscripts to the Army of Northern Virginia, to Lee's army. More than 3 of every 5 (61.0%) went to the infantry. From February through December 1864, another 7,732 conscripts were assigned to the army from Camp Lee. Almost 3 of every 4 (73.1%) were designated for the infantry, indicating the army's greatest need. Unfortunately, the long marches on foot, the extensive duty, the extreme hazards, and the excessive work demands to replace those who had fallen in battle made infantry the physically toughest branch on soldiers old and young.[10]

The spotty records show that 1 in every 12 infantrymen (8.7%) went AWOL at some time. The average length of their absence was 3.9 months. Until Longstreet's movement to the Western theater, virtually all of the soldiers who left their unit without authorization were from Virginia or North Carolina.[11]

According to incomplete records, between 1–6 and 1–7 (15.3%) infantrymen deserted during the course of the war. Of those deserters, only 1 in every 6 (17.4%) returned to the army. Ferdinand Wiley, a private in the 1st Battalion Virginia Infantry, decided in June 1862 to go home temporarily—what soldiers referred to as "French leave." Even though he returned one month later, Wiley had missed the Seven Days' fight, and authorities levied charges against him before a general court-martial. The court sentenced him to a year in jail, but Wiley escaped and remained at liberty for the rest of the war.[12]

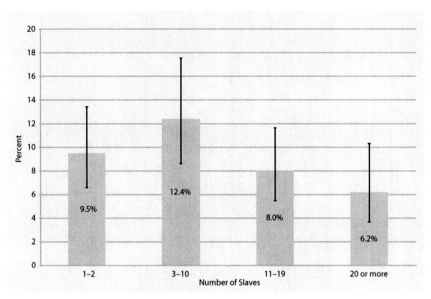

FIGURE 2.7. Personal and family slaveholding of infantrymen*
*The total equals the percentage of personal and family slaveholding.

Infantry deserters tended to be much poorer than nondeserters. Their median wealth, both personal and family if they lived with relatives, totaled $533, barely 40% of those who remained with the army ($1,350). Five of every 9 (53.8%) deserters possessed less than $800 in wealth, compared to slightly greater than 4 in 10 (41.4%) nondeserters. More than 3 in 10 (31.4%) nondeserters or their families boasted total wealth of $4,000 or more. Only 1 in every 45 (2.2%) infantrymen valued at $4,000 or more deserted. Moreover, nondeserters owned slaves far more often. Two of every 9 (23.1%) deserters or their families with whom they lived owned slaves, while nearly 7 of every 9 deserters did not possess slaves. One in 11 (9%) slaveowners or men from slaveholding families deserted; 1 of every 6 (17.1%) of all nonslaveowners deserted. Thus, an individual from a family that did not own slaves was almost twice as likely to desert as one whose family had at least one bondsman or bondswoman.

The sample indicated little connection between desertion and illness or combat injuries. Slightly less than 1 in 5 (19.6%) infantry deserters was wounded, compared to almost 1 in 3 (32.3%) nondeserters who sustained wounds. Although 37% of all deserters from the infantry were sick at least once during their service, nearly half of all nondeserters suffered a serious illness.[13]

Marital status and children proved to be a powerful consideration. Although a slightly higher percentage of infantry deserters were married (42.1% compared to 38.9%), children at home became a telling factor. Every married infantryman who deserted had children at home, even though 1 in every 6 (16.8%) infantrymen in the army who was married had no children at home. One additional single deserter was a widower who had left three children behind. Nearly 1 in 3 (32.9%) infantrymen was a father, but almost 4 of every 9 (43.6%) deserters had children. Less than 1 in 7 (13.8%) nondeserters had children, whereas more than 1 in 6 (17.1%) deserters had offspring whom they left behind. While the issue of having children did not determine whether infantrymen deserted or not, it was a major factor in the decision of some men to leave the army. Among married deserters with children, poverty enhanced their concern for loved ones at home. The median wealth of married deserters with children was $211 (personal and family), less than one-sixth of those who did not desert. In fact, more than 5 of every 9 (56.3%) deserters had a total wealth below $275. Three of every 4 (75.0%) had a total wealth of $950 or below.

Married nondeserters certainly suffered financially during the war, but nothing like married deserters. Married nondeserters in the infantry had a median wealth (personal and family) of $800, the borderline between poor and middle brackets. Whereas 5 of every 9 (56.3%) married deserters owned less than $275 in property, fewer than 5 of 13 (37.4%) married nondeserters did. Even among nondeserters who were married with children, less than 4 in 10 (39.7%) had total wealth under $275, and their median wealth was $700, more than triple that of married deserters with children ($211). Poorer men may not have maintained the same attachment to the community and its values as more well-to-do people. It is possible that while some may not have been committed to the cause of secession and slavery, others may have, but that sentiment was not strong enough to keep them at their post in the face of prolonged brutality and hardship. A war of that magnitude imposed huge burdens on most families, but no one suffered as harshly as the poor. The combination of children at home and poverty weighed heavily on the minds of lower-class infantrymen and no doubt compelled a number of them to desert.

Married deserters with children tended to be considerably older than other deserters or nondeserters, and the physical and emotional strain of combat may have affected them as well. The median birth year for married deserters with children was 1828, which meant that half of them were 33 years of age or older in 1861. By contrast, the median birth year for single deserters was 1839 and for nondeserters it was 1838. Private John Lovvorn of the 44th Alabama Infantry, for example, entered military service in 1863 at age 33. Lovvorn, a prewar farmer with a wife and four children, was worth only $70. After suffering wounds at Gettysburg and again at Chickamauga, Lovvorn had enough. He slipped away from the army in northern Georgia and made his way back to Lebanon, Alabama. He never returned to the army.

Because infantrymen bore the brunt of combat, they suffered the overwhelming number of casualties. In the sample, 1 in every 7 (13.7%) infantrymen was killed in action or died of their wounds. They constituted 92.4% of all soldiers who were killed in action in Lee's army. More than 3 in every 10 (30.7%) sustained combat wounds. By merging the two categories, more than 2 of every 5 (41%) infantrymen who ever served in Lee's army were wounded at least once or killed in action. Nine of those in the sample who were wounded subsequently recovered, only to be killed in another battle; 1 in every 5 (20.7%) who sustained an injury was later wounded again at least once. Two in every 13 (15.3%) infantrymen who were not killed or wounded in action were taken prisoner prior to the surrender at Appomattox Court House in April 1865. Thus, more than 5 of every 9 (56.7%) infantrymen were combat casualties at least once. Another 1 in 8 (12.7%) was never a battlefield casualty but died of disease. The combined tally of combat casualties or death by disease totaled more than 2 of every 3 (67.7%) infantrymen. Two soldiers in the sample were killed accidentally, and another 15 who were discharged for disability were neither wounded nor captured. When these men are included in the calculation, 3 of every 4 (76%) infantrymen were either killed, wounded, captured, died of disease, or discharged for a disability. An additional 1 in every 13 (7.7%) deserted the army for the duration of the war who were neither casualties nor disabled. By factoring them out of the data (it was difficult to suffer a battlefield casualty, die of disease while in the army, or be discharged for disability if one deserted permanently), the statistics soar to 4 of every 5 (79.4%).[14]

Figure 2.8 breaks down the infantry's total losses.

Infantrymen who entered military service early in the war suffered disastrously. Almost 3 of every 4 (74.4%) soldiers who first volunteered in 1861 were either killed, wounded, POWs, discharged for disability, or they died of disease. Those who joined the army the following year endured an even more brutal experience, with almost 8 of every 10 (83.1%) encountering the same fate. Despite a much briefer term of service, more than 7 of every 11 men who entered the infantry in 1863 (52.7%) or 1864 (66.7%) were similarly victimized by the war.

Figure 2.9 highlights infantry losses by year of enlistment.

Infantrymen who were killed or wounded tended to be more affluent than those who did not receive a battlefield injury. The combined personal and

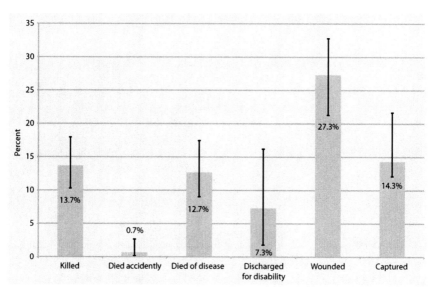

FIGURE 2.8. Losses among infantrymen

family median wealth for killed or wounded was $1,275, compared to $1,022 for noncasualties, a full 25% higher. Almost 5 of every 9 (54.7%) infantrymen with a combined personal and family wealth of more than $10,000 was either killed or wounded. The distinction in slave ownership was even greater. Of those infantrymen who did not suffer battlefield injuries, only 3 of every 10 (30.4%) of them — or their families if they resided with them — owned slaves. Among those who were killed or wounded, more than 4 of 10 (41.5%) were slaveholders themselves or the family members with whom they lived were, a 36.4% higher rate.

The inverse was true for those who died of disease. The median wealth of soldiers or their families who succumbed to illness was $650; for those who did not perish from sickness and their families, the median wealth was $1,250. Only 28% of the disease victims owned slaves or their families did, while more than 36% of the survivors of illness did. Wealth offered a superior diet both before and early in the war, when soldiers could purchase additional food or receive care packages. It also provided a more reliable means of replacing clothing during wartime when it wore out.

As the war dragged into its last year, the infantry remained an effective fighting force, but the grind took its toll. More than 3 of every 5 (63.1%) infantrymen who fell into Union hands did so in 1864 or 1865. Casualties were staggering. Ranks thinned. Reliable soldiers were killed, wounded, captured, or broke down from the continual strain of fighting and poor diet. Replace-

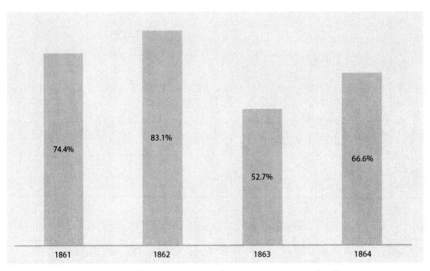

FIGURE 2.9. Total losses among infantrymen by year of enlistment

ments consisted of conscripts who were not especially prepared or suited to the rigors of combat. Quality officers were lost; their successors may have been good combat soldiers, but they lacked the necessary skills and discipline to lead and manage soldiers. In October 1864, the absence of enthusiasm and aggressiveness among the Confederates in the First Corps shocked Brigadier General Porter Alexander, who had recently returned to the army after several months away recuperating from a wound. "Our troops have fought so long behind breastworks," he thought, "that they have lost all spirit in attacking or would have carried it easily." The army commander himself witnessed the halfhearted attacks. "Gen Lee was more worried at this failure," Alexander wrote his wife, "than I have ever seen him under similar circumstances." They fulfilled President Jefferson Davis's strategy of delivering powerful blows against the enemy to discourage them from pursuing the war, but the costs of that strategy proved to be the infantry's undoing.[15]

CHAPTER THREE

The Cavalry

At the Battle of First Manassas on 21 July 1861, the Union army feigned a frontal attack and skillfully maneuvered a flanking force that turned the Confederate left wing and began rolling up the Rebel defenders' line. Stout infantry resistance, timely reinforcements from the Shenandoah Valley, and Federal exhaustion combined to turn the tide. What looked like a Union victory transformed into a Confederate rout.

Although the Union commander, Major General Irvin McDowell, had positioned three brigades at Centreville, Virginia, to prevent a retreat from becoming a disaster, the Confederate army could have exploited its victory better. Its infantry was too tired from fighting all day and too disorganized in triumph to take advantage of the Union collapse. Joseph E. Johnston needed cavalry, the arm that traditionally pursued an enemy, to crush any resistance and to capture large numbers of fleeing soldiers and equipment. But the Confederate army boasted only a few regiments, not nearly enough to effect the kind of speed and shock to carve up retreating forces.

According to the sample used in this study, fewer than 1 in every 4 (23.3%) cavalrymen in Lee's army enlisted in 1861. During the second year of the war, more than 4 of every 9 (45.3%) horsemen signed up for military service. Confederate authorities realized that the army in Virginia needed to increase the number of cavalry regiments, and word had spread from the army to the civilian world about the benefits of cavalry duty over the infantry and artillery. In 1863, 2 in every 9 men (22.7%) who served in cavalry units entered the army. Only in 1864, when pressing manpower needs for the infantry dictated military assignments, did the numbers dip to below one-eleventh (8.7%).

The sample included only 6 cavalry officers (4.0%), with Foxhall A. Daingerfield of the 11th Virginia Cavalry holding the highest rank as captain. A lawyer before the war, Daingerfield rose from his original rank of private, suffering wounds in the head, shoulder, and foot. More than 4 of every 5 cavalrymen (81.3%) held the exclusive rank of private, and 93.3% were at one time privates.

Just under 1 in every 8 (12.0%) was a noncommissioned officer (corporal or sergeant) at some time during the war.[1]

Cavalrymen had the same median birth year—1838.0—as their infantry counterparts, and their average birth year—1835.2—was six months earlier, no consequential distinction. Where cavalrymen exhibited interesting differences was in the lower and upper birth years. One in every 14 (7.1%) horsemen was born before 1821, compared to 1 in 17 (5.8%) foot soldiers. One of every 4 cavalrymen (25.2%) was born by 1830; in the infantry, the proportion was just more than 2 of 9 (22.6%). Mounted men were also younger, with nearly 4 of every 11 (35.3%) born after 1840, whereas 3 of 11 (27.7%) infantrymen fit into that category. Soldiers in their forties, as men born before 1821 were, preferred the ease and reduced physical hardship of riding, rather than walking. The thrill of speed on horseback and the prewar and wartime perception of the glamorous mounted arm enticed impressionable young volunteers—men or teenagers who were 20 and under when the war broke out—to join the "chivalry," as infantrymen and artillerymen often derisively referred to that branch.[2]

Figure 3.1 depicts the year of birth of cavalrymen.

Cavalrymen primarily claimed Virginia, South Carolina, and North Carolina as their birth state. Five of every 9 (55.3%) originally hailed from the Old Dominion. In the sample, slightly less than 1 in 6 (16.3%) was born in South Carolina, followed by 1 in 8 (12.8%) in North Carolina. Georgia was next at exactly one-half of North Carolina's total (6.4%). By far, the mounted arm had the highest percentage of men from the Upper South with more than 3 of 4 (76.3%). Just under 1 in 12 (7.8%) was Northern-born, and fewer than 1 in 100 (0.7%) was born abroad.[3]

Only selected states fielded cavalry units in Lee's army; the sample thus represents soldiers who resided in only a handful of slaveholding states. More than 3 of every 5 (61.7%) of these horsemen lived in Virginia at the time of the war. Barely more than 1 in 6 (16.8%) were South Carolinians, followed by inhabitants of North Carolina (12.8%), Georgia (6.0%), and Maryland (2.7%). More than 2 of every 9 (22.6%) cavalrymen resided in a state that was not their birth state.[4]

Soldiers who joined the cavalry were the least likely of the three arms to have resided in urban areas before the war. One in every 25 (4.0%) came from a city in the top 100 in population in 1860, compared to more than 1 in 17 (5.9%) for the army as a whole. Their occupations reflected that rural lifestyle, as nearly 5 of every 9 (54.5%) were farmers. The cavalry also had the fewest unskilled workers at 1 in 16 (6.7%). In the Confederate army, cavalrymen had

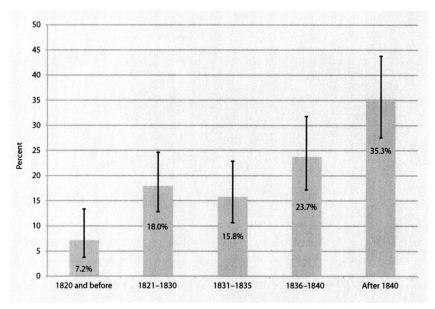

FIGURE 3.1. Year of birth of cavalrymen

to provide their own mounts. Most single men living on their own probably owned a horse already; still, unskilled workers held the lowest-paying jobs and therefore were the least likely to have horses to spare.

Figure 3.2 breaks down the prewar occupations of cavalrymen.

The most intriguing occupational statistic was the extremely large number of students who entered the cavalry. It had the largest proportion of students at more than 1 in 5 (21.6%), about 60% higher than the infantry. Both family wealth and youthful enthusiasm influenced these recruits. In the sample, only 2.1% of the mounted men were born in 1847 or later, which meant that almost 98% of all cavalrymen were 15 years of age or older at the time the fighting erupted. Families had to be comfortable financially to afford young males of 15 or older to be in school, and the cavalry was by far the most expensive branch of service. Opie N. Watson, for example, was a 17-year-old student when the war began. The son of a very wealthy slaveowner, Watson rushed off to enlist in the 8th Virginia Cavalry. Students were also likely to possess that youthful exuberance and naïveté and be more susceptible to romantic notions of cavalry service.[5]

Like infantrymen, cavalrymen tended to come from areas with a dense slave population. Mounted troops resided in counties in which the ratio of slaves to whites averaged 782 slaves for every 1,000 whites. Compared to the states that sent men into Lee's army, the ratio was almost 50% greater.[6]

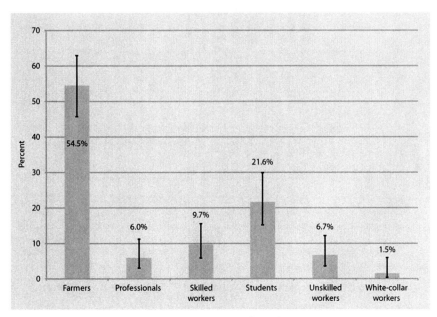

FIGURE 3.2. Occupation of cavalrymen

More than 2 of every 3 (67.6%) cavalrymen were single. Of the married men, more than 3 in 11 (28.1%) had no children in 1860. The average number of children for cavalrymen was 2.58. Private John S. Hite of the 14th Virginia, a middle-class farmer from Gilmer County, had the most children in the sample at nine. Hite died of a stomach ailment in February 1863.[7]

Compared to infantrymen, soldiers in the cavalry tended to come from wealthier backgrounds. Eight of 11 (72.7%) horse soldiers owned less than $800 in personal property, while 8 of 10 (79.6%) infantrymen fit into that bracket. The two branches had roughly the same percentage of men in the middle categories of wealth—10.1% for cavalry and 10.6% for infantry—but far more mounted men possessed considerable wealth. More than 1 in every 6 (17.3%) cavalrymen were valued at $4,000 or more, compared to 1 in 10 (9.9%) infantrymen.

Figure 3.3 traces the personal wealth of cavalrymen.

The starkest distinction emerges when we examine the combined wealth of soldiers and their families if they lived with their families. Mounted troops and their families possessed a median wealth of $2,800, a figure that more than doubled the median infantry wealth of $1,225 and placed over half of them in the upper middle class or higher. Fewer than 1 in 3 (32.4%) cavalry-men fell into the poor categories, compared to slightly less than 4 of 9 (42.3%)

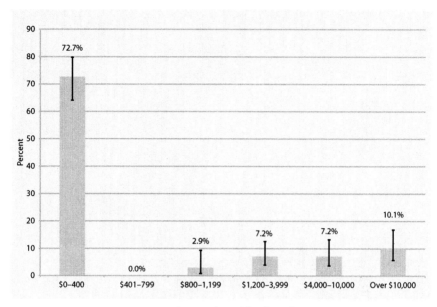

FIGURE 3.3. Personal wealth of cavalrymen

infantrymen. More than 9 of every 20 (46.8%) mounted men had a combined accumulation of $4,000 or more, while one-third (33.9%) of all foot soldiers qualified for these categories. Only in the upper middle bracket, between $1,200 and $3,999, did the percentage of infantrymen (17.2%) exceed cavalrymen (14.4%).

Figure 3.4 indicates the combined personal and family wealth of cavalrymen.

In cavalrymen's households, the median wealth nearly tripled those of foot soldiers, $5,700 to $2,100. Three of every 5 (59.3%) mounted men lived in households with total property valued at $4,000 or more, and 3 of 8 (37.4%) resided amid property worth more than $10,000. By comparison, 2 of 5 (41.2%) infantrymen resided in households valued at $4,000 or more, and fewer than a quarter (24.5%) were worth over $10,000.[8]

Figure 3.5 gives the household wealth of cavalrymen.

With such high levels of wealth among cavalrymen and their families, it is not surprising that their slave ownership was extensive as well. More than 1 of every 6 (17.3%) cavalrymen personally owned slaves, and more than 4 of every 9 (44.6%) horsemen or their families, if they lived with them, owned slaves. By comparison, 1 in 8 infantrymen (12.8%) owned slaves, and fewer than 4 of every 11 (36.1%) of them or their families had slaves. Nearly 5 of every 9 (54.0%) cavalrymen came from slaveholding households. This propor-

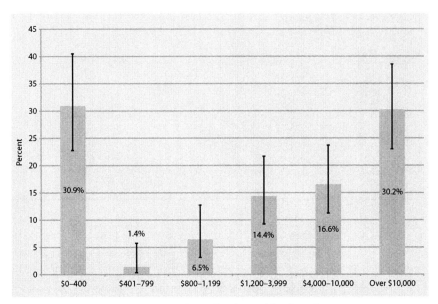

FIGURE 3.4. Personal and family wealth of cavalrymen

tion more than doubled the percentage of the South as a whole in 1860 and was 27.5% higher than that of the infantry. A future soldier like Samuel J. Hunt of the 3rd Virginia Cavalry grew up in a middle-class home in Prince Edward County. In 1860, he was on his own, worth nothing, and with a young wife. But Hunt worked as an overseer for Thomas Hickson, who possessed 16 slaves and enjoyed a net worth of nearly $35,000. Hunt and his bride lived in the big house and enjoyed the many niceties of a wealthy household and the benefits of slave labor without owning any of them. Among cavalrymen, more than 1 in every 8 (13.0%) came from the planter class—either they or their family with whom they lived owned 20 or more slaves—and 1 in 7 (14.4%) lived in planter households.

Figure 3.6 categorizes slave ownership among cavalrymen.

Throughout the period of conscription, the percentage designated for the cavalry changed little. From December 1862 through January 1864, authorities at Camp Lee ordered 1,032 men, slightly over 1 in every 5 (20.9%) conscripts, to the cavalry. From February through December 1864, some 1,585 conscripts were assigned to cavalry units, once again one-fifth (20.5%) of all conscripted men who went into the field.

Only three cavalrymen in the sample for this study were definitely conscripted. Private Hersey B. Parker of the 16th Battalion, North Carolina Cavalry, came from a planter family. Parker was a student when the war broke out.

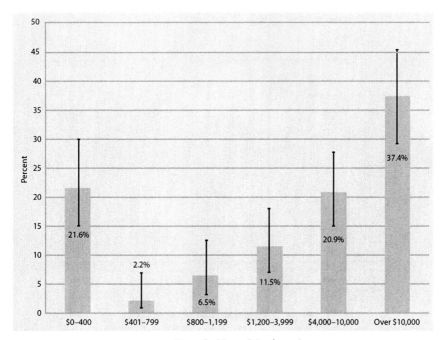

FIGURE 3.5. Household wealth of cavalrymen

Later, he transferred to the 54th North Carolina Infantry and was captured near the end of the war. Private Flavious J. Wrenn of the 13th Virginia Cavalry grew up in a poor farming household. He was conscripted in 1863 and served for the rest of the war, surrendering at Appomattox Court House. The final conscript in the sample, John R. Thompson, enlisted in the 1st Virginia Cavalry in 1862. He was released as underage in 1863 and then conscripted the next year and assigned to the 12th Virginia Cavalry.[9]

Despite poor record keeping and the loss of many documents, we know that almost 1 in every 11 (8.7%) cavalrymen was absent without leave. Because these men were mounted, they could more readily depart temporarily, return home, then make their way back to the army to face punishment. Private Opie N. Watson, the 17-year-old who enlisted in the 8th Virginia Cavalry, left his comrades for three months before returning to the regiment. Due to spotty records, his punishment is unknown.[10]

Desertion proved a much more serious problem for the cavalry. According to the sample, close to 1 in every 5 (18.7%) horsemen deserted at least once during his term of service, a staggering statistic. Worse still, not one of them returned to his unit. Yet despite their affluence, cavalrymen from richer backgrounds tended to stay with the army. The median wealth of mounted

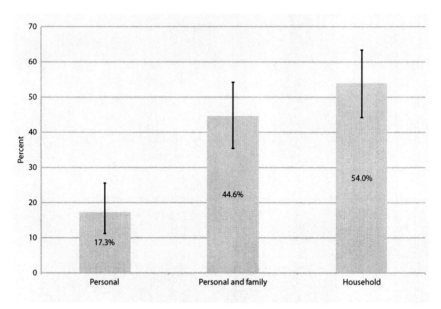

FIGURE 3.6. Slaveholding of cavalrymen

deserters at $1,468 was well above the army median. A fair proportion of the men worth between $1,200 and $10,000 deserted. But mounted men who remained with the army had accumulated nearly triple that wealth, or their families with whom they resided had, at $4,300. More than half (51.3%) of all nondeserters or their families owned slaves, and more than 3 of every 5 (61.1%) lived in slaveholding households. By contrast, less than 1 in every 6 (15.4%) cavalrymen or their families owned slaves, and fewer than 1 in 4 (23.1%) lived in the homes of slaveholders. By and large, wars hurt poor people more than richer folks, because those with money had a greater margin of comfort and could sustain greater losses without lacking necessities.[11]

Figure 3.7 compares the wealth of deserters and nondeserters among cavalrymen.

Five of every 13 (38.5%) cavalry deserters in the sample were married, but all of those married soldiers plus a single deserter had children at home. Even more striking, 1 in every 4 (24.7%) nondeserters was a father, but nearly 4 in 9 (42.3%) deserters were as well. As in the infantry, deep concern for the well-being of their children at home appeared to be a powerful motivator in desertion from the cavalry. And although cavalry duty may not have been as physically taxing or as dangerous as service in the infantry or artillery, mounted men could more easily slip away and desert.

Standard jokes circulated throughout the army of infantry officers offer-

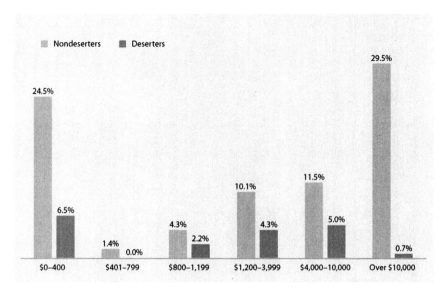

FIGURE 3.7. Desertion among cavalrymen by wealth

ing money for sighting a cavalryman killed in battle because it was so rare. Statistics tend to bear this out. One in every 21 (4.7%) mounted men in the sample was killed in action, and another 1 in 7 (14.7%) was wounded. The infantry, by contrast, was triple (2.9 times) that ratio in killed in action and more than double (2.1 times) that that ratio in wounded. Only in POWs did the cavalry approach the percentage of infantrymen (27.7%), with just less than 1 in 4 (24%) horsemen suffering that fate. Another 1 in 14 (7.3%) succumbed to disease, and 1 in 30 (3.3%) was discharged for disability. All together, more than 4 of every 9 (45.3%) cavalrymen were killed in action, wounded, taken prisoner, died of disease, or discharged for disability. By factoring out those who deserted for the remainder of the war, the cavalry statistic rose to 5 of every 9 (55.7%). Among infantrymen, 73.3% were killed, wounded, captured, died of disease, or discharged for disability, and when deserters were removed from the equation, the statistic rose to 79.4%.[12]

Figure 3.8 breaks down total losses within the cavalry.

Like infantrymen, wealthier cavalrymen tended to suffer the preponderance of combat fatalities and injuries. The median wealth of those cavalrymen and their families, if they lived with them, who were wounded at least once or were killed in action was $7,800. For those horsemen who were neither killed nor wounded, the median wealth was $2,358. Five of every 9 (55.2%) cavalrymen who suffered combat deaths or wounds owned slaves, or family members with whom they resided did; the combined personal and family slaveholding

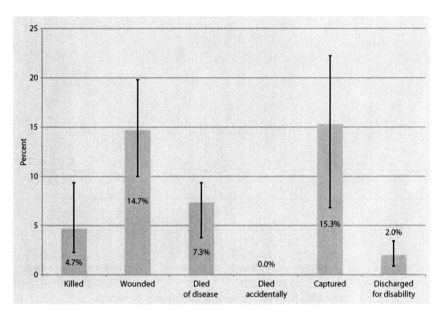

FIGURE 3.8. Losses among cavalrymen

for those who escaped battlefield injury or death was just less than 3 of every 7 (38.2%). In general, wealthier soldiers had more at stake in the war. They remained at their posts more consistently, incurred greater risks, and suffered more battlefield tragedies than their less well-to-do comrades.

Once again, horse soldiers who died of disease tended to be poorer than those who did not fall to illness. The combined median wealth for cavalrymen and their families if they yielded to disease was $1,100, while those who fought off illness had a combined personal and family wealth of $3,378.

Compared to the infantry, service in Lee's mounted branch proved far less lethal and much less demanding. Cavalrymen rode most of the time, had mobility to scavenge food and to seek relief from the humdrum of camp life, and did not shoulder the burdens of combat that infantrymen and artillerymen regularly did. But to dismiss their service as light duty ignores the huge sacrifices they endured. They largely ate the same rations as soldiers from the other branches of service, and as the war extended into the second, third, and fourth years, they worried more and more about feeding their animals.

In the early stages of the war, Lee's cavalrymen rode on powerful mounts and exhibited extraordinary skills in horsemanship, giving the Confederates a decided advantage. In time, however, the tide shifted to the Federals, who secured good-quality animals, fed them well, and improved their own riding skills. More importantly, Union cavalrymen switched from single-shot weapons to repeating rifles. Confederates armed with musketoons, even Enfields, were no match for the increased firepower of Yankee cavalrymen. The overwhelming strength of Union cavalry in the Shenandoah Valley during the fall of 1864 demonstrated this tremendous superiority.

The decline in the quality of mounts, the inferiority of weapons, and the prolonged hardships of war damaged the Confederate cavalry. More than 3 of every 5 horse soldiers (60.7%) who fell into Union hands during the war did so in the last two years.

Regardless, the Confederate cavalry continued to contribute vitally to the army. Major General Wade Hampton, who succeeded to the post of cavalry commander when J. E. B. Stuart was killed, launched a daring cattle raid in September 1864. The 2,468 heads of beef that were seized provided Lee's army with meat for the next month. More decisively, Hampton utilized mobility brilliantly in the Petersburg campaign, arriving at critical moments with sufficient firepower to slow the Union army and allow Confederate infantry and artillery to reach essential crossroads and positions. Thus, it was not just the cavalry's scouting and raids but its mobility and firepower in the face of Union infantry that achieved vital results.

CHAPTER FOUR

The Artillery

No branch of Lee's army underwent more organizational changes than the artillery. In the Battle of First Manassas, the Confederacy barely had two dozen field guns, which it parceled out among various brigades, severely limiting its effectiveness. Over the next year the army saw a substantial increase in the number of guns, but there were two major drawbacks. First, the way the Confederacy organized its artillery did not exploit its new batteries, and, second, the quality and caliber of guns did not match Federal artillery. Thus, not only were the Confederates outgunned, the dilution of artillery firepower by scattering guns throughout the army worsened the problem.

Under the slow, unsteady hand of clergyman-turned-chief-of-artillery William Nelson Pendleton, Lee's artillery implemented two series of changes, one in October 1862 and the other in mid-February 1863. In both instances, they were products of prodding by young, talented artillerymen. After heavy losses during the summer and fall of 1862, Pendleton ordered the consolidation of artillery batteries, culled the officer corps of incompetents, and reduced the required number of animals, thereby easing the burden on army logistics. Around the same time, Lee requested that the army produce far more Napoleon 12-pounders and eliminate other guns. He considered Napoleons the most serviceable on the wooded battlefields of Virginia.

Then, in mid-February 1863, again after consultation with various talented artillerymen, Pendleton made a far-reaching change. In the past, the Confederacy had assigned an artillery battery—four or six guns—to each brigade and kept the rest of the artillery in an army reserve. The artillery chief now directed the formation of battalions consisting of four batteries each, with each battalion assigned to a division. The battalion commanders would report to the corps chief of artillery and the division commander, and the corps chief would answer to Pendleton and the corps commander. In addition, each corps would have an artillery reserve consisting of two battalions. This reorganization improved unity and the concentration of firepower.

Although artillerymen had the same median birth year as soldiers in the

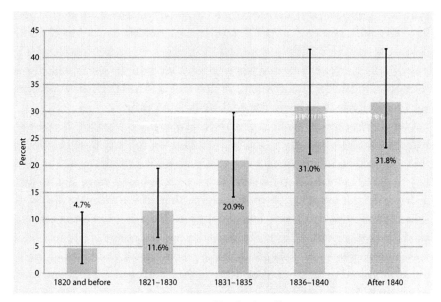

FIGURE 4.1. Year of birth of artillerymen

other two branches of service, they were on average the most youthful (1836.3)
—more than a year younger than cavalrymen (1835.2) and seven months
younger than infantrymen (1835.7). One in 6 (16.3%) artillerymen was born
before 1831, compared to more than 2 of 9 (22.6%) infantrymen and more than
1 in 4 (25.2%) mounted men. Artillery had the highest percentage (20.9%) of
soldiers born between 1831 and 1836, as well as the highest percentage of men
born after 1836 by a slight margin (0.8%) over infantry.

Figure 4.1 tracks the age of artillerymen by year of birth.

A majority of the sample (51.1%) of artillerymen were born in Virginia, followed by more than 1 in 9 (11.5%) from South Carolina and fewer than 1 in
12 (7.9%) from Georgia. Surprisingly, greater than 1 in every 9 (11.5%) was
foreign-born. Pat McGlown, a 35-year-old Irish native, enlisted in the Macon
Light Artillery in May 1862. A single laborer worth $40 in 1860, McGlown
lived in Atlanta before the war. Foreigners by birth like McGlown combined
with Northerners (2.9%) to make up 1 in every 7 (14.4%) soldiers in the artillery.

Virginia, South Carolina, Georgia, and Louisiana supplied most of the artillerymen for Lee's army, and it is not surprising that the soldiers resided in
those states when the fighting began. More than 5 of every 9 (57.1%) artillerymen lived in Virginia, with almost 2 in 13 (15.0%) coming from South Carolina
and close to 1 in 8 (12.2%) from Georgia. Slightly more than 1 in 20 (5.4%)

resided in Louisiana, and just fewer than 1 in 20 (4.7%) came from North Carolina. All told, 1 of every 3 (33.3%) artillerymen resided in the Lower South before the war. Even with foreign- and Northern-born soldiers excluded, 1 in 5 artillerymen enlisted in a unit from a state other than the one in which they were born, much like infantrymen. Artillerymen also had the highest percentage (3.4%) of men who crossed state boundaries to enlist.

Compared to other branches of service, artillerymen were much more urbanized. Almost 1 in every 5 (19.4%) lived in a top 100 city in population, 4 times more than infantrymen and 5 times more than cavalrymen. The artillery required individuals to function as a precise team, to move and unhitch or hitch the guns quickly. Once in position, they had to estimate distances, select ammunition, load, aim, fire, and then swab the piece to extinguish any sparks before reloading. They acted as a team and frequently performed these tasks under enemy fire. One glitch in the process and a gun failed to fire or did so very slowly, placing everyone's life in the battery and many infantrymen in jeopardy. People from urban areas were much more comfortable working in close proximity with others. In cities, they grew accustomed to seeing and interacting with people all the time. Individualism naturally broke down a bit in urban areas, which made working as a group, which the artillery necessitated, more ingrained. Cities were also home to more prewar militia batteries. With a considerable number of men who knew how to service field artillery, it was natural for these organizations to form the cadre for multiple wartime batteries. The high urbanization rate—in the seceding states, only 5% lived in the top 100 cities—would also explain the high numbers of foreigners by birth in the artillery. Individuals like Private McGlown had migrated to cities, where employment for the unskilled was readily available. Quite a number of immigrants, such as William Forner of the 2nd Maryland Artillery, possessed skills as well. It was much easier for Forner to ply his trade as a butcher in an urban area like Baltimore than in a farming community.

With such a high proportion of urbanites, it is not surprising that the prewar occupations of artillerymen varied significantly from their comrades-in-arms. Barely more than 3 in 10 (30.6%) men in the artillery worked on farms; the infantry (55.4%) and the cavalry (54.5%) nearly doubled that percentage. The artillery had more prewar professionals, skilled, unskilled, and white-collar or clerical jobs than the other branches. For every 3 farmers in the artillery there were 2 (20.7%) skilled workers, a stunning statistic in light of the overwhelming rural influence in the seceding states. Skilled workers were more than twice as prevalent in the artillery as in the other branches (8.2% for infantry and 9.7% for cavalry). The percentage of white-collar and clerical posi-

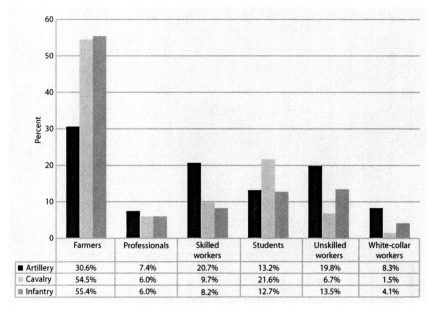

	Farmers	Professionals	Skilled workers	Students	Unskilled workers	White-collar workers
■ Artillery	30.6%	7.4%	20.7%	13.2%	19.8%	8.3%
Cavalry	54.5%	6.0%	9.7%	21.6%	6.7%	1.5%
Infantry	55.4%	6.0%	8.2%	12.7%	13.5%	4.1%

FIGURE 4.2. Occupation by branch

tions—jobs that were much more common in cities and towns than in the countryside—in the artillery (8.3%) was double that of the infantry (4.1%) and almost 6 times greater than that of the cavalry (1.5%). Unskilled workers, too, were significantly more common in the artillery (19.8%) than in the infantry (13.5%) and the cavalry (6.7%). The artillery attracted fewer students (13.2%) than the cavalry (21.6%) and slightly more (12.7%) than the infantry.[1]

Figure 4.2 surveys prewar occupations by branch of service.

The high percentage of clerical positions in the artillery affected the statistics on marital status. Young, single males often held these clerical positions, which were a kind of apprenticeship for professional jobs. In the sample, the median birth year for artillerymen who held clerical positions before the war was 1840, making them 21 years old during the first year of the conflict. Ninety percent of them were not married. Thus, more than 3 of every 4 artillerymen (75.8%) were single. By comparison, in the cavalry, a bit more than 2 of every 3 (67.4%) soldiers were unwed and in the infantry, slightly more than 3 of 5 (61.2%).[2]

Married artillerymen had significantly fewer children than rifle toters or horsemen. While fathers in both the infantry and the cavalry averaged approximately 2.7 (infantry at 2.72 and cavalry at 2.58) children, parents in the artillery had on average 2.13 children. One in three married artillerymen had no

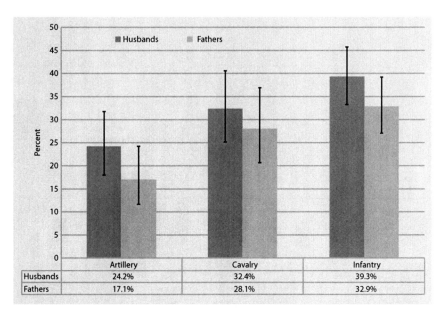

	Artillery	Cavalry	Infantry
Husbands	24.2%	32.4%	39.3%
Fathers	17.1%	28.1%	32.9%

FIGURE 4.3. Husbands and fathers by branch

children in 1860. Private William H. Woody of Kirkpatrick's Artillery held the artillery sample's crown of virility (or fertility) at 9.[3]

Figure 4.3 compares the percentage of husbands and fathers in the three branches of service.

Despite their urban influence, artillerymen lived in counties with denser slave populations than either infantrymen or cavalrymen and many more slaves than in the states from which Lee's army drew its troops as a whole. For every 1,000 whites in counties in which artillerymen resided, there were 873 blacks. In the cavalry that ratio was 1,000 whites to 782 blacks, and in the infantry it was 1,000 to 744. The ratio for states tapped by the Confederate government for military units in the Army of Northern Virginia was 1,000 to 560.[4]

Among the three branches, artillerymen were by far the poorest. Seventeen of every 20 (85.3%) artillerymen owned less that $800 in property, well below cavalrymen (55.4%) and infantrymen (56.2%). The median wealth of all artillerymen and their families, if they lived with them, was $800, the minimal figure for the middle class. Fairly typical was William D. Kennon, a prewar clerk in Richmond. Kennon possessed very little personal wealth and resided in a boardinghouse. By contrast, infantrymen totaled 50% more at $1,225 and cavalrymen more than tripled that wealth at $2,800. Four of every 9 (44.2%) artillerymen and their families had a total wealth of $400 or less.

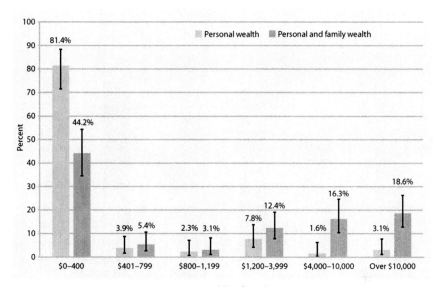

FIGURE 4.4. Wealth of artillerymen

Figure 4.4 traces the personal and combined personal and family wealth of artillerymen.

Yet the artillery was also an organization of extremes. It had not only the highest percentage (49.6%) of soldiers in the lower class and the smallest percentage (15.5%) in the middle class, but also a fairly substantial percentage (34.9%) in the upper class. More than 1 in every 3 (34.9%) artillerymen were worth more than $4,000, a difference that was statistically insignificant from infantrymen (33.9%) but well below cavalrymen (46.8%). Greater than 1 in 6 (18.6%) possessed over $10,000 in real and personal property, well below cavalrymen (30.2%) but little different from foot soldiers (19.3%).[5]

Figure 4.5 tracks economic class among the three branches of service.

Those same distinctions appeared in slave ownership among artillerymen. Slightly more than 1 in 11 (9.3%) personally owned slaves, the lowest percentage of all three branches of service. With family ownership, if soldiers lived with family, factored into the equation, however, the figure leaped to just below 2 in 5 (38%), reflecting the large number of younger soldiers who still resided at home. But the greatest difference among artillerymen was the number of men who lived in nonfamily slaveholding households. More than 1 in every 7 artillerymen were similar to Private Robert C. Thompson in the Surry Light Artillery. Before the war, Thompson was a teamster for a merchant named Nicholas Savage. Although he owned virtually nothing, Savage claimed a total wealth of $9,000, including five slaves, and Thompson lived

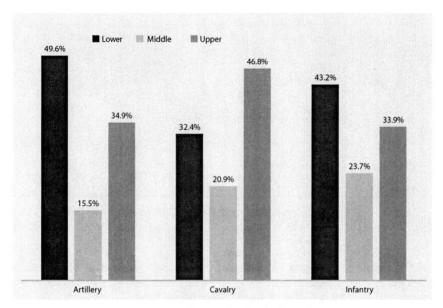

FIGURE 4.5. Economic class by branch

in the Savage home. Even though 38.0% of all artillerymen or their immediate families with whom they lived owned slaves, 53.5% resided in slaveholding households. The median household worth soared to $3,300, compared to $800 for the median artilleryman and his family, and more than 2 of every 5 lived in households worth more than $5,000. Slightly more than 1 in 18 (5.5%) artillerymen, or their families with whom they lived, qualified for planter status (20 slaves or more). One in every 13 (7.8%), however, resided within a planter household.[6]

Figure 4.6 highlights slave ownership among the three branches.

More than half (52.0%) of all artillerymen in the sample enlisted in 1861, and nearly a third (31.3%) more joined the army in 1862. By the late stages of the war, veterans with extensive combat experience dominated the artillery ranks. Only 1 in 14 entered military service in 1863 and another 1 in 10 the following year.[7]

Figure 4.7 compares the year of enlistment among the three branches.

Within the sample, fewer than 1 in 12 (8.0%) were officers, with Captains Wiley Coleman of Neblett's Heavy Artillery Battery, James W. Dickerson of the Lynchburg Artillery, and William B. Jones of the Peninsula Artillery holding the highest rank. More than 3 of every 4 artillerymen (76.7%) maintained the rank of private throughout the war. Better than 1 in every 8 (13.4%) was a noncommissioned officer in his highest rank.[8]

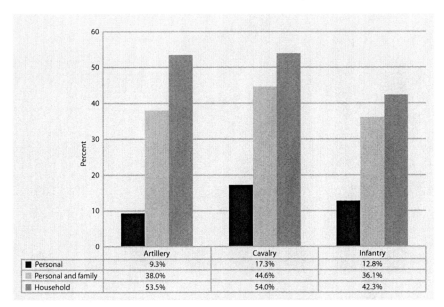

	Artillery	Cavalry	Infantry
■ Personal	9.3%	17.3%	12.8%
Personal and family	38.0%	44.6%	36.1%
Household	53.5%	54.0%	42.3%

FIGURE 4.6. Slaveholding by branch

From December 1862 through December 1864, 1,387 conscripts who passed through Camp Lee were assigned to the artillery, comprising 10.9% of all soldiers sent to combat units. Records indicate only four (2.7%) artillerymen in the sample who were conscripted into service. Irishman Philip Brady enlisted in April 1861 in the 1st Louisiana Infantry and served until July 1862, when he was released from service. The Confederate government conscripted him in 1864 and assigned him to the 2nd Richmond Howitzers, where he served out the war. John David Pugh, a daguerreotypist in Bibb County, Georgia, was conscripted in 1862 and assigned to the Macon Light Artillery. Pugh was taken prisoner around Petersburg in the last days of the war. Thirty-five-year-old Benjamin W. Vaughn suffered the fate of conscription in 1863 and went to the 1st North Carolina Artillery. He was captured in September 1863, took the oath of allegiance to the Union, and later served in the Federal army. A well-to-do farmer who leased one slave, William J. Hope was conscripted in 1862 and served in the Lynchburg Artillery until he was discharged for chronic diarrhea in 1864.[9]

Despite coming predominantly from Virginia, only 1 in 14 (7.3%) artillerymen went absent without leave, according to military service records. This was the lowest AWOL percentage per branch of service, with both infantry and cavalry tabulating more than 1 in 12 (8.7% each). The average length of absence was 2.5 months, and the median absence 1.0. Cavalrymen averaged an

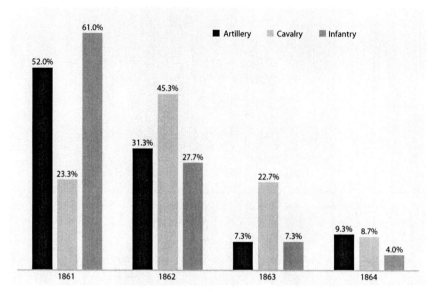

FIGURE 4.7. Year of enlistment by branch

absence of 2.1 months, but the median was 3.0 months; infantrymen on average stayed away from the army the longest at 3.6 months and had a median absence of 3.0 months as well.[10]

Like men who were AWOL, artillerymen were far less likely to desert the service than soldiers in the other branches. Less than 1 in 8 (11.9%) artillerymen deserted Lee's army. By comparison, infantrymen were 29.0% more likely to desert than artillerymen, and horsemen were 57.0% more likely to do so.[11]

Armywide, proximity to home played a powerful role in desertion. Except in instances when they deserted to the Union late in the war, soldiers seldom abandoned the army unless they had a reasonable chance of making it home. Yet more than 5 of every 9 (57.1%) artillerymen were residing in Virginia when they joined the army, and another 2 of 9 (22.4%) lived in North Carolina, South Carolina, or Maryland. By contrast, cavalrymen fled from the ranks in the highest percentage, and more than 3 in every 5 came from Virginia and another one-third (32.3%) lived in South Carolina, North Carolina, or Maryland. Cohesion most likely acted as a deterrent to desertion. More than any other branch of the service, artillerymen functioned as a team. To desert meant not only abandoning the Confederate army but also leaving comrades without a valuable component in the gunnery system. Each gun team depended on every member to perform a vital function. The desertion of one man hurt all the others who serviced that gun. This kind of powerful support network discouraged artillerymen from abandoning their post.

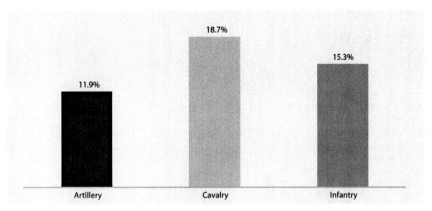

FIGURE 4.8. Desertion by branch

Figure 4.8 indicates the rate of desertion among the three branches of Lee's army.

Those artillerymen who did desert were the poorest soldiers among the three branches of service. The combined median personal and family wealth for artillery deserters was $25. For infantrymen that combined median wealth was $533, and for cavalry it leaped to $1,468. As the poorest servicemen, artillerymen who refused to desert had a combined median personal and family wealth of $1,150, solidly in the middle bracket and 46 times greater than their comrades who did desert. Infantry nondeserters held property worth $200 more than their comrades in the artillery, and cavalrymen who stayed with the army had a whopping $4,300 in median wealth. Those artillerymen who did desert the Confederate flag were extremely poor. Pressing financial needs and a weaker attachment to their community and the Rebel cause most likely influenced their decision to flee the army.

Only 15.4% of all deserters or their families with whom they resided owned slaves, compared to 50.8% for nondeserters. And while almost 5 in every 9 (54.3%) nondeserters lived in slaveholding households, nearly half (46.2%) of all deserters, surprisingly, did so as well. Evidently, the clear distinction between owning slaves and working for and living with a slaveholding employer also influenced the decision to desert.

Both children at home and marital status affected desertion rates in this branch. Among all artillerymen, 1 in 6 (17.1%) had children at home. Three of 8 deserters (38.5%) left children behind, while 1 in 7 (14.7%) nondeserters claimed offspring. Just below 1 in 4 (24.2%) artillerymen were married, and 7 of 10 (71.4%) married men had children. Only 1 in 5 (20.9%) nondeserters left behind spouses, compared to nearly 5 of 9 (53.8%) deserters in the long arm.

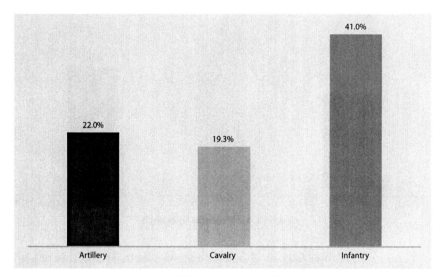

FIGURE 4.9. Killed and wounded by branch

After infantrymen, soldiers in the artillery suffered the most combat casualties. One in every 19 (5.3%) artillerymen in the sample was killed in battle, and another 1 in 6 (16.7%) was wounded. Three artillerymen in the sample were wounded twice and three who were killed in action had been wounded previously.

Figure 4.9 contrasts the percentage of killed or wounded by branch.

In addition to those artillerymen who were killed or wounded, 1 in 8 (12.0%) who were neither killed nor wounded were taken prisoner, bringing the total percentage of artillerymen who were casualties to slightly more than 1 in 3 (34.0%). Greater than 1 in 17 (6.0%) died of disease or injury, and another 1 in 14 (7.3%) were discharged for disability. Thus, nearly half of all artillerymen (47.3%) endured one of the following fates: killed, wounded, captured, died of disease, or discharged for disability.

Figure 4.10 breaks down the losses among artillerymen.

Although these casualties did not compare with those suffered by infantrymen, more artillerymen were killed or wounded in battle than horsemen. Yet the cavalry's numbers exceeded the artillery in prisoners of war and death from disease.[12]

Figure 4.11 compares total losses among the three branches.

Like infantrymen and cavalrymen, artillerymen who were killed or wounded tended to be wealthier than their comrades who endured no battlefield injuries, but, among the three branches, that distinction was weakest for artillery-

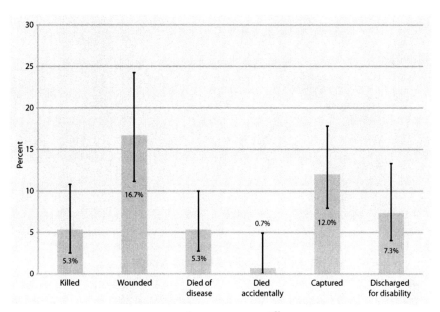

FIGURE 4.10. Losses among artillerymen

men. The combined median personal and family wealth for artillerymen who were wounded or killed in battle was $800, while those who suffered no combat injuries or deaths had a combined median wealth of $757. Killed and wounded artillerymen were much more likely to own slaves or live with family members who did. Nearly half (48.3%) of the battlefield victims or their families owned slaves, compared to a bit more than 1 in every 3 (35.0%) of the noncasualties.

Once again, artillerymen who died of disease tended to be poor, but the statistics indicated a wide variation. The combined median personal and family wealth of artillerymen who perished from illness was only $100, although one man came from a family worth $23,490 and another with assets of $6,665. The average combined wealth of disease victims was $4,700.

Compared to other branches, the artillery had less mobility in rank. Certainly, soldiers in the artillery suffered nearly 50% killed, wounded, captured, died of disease, or discharged for disability. Its low desertion rate, based primarily on a high degree of cohesion, ensured that its total losses from the ranks were far below those of the infantry and fewer than those of the cavalry, which had a desertion rate of nearly 1 in every 5 horsemen (18.7%). More than 3 of every 4 artillerymen, as previously noted, retained the rank of private throughout their entire length of service.

In the late stages of the war, the artillery suffered disastrously. Food short-

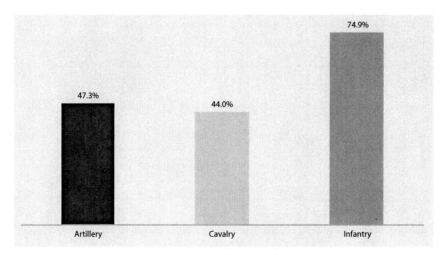

FIGURE 4.11. Total losses by branch

ages plagued the long arm, with soldiers receiving meager rations amounting to 900–1,200 calories per day and the animals living on an even more inadequate diet. Almost 4 of every 5 artillerymen (78.3%) who fell into Union hands during the war did so in 1864 or 1865. Prolonged hardships, heavy fighting, and declining morale influenced those numbers.

Although artillerymen in Lee's army exhibited extraordinary courage and achieved striking results on several battlefields, over the course of the war Union gunners largely outclassed them. The Federals had more and better guns, superior ammunition, and bigger and stronger animals. And while Confederate artillerymen suffered nowhere near the hardships and losses of infantrymen, they fought at a time of change in warfare, when the range of rifled muskets and the accuracy and firepower of enemy artillery placed them at much greater jeopardy than in the previous decades. Life for soldiers of the long arm may have lacked the grueling and savage experiences of infantrymen, but it was more demanding and risky than cavalry service.

CHAPTER FIVE

Northern- and Foreign-Born Soldiers

Twenty-six-year-old Peter Vanname was a sailor by trade when Virginia seceded. Born in New York, he drifted southward with his family and settled in York County, Virginia. Although neither he nor his immediate kin owned slaves, the move to Virginia had been financially lucrative. Vanname boasted $2,000 in wealth and his family claimed an additional $7,000. His loyalty resting with his adopted state, he enlisted in the 2nd Company of the Richmond Howitzers in 1861. Vanname fought the entire war as a private and was paroled in 1865. He lived his remaining years in Virginia, where he died in 1901.

The tall, dark-complexioned Peter E. Gillman also served for his adopted state as well as for his adopted country. The 26-year-old had migrated from Ireland and settled in Holly Springs, Mississippi, as a laborer. Military service looked attractive to the single Irishman, who had accumulated no appreciable wealth, and he, too, enlisted in 1861 as a private in Bradford's Confederate Guards, an artillery battery. Gillman served creditably, rising in rank to corporal. He overcame a bout of dyspepsia, only to be taken prisoner in the final stages of the war.

Although Northern-born or foreign-born soldiers did not dominate the Confederate ranks, taken together they did comprise a significant portion of the Army of Northern Virginia.[1] Almost 1 in 28 (3.4%) was born in a foreign country, and another 1 in 25 (4.0%) originally came from a Northern state. Northern- and foreign-born Confederates together made up 1 in every 13 soldiers (7.4%) in Lee's army. By contrast, 3 of every 4 soldiers in his army (75.1%) were born in Virginia, North Carolina, South Carolina, or Georgia, and 5 of every 9 (54.7%) Southern-born soldiers in the army lived in the Upper South in 1860. A majority (54.8%) of the foreign-born men resided in the Deep South before the war. Northern-born troops, by contrast, migrated overwhelmingly (69.8%) to the Upper South.

The backgrounds of these adopted Confederates differed dramatically from those of their native-born comrades. When the war broke out, Northerners could return home, and those of military age who elected to remain in the

Confederacy would have to serve in military units. Foreigners by birth who were not citizens had no such military obligation, yet they volunteered in considerable numbers for their new homeland. Half of them had emigrated from Ireland, and more than another quarter were from the various German states. Northerners in Lee's army came heavily from the border states. Nearly 4 in 9 (43.3%) were born in states that abutted the Confederacy, and 1 in 3 alone were native Marylanders. An additional 2 of every 5 hailed from either New York (26.7%) or Pennsylvania (13.3%).

Northern- and foreign-born soldiers tended to be significantly older than their Southern-born comrades. While the median year of birth for Southern-born soldiers was 1838, those from the North had a median birth year of 1832 and those from foreign lands had a median birth year of 1836. The average age varied much less, with Southern-born Confederates nearly two years younger (1835.7) than Northern-born (1833.3) men and almost one and a half years younger than foreign-born (1834.3) troops.

Figure 5.1 examines year of birth among foreign-born, Northern-born, and Southern-born soldiers in Lee's army.[2]

Despite their more advanced years, both Northern-born and foreign-born men were less likely to be married and a smaller percentage of them had children. Less than 2 in 9 (21.2%) Northern-born men were married. The proportion of foreign-born troops who were married was significantly higher than that of their Northern-born peers at almost 1 in 3 (31.8%), but it was still below the rate of the Southern-born soldiers in Lee's army (38.4%). Five of every 6 (83.3%) foreigners married a fellow countrywoman, while 3 of every 5 (60.0%) Northerners wedded a Southern woman. Thus, Northerners seemed to integrate into Southern society more easily than foreigners.

Southern-born soldiers were also much more likely to have children than their Northern- or foreign-born comrades. Nearly 1 in every 3 (31.7%) soldiers who was born in a future Confederate state had children, whereas 1 in every 7 (21.2%) Northerners by birth and less than 1 in every 3 (29.4%) immigrants claimed children at home.

Both the foreign- and Northern-born gravitated toward urban areas, especially compared to native Southerners. At the time of the war half of all immigrants (49.8%) in Lee's army resided in the 100 largest cities, and more than 1 in 6 (17.8%) Northerners by birth did so as well. Foreigners were 13.5 times more likely to live in urban areas than those soldiers who were born in the South (3.7%), while Northerners by birth were 4.5 times as likely to reside in cities.

With such a powerful urban influence and given the cost of purchasing land,

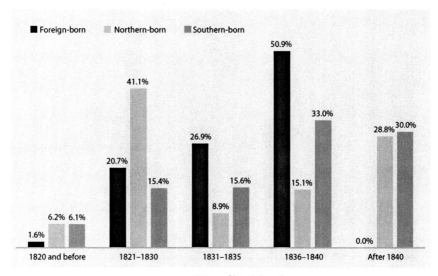

FIGURE 5.1. Year of birth by place

equipment, and seed for agriculture, it is not surprising that few foreigners embraced farming. Only 1 in 38 (2.6%) tilled the soil. More typical urban pursuits dominated the prewar occupations of foreigners by birth. One-third (33.9%) were skilled workers and nearly 5 of every 9 (53.9%), the largest block, held unskilled positions. One in 10 (9.6%) maintained professional or entre-preneurial jobs, a high ratio and again one that reflected the sizable propor-tion of urbanites among the immigrant population. None in the sample was a student or held a white-collar or clerical position.

By contrast, Northern-born soldiers in Lee's army gravitated toward skilled jobs, farming, and white-collar or clerical positions. Skilled workers com-prised 2 in 9 (21.2%). Farmers made up just less than 1 in 3 (30.8%), and slightly fewer than 1 in 6 (15.1%) held white-collar or clerical positions. Only 1 in 6 (17.1%) Northerners by birth were unskilled laborers, and 1 in 9 (11.7%) still pursued some form of schooling.

Among Southern-born soldiers, the rural influence predominated. More than 5 of every 9 (56.5%) were farmers, while less than 1 in 12 (7.8%) were skilled workers—jobs that were concentrated in towns and cities. More Southern-born troops were students (14.4%) than unskilled laborers (11.6%), and fewer than 1 in 25 (3.8%) held white collar or clerical posts. About 1 in 17 (6.1%) were professionals.[3]

Figure 5.2 surveys the prewar occupations of the three birth groups.

In a comparison by personal wealth, Northern-born soldiers were signifi-

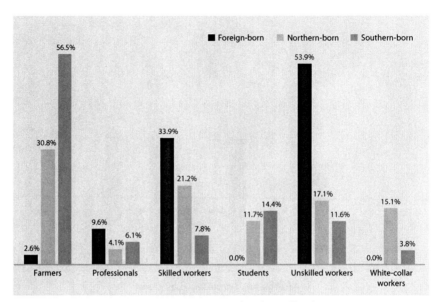

FIGURE 5.2. Occupation by place of birth

cantly poorer, with more than 4 of every 5 (81.5%) worth under $400 and 9 of 10 (89.1%) in the lower class. Foreign- and Southern-born Confederates had essentially the same percentage of men with personal wealth below $400: 73.74% versus 73.79%. So many Southern-born troops were young and still lived with their parents that they skewed personal wealth statistics, particularly in comparison with immigrants. Nearly 1 in 9 (10.7%) Southern-born soldiers had a personal wealth of $4,000 or more, and Northern-born troops were close behind at 1 in 10 (9.6%). No foreign-born soldier in the sample fit into the upper class—that is, those with total assets of $4,000 or more.[4]

Figure 5.3 depicts the personal wealth of the three birth groups.

Combined personal and family wealth reflected the superior jobs and connections of native Southerners over the foreign- and Northern-born. The median property value of the soldiers in Lee's army who grew up abroad and emigrated to the Confederacy was only $100. The wealthiest in the sample, German immigrant Jacob Harris of the 8th Georgia Infantry, had personal assets of $3,500. Northern-born rebels quintupled the combined wealth of immigrants at $500, yet they too were poor. Southern-born Confederates, however, were quite comfortable financially. The combined median personal and family wealth was $1,500, solidly in the middle class.

Figure 5.4 surveys the combined personal and family wealth of the three birth groups.

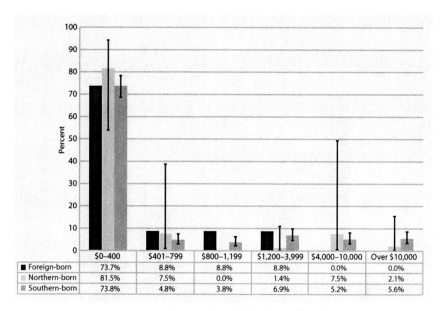

	$0–400	$401–799	$800–1,199	$1,200–3,999	$4,000–10,000	Over $10,000
■ Foreign-born	73.7%	8.8%	8.8%	8.8%	0.0%	0.0%
Northern-born	81.5%	7.5%	0.0%	1.4%	7.5%	2.1%
▤ Southern-born	73.8%	4.8%	3.8%	6.9%	5.2%	5.6%

FIGURE 5.3. Personal wealth by place of birth*
*The size of the foreign-born sample was too small for the calculation of confidence levels.
Because the size of Northern-born soldiers is so small, the confidence intervals are large.

Total household wealth indicated similar discrepancies by place of birth. Foreign-born troops had a total household wealth of only $450, indicating that few wealthy Confederates allowed immigrants to live in their homes. In fact, only 1 in every 9 (11.1%) resided in households with a combined value of $4,000 or more. By contrast, more than 3 of every 5 (62.3%) Northern-born Confederates lived in upper-class households. The median household wealth for Northerners by birth was $5,000, considerably more than Southern-born Confederates at $2,500.

The same proved true of slaveholding. No immigrants or their resident family members owned slaves, and 1 in 8 (12.7%) lived in slaveholding households. Among Northern-born soldiers in the sample, none owned slaves as well, but 1 in 10 (9.6%) of them or their families did. Slightly less than 1 in 3 (32.2%) lived in households with slaves. Among Southern-born soldiers, the picture was vastly different. One in 7 (14.1%) personally owned slaves; 2 of every 5 (39.8%) owned slaves, or their families with whom they resided did, and close to half (46.2%) lived in slaveholding households. Newcomers clearly struggled to make an economic and social mark in the seceding states, while those from established Southern families succeeded much more easily.[5]

Figure 5.5 tracks slave ownership among the three birth groups.

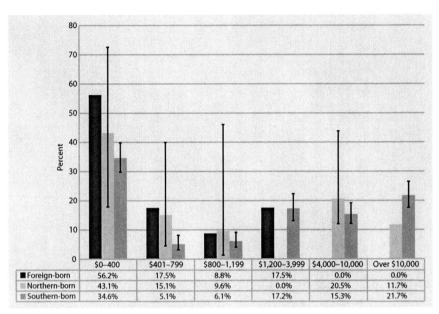

	$0–400	$401–799	$800–1,199	$1,200–3,999	$4,000–10,000	Over $10,000
■ Foreign-born	56.2%	17.5%	8.8%	17.5%	0.0%	0.0%
Northern-born	43.1%	15.1%	9.6%	0.0%	20.5%	11.7%
Southern-born	34.6%	5.1%	6.1%	17.2%	15.3%	21.7%

FIGURE 5.4. Personal and family wealth by place of birth

When states trumpeted a call to arms, adopted Confederates rushed to the forefront. Two of every 3 (66.4%) Northern-born soldiers enlisted in 1861, and another 1 in 7 (13.7%) entered the service the following year. Thus, 4 of 5 (80.1%) joined in the first two years and the remainder in 1863. Among the foreign-born, 4 of every 5 (81.0%) volunteered in 1861 and another 1 in 5 (19.0%) joined the army the very next year. By comparison, 5 of every 9 (56.5%) Southern-born soldiers enlisted in 1861 and 3 in 10 (30.5%) entered military service in 1862. Almost 8 of every 9 (87.0%) Southern-born men joined during the first two years. In an effort to demonstrate their loyalty to the Confederate states, Northern- and foreign-born males may have rushed to arms. With few financial assets, soldiering also may have been an appealing prospect. Pay even as a private would have been competitive and more reliable than their civilian wages, and few in 1861 believed the war would last all that long. Military service would also enable them to rub shoulders with wealthier folks, who might offer preferential consideration to their families during wartime and to old army buddies when it came to postwar business and hiring.

Figure 5.6 compares year of enlistment among the three birth groups.

Opportunities to gain a higher rank in Lee's army were few for anyone. Only 1 in 14 Southern-born soldiers acquired commissions as officers. Foreign-born officers were rare, but native Northerners, who already possessed English-language skills, fared better. The only foreign-born officer in the sample was

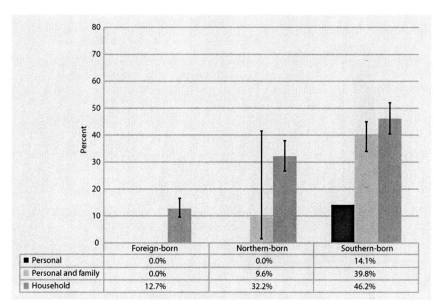

	Foreign-born	Northern-born	Southern-born
■ Personal	0.0%	0.0%	14.1%
▨ Personal and family	0.0%	9.6%	39.8%
▤ Household	12.7%	32.2%	46.2%

FIGURE 5.5. Slaveholding by place of birth

Daniel Girand Wright. Wright came from a well-connected Baltimore family but happened to be born in Brazil. When the war began, the 20-year-old Wright was studying law. He held the rank of first lieutenant in the 1st Maryland Infantry and later worked as a staff officer. Wright survived the war and eventually became a distinguished jurist. Three Northerners by birth earned commissions, but only one originally hailed from a free state. Twenty-two-year-old John F. Groshen of Frederick, Maryland, rose from corporal to captain in the 1st Maryland Infantry. Like Groshen, Elwood M. Bean was a Marylander. He emigrated to Texas and was eventually elected second lieutenant in the 5th Texas. Bean suffered wounds at Gettysburg and Petersburg, endured ten months in Union prison camps, and was discharged for permanent disabilities. Only one man in the sample who was born in a nonslaveholding state, James E. Clute, held an officer's commission. A native New Yorker, Clute moved to Texas and became second lieutenant in the 5th Texas Infantry before he was killed in action assaulting the Union defenses at Gaines's Mill in June 1862.

For Southern-born soldiers, the conscription rate was 3%, a vast undercount due to poor record keeping. All adopted Confederates in the sample, whether Northern- or foreign-born, enlisted except one, and his case was unusual. Irish-born U.S. citizen Philip Brady of New Orleans enlisted in the 1st Louisiana Infantry in 1861 and served a year. Brady then left the service

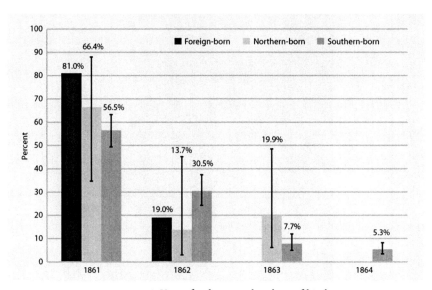

FIGURE 5.6. Year of enlistment by place of birth

and evidently worked in Richmond until he was conscripted in July 1864 and assigned to the 2nd Richmond Howitzers.

Even though the numbers were small, more than 2 of 9 (23.0%) immigrant soldiers went absent without authorization. By comparison, only one Northerner by birth, 33-year-old private W. L. Dewyer, a native Marylander, went AWOL. Dewyer later deserted for the rest of the war. Fewer than 1 in 12 (8.2%) Southern-born troops left their unit without permission.

Despite their initial motivations to serve in the Confederate army, hardships and sacrifices took their toll on both immigrants and Northern-born soldiers. Over time, the burdens of war weakened their commitment to the rebellion, driving many to abandon the flag or forcing others to leave the army to look after loved ones. More than 1 of every 4 (26.3%) foreigners and 1 of every 7 (15.1%) Northerners by birth deserted during the war, compared to less than 1 in every 7 (14.0%) native Southerners. Among the immigrant deserters in the sample, the wealthiest was John Mulqueen, a married father and private in the 3rd Battalion Louisiana Infantry from New Orleans. Mulqueen's total property was valued at $100. He was the only married deserter among foreign-born troops.

The assets of Northern-born deserters in the sample diverged considerably. Conrad Remly, a Pennsylvanian by birth, boasted a family wealth of $7,000, and a young Marylander named John L. Slingluff, a prewar student, lived with his mother, who enjoyed a net worth of $5,000. Others, however, possessed

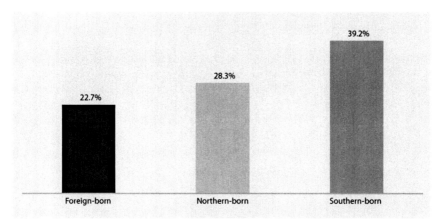

FIGURE 5.7. Killed and wounded by place of birth

no appreciable wealth. Three of 9 (42.9%) Northern-born deserters were married with children, but 2 of the 3 (66.7%) were over 40 years of age when they abandoned the ranks.

Both foreigners and Northerners by birth endured heavy losses, but not nearly as severe as Southern-born soldiers in Lee's army. Slightly less than 1 in 5 (19.1%) immigrants was killed in action and another 1 in 14 (7.1%) was wounded. An additional 1 in 5 who was never killed or wounded ended up dying of disease (0.4%) or was captured (19.5%), and 1 in 11 (9.1%) was discharged for disability. In total, slightly less than 5 of every 9 foreigners by birth suffered at least one of the following: killed in action, wounded, died of disease, imprisoned by the enemy, or discharged for disability.

Northerners by birth did lose severely, but not quite as badly as their comrades. One in 15 (7.5%) was killed in action and another 1 in 7 (13.7%) endured at least one combat wound. Nearly 1 in 7 (13.6%) died of disease and 1 in 10 (9.5%) was captured. This tabulated a loss in killed, wounded, death from disease, and prisoners of war at more than one-half (51.4%). No Northerners by birth in the sample were discharged for disabilities.

Figure 5.7 compares the percentage killed and wounded among the three birth groups.

Although these statistics were staggering, they paled in comparison to the losses of native Southerners in Lee's army. One in every 8 (12.3%) Southern-born soldiers in the sample was killed in action, and nearly 3 in 10 (27.6%) more were wounded. One in 8 (12.6%) who had never been wounded in the field died of disease or was killed accidentally, and 1 in 7 (14.6%) who never suffered a wound spent time in Union hands as a POW. An additional 1 in 20

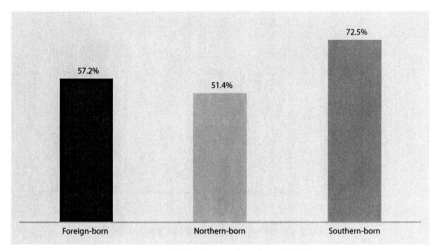

FIGURE 5.8. Total losses by place of birth

(4.8%) who avoided those misfortunes was discharged for disability. Among native Southerners who ever served in Lee's army, almost 3 of every 4 (72.5%) men died, suffered wounds, were captured, or were discharged for a disability, and many soldiers endured multiple afflictions.

Figure 5.8 compares total losses among the three birth groups.

By and large, foreigners and Northerners by birth were poor, and casualties reflected that lack of wealth. The richest foreigner who was killed or wounded, Canadian-born private Daniel McCaskill of the 26th North Carolina Infantry, came from a family worth only $450. McCaskill was severely wounded at Gettysburg and lingered for four months before he died. Private John Slingluff, whose widowed mother was worth $5,000, was the wealthiest Northerner by birth to suffer a wound. The 19-year-old Slingluff received his injury at the Second Battle of Winchester in June 1863.

Despite their modest wealth and limited roots, foreign- and Northern-born soldiers incurred huge losses and endured terrible hardships on behalf of their adopted nation. Evidence of when and how they joined the service and surviving wartime writings suggest they did so more out of commitment and pecuniary rewards than compunction. Dewees Ogden, who was born and raised in New York, had moved to Mississippi in the 1850s. When the secession crisis struck, he was visiting family in New York; slipping down to Virginia, he joined the Richmond Howitzers as a private. He fully understood that it was the "verdict of the 'whole family'" that he was an outcast for his "treason, desertion and ingratitude." Ogden refused to change his mind. He thought abolitionism was an abomination, and he was plenty tough enough to endure his family's barbs. Ogden was killed in action at Gettysburg.[6]

Lewis Leon was born in the German duchy of Mecklenburg in 1841, but as a young boy he immigrated with his family to New York. In 1858, he moved to Charlotte, North Carolina, where he quickly established his roots. On April 20, 1861, more than two weeks before his adopted state seceded from the Union, 19-year-old Leon enlisted in the 1st North Carolina Infantry. He fought in the Battle of Big Bethel, and when his six-month term expired, Leon reenlisted in the 53rd North Carolina Infantry. During the war, he sustained a minor wound at Gettysburg and was taken prisoner at the Battle of the Wilderness in May 1864. He spent the rest of the war in Point Lookout and Elmira Prison camps until he received a parole in June 1865. A clerk before the war and a member of the Jewish faith, Leon returned to Charlotte, where he raised a family and accumulated substantial wealth. His commitment to Southern independence was so strong that in his early seventies, he wrote: "I still say our Cause was just, nor do I regret one thing that I have done to cripple the North."[7]

Most Northern- and foreign-born troops, whether motivated by money or by a desire to demonstrate their commitment to the Confederacy, embraced arms with vigor. As the war dragged on, however, their commitment was more likely to waver. Their pain was not proportionate to that of Southern-born soldiers, who were fighting for their way of life and their loved ones, and they tended to abandon the army at significantly higher rates. Yet there were enough stalwart Confederates born abroad or in the North who fought, suffered, and died valiantly to ensure that the disproportionate casualties endured by their Southern-born comrades never triggered a powerful reaction toward them during or after the war.

CHAPTER SIX

Upper and Lower South

Over the course of the war, Lee's army became a symbol of the Rebel independence movement in the eyes of Confederates and Unionists alike. That image emerged primarily because of its staggering successes in the face of vastly superior Federal numbers and resources. But it also developed because the Army of Northern Virginia drew soldiers from across the Confederacy. Had all those troops come from the East—Virginia, North Carolina, South Carolina, and Georgia—the army would have appeared to be regional rather than national. By tapping regiments from Maryland to Texas, Lee's force was nationwide in scope. Southerners throughout the Confederacy took a personal interest in his army because part of it came from their home state.

Initially, Confederate officials simply banded regiments into brigades as they arrived in Virginia, regardless of the mix. President Davis, however, believed the creation of brigades from a single state would benefit the Confederacy. Civilians would take greater pride in those brigades from their own state, motivating their men to volunteer and keeping manpower at a high level. Single-state brigades would thus generate attention and enthusiasm at home from an army hundreds, sometimes more than a thousand, miles away. Davis also realized this approach would ensure that general-officer slots went to individuals from different states. The Confederate president knew that generalships were prized patronage positions and that each state wanted to share in these appointments. If all the regiments in a brigade came from a single state, at least one brigadier general—the rank of a brigade commander—would come from that state. Otherwise, wartime attrition might lead to a situation where some states had no generals in the field, even though those states sent thousands of soldiers to Lee's army.

Lee's predecessor, Joseph E. Johnston, refused to comply with Davis's requests and then directives to realign brigades by states, believing that the transfer of units would reduce army readiness. The matter became a bone of contention between the commander in chief and one of his principal army commanders. At the same time, P. G. T. Beauregard adjusted his command structure promptly, in accordance with the president's wishes. Shortly after Lee took command of the army, Davis reminded him of those wishes. Lee admitted, "I fear the result nor do I think it the best organization." Personally, Lee preferred to command troops from different states. "I think it could be better controuled, more emulation would be excited, there would be less combination against authority," he told Davis. He did recognize the importance of political patronage and the fact that the soldiers themselves might prefer it. "The latter consideration has much weight with me," he conceded. More significantly, it was the president's desire and required Lee's compliance. In the midst of an active campaign, however, he explained that the consolidation "must necessarily be slow & will require much time." Nevertheless, Lee assured the president that all new brigades would be organized by state.[1]

Even with the new policy of consolidation, it was understood that Lee could not merge all regiments from a specific state into state brigades. Brigades needed to be a minimum size and, ideally, approximately of equal size. Yet states did not contribute the same number of regiments and batteries to the Army of Northern Virginia. Thus, an inevitable mixing of some states in brigades was a simple matter of arithmetic. But in accordance with Davis's directive, Beauregard and then Lee consciously attempted to reassign regiments into state brigades whenever they could. As a result, Lee's army had brigades from every Confederate state except Arkansas, and the 3rd Arkansas Infantry was part of the acclaimed Texas Brigade.

Still, soldiers came more heavily from the Upper South—Maryland, Virginia, North Carolina, Kentucky, Tennessee, and Arkansas—than the Lower South—South Carolina, Georgia, Florida, Alabama, Mississippi, Louisiana, and Texas. In 1860, 4 of every 9 troops (44.5%) in the sample lived in the Lower South, while 5 of every 9 (55.5%) resided in the Upper South.[2]

With New Orleans, Charleston, Savannah, Augusta, Columbus, and Atlanta among the 100 largest cities in the United States in 1860, the Lower South boasted a disproportionate number of soldiers from urban areas, 2.3 to 1.0. Despite the larger number of men from the Upper South in the sample, more artillerymen and almost 4 times as many infantrymen who resided in urban areas came from the Lower South. The two regions had roughly an equal percentage of urban cavalrymen.[3]

With the exception of Arkansas, the newer states in the old Union, those areas that became states in the nineteenth century, comprised the region called the Lower or Deep South. Hence, the Lower South had substantially more soldiers who were born in a state other than the one in which they had enlisted. During the course of two or three decades before the outbreak of war, people in the Northern and Eastern states of what became the Confederacy migrated to the West and South. Typical was Cicero Farrar, who was born in Tennessee but made his way to Mississippi, where he and his wife settled. Thus, in the Lower South 1 in 3 (32.7%) soldiers were born in a state other than their resident state at the time of enlistment, compared to 1 in 5 (20.7%) in the Upper South.[4]

According to the sample, men from the Lower South tended to be slightly older than those from the Upper South. Farrar, for example, was 31 when he joined the 42nd Mississippi Infantry as a private in May 1862. The median birth year for soldiers from the Lower South was 1837, one year earlier than those from the Upper South. The average age was almost identical, with year of birth at 1835.65 versus 1835.60. A slightly more pronounced difference was evident in the percentage of men who were born before 1836, with 42% in the Lower South compared to 35.2% in the Upper South.

Figure 6.1 compares the percentage of soldiers from the Upper South and Lower South by year of birth.

Despite the subtle age difference, soldiers in both regions married at almost identical rates: 38.0% for the Lower South and 37.1% for the Upper South. Slightly less than a third (32.0%) of all servicemen from the Lower South had children, marginally eclipsing the ratio of representatives from the Upper South at 3 of 10 (30.6%). Eight of 10 (82.1%) married men from the Lower South were fathers, again almost identical to the rate (82.2%) from the Upper South.[5]

More than half of the soldiers in both the Upper (53.7%) and Lower (53.7%) South were farmers before they entered military service. Typical were Julius A. Vick of Clark County, Mississippi, and William H. Seavey of Greenbriar County, Virginia. Both men, in their early twenties, embraced the life they had known. Their fathers had tilled the soil, and so did they. The most pronounced regional differences in prewar occupations were among professionals, students, and unskilled workers. Soldiers from the Lower South were almost 50% more likely (7.4% compared to 5.0%) than their Upper South counterparts to hold professional positions before the war. Prewar merchant William A. Evans of Chesterfield County, South Carolina, represented that body of soldiers. This was certainly one reason why men from the Lower South reflected the slightly older population in the army. Evans was 28 when he enlisted in 1861. According to the 1860 census, male residents of the Lower South were also 60.0% more likely (17.3% compared to 10.8%) to be students than men from the Upper South, a factor that operated against the age distinction. By contrast, Upper South men in Lee's army were nearly twice as likely (16.7%

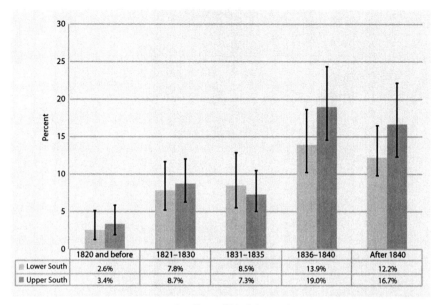

	1820 and before	1821–1830	1831–1835	1836–1840	After 1840
Lower South	2.6%	7.8%	8.5%	13.9%	12.2%
Upper South	3.4%	8.7%	7.3%	19.0%	16.7%

FIGURE 6.1. Year of birth by region

compared to 8.9%) as men from the Lower South to hold unskilled jobs. With a higher percentage of urbanites from the Deep South and the large number of unskilled jobs available in cities as opposed to rural areas, this is an unusual statistic. Men such as William Linticum of the 48th Virginia Infantry worked as a laborer before the war. The 25-year-old Linticum had recently married and possessed a total wealth of $100 in 1860. He was wounded twice in combat and rose to the rank of sergeant.[6]

Figure 6.2 highlights occupational similarities and differences among soldiers from the Upper and Lower South.

The high percentage of unskilled workers in the Upper South and of students and professionals in the Lower South suggest that there may have been marked distinctions in wealth by region of residence. In the category of personal wealth, little separated men from the Lower and Upper South. In both instances, the median wealth was $0, and the average wealth slightly favored soldiers from the Lower South, $1,759 to $1,703. More than 3 of every 4 soldiers (76.1%) from the Lower South and more than 4 of 5 (81.7%) from the Upper South claimed total wealth under $800. Less than 1 in every 8 (11.9%) in the Lower South was an individual like Charles H. West, of South Carolina, who boasted wealth greater than $4,000, while 1 in 11 (9.1%) from the Upper South, such as Thomas Farrar of Virginia, qualified for that level of affluence.

Figure 6.3 examines soldiers' personal wealth in the two regions.

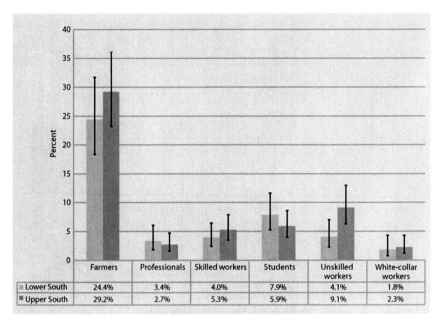

	Farmers	Professionals	Skilled workers	Students	Unskilled workers	White-collar workers
Lower South	24.4%	3.4%	4.0%	7.9%	4.1%	1.8%
Upper South	29.2%	2.7%	5.3%	5.9%	9.1%	2.3%

FIGURE 6.2. Occupation by region

Yet the combination of personal and family wealth when soldiers lived in the home of immediate relatives indicates important differences. Private Robert E. Pennal was a prewar clerk in Charleston, South Carolina, who had no wealth of his own. But he still lived with his mother, and she owned an estate worth $32,000, including three slaves. For soldiers like Pennal who resided in the Lower South, the combined median wealth was $1,700, nearly double the $900 in the Upper South. The average combined wealth, a less useful statistic, placed men from the Lower South at $10,565, while those from the Upper South lagged far behind at $6,892. One in every 3 (34.2%) soldiers from the Lower South had wealth in the poor category ($799 or less), and nearly 2 in every 5 (39.2%) possessed at least $4,000 worth of real and personal property. Among the soldiers from the Upper South, nearly 1 in every 2 (47.9%) had a combined wealth of $799 or less, and approximately one-third (32.4%) boasted a combined total worth of $4,000 or more.

Figure 6.4 examines soldiers' combined personal and family wealth in the two regions.

Household wealth escalated to a median of $3,750 in the Lower South and $1,700 in the Upper South, both figures in the middle range yet at a very comfortable level. Slightly more than 1 in 4 (25.9%) soldiers from the Deep South had a household wealth of below $800, whereas nearly 2 of 5 (38.9%)

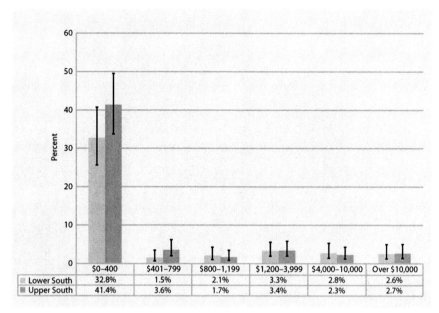

	$0–400	$401–799	$800–1,199	$1,200–3,999	$4,000–10,000	Over $10,000
Lower South	32.8%	1.5%	2.1%	3.3%	2.8%	2.6%
Upper South	41.4%	3.6%	1.7%	3.4%	2.3%	2.7%

FIGURE 6.3. Personal wealth by region

men from the Upper South were in that category. At the same time, nearly half (47.5%) of those from the Lower South lived in households worth $4,000 or more. Private A. P. Dickert of the 14th Alabama Infantry was just such a beneficiary. He had no personal wealth, yet he worked as a laborer and lived in the house of David Folk, who was worth $21,500. In the Upper South, the ratio exceeded 2 of 5 (40.6%), an extremely high percentage.[7]

Figure 6.5 compares the household wealth of Confederate soldiers in the two regions.

Slave ownership reflected those patterns of wealth accurately. Among personal slaveholding, some differences appeared in soldiers from the two regions of the prewar South. Slightly more than 1 in 7 (15.0%) troops from the Lower South owned slaves themselves, while a bit more than 1 in 9 (11.4%) men from the Upper South did. Less than one-half of 1.0% (0.4%) of the soldiers from the Lower South qualified as members of the planter class (owned 20 or more slaves); 1 in every 90 (1.1%) from the Upper South were planters.

Much like soldiers' wealth, the combination of personal and family slaveholding marked a substantial distinction between the two regions. Nearly 4 in every 9 (43.0%) soldiers from the Lower South owned slaves themselves or their family with whom they resided owned slaves, whereas just less than 1 in every 3 (32.5%) men from the Upper South did. In 1860 David Henry Deahl, a

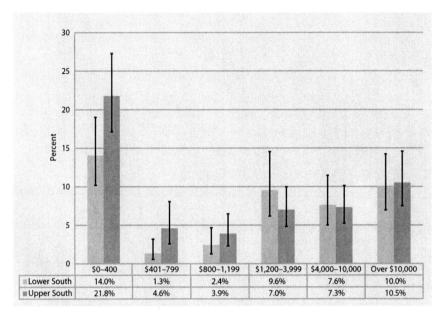

	$0–400	$401–799	$800–1,199	$1,200–3,999	$4,000–10,000	Over $10,000
Lower South	14.0%	1.3%	2.4%	9.6%	7.6%	10.0%
Upper South	21.8%	4.6%	3.9%	7.0%	7.3%	10.5%

FIGURE 6.4. Personal and family wealth by region

future private in Chew's Battery, was fifteen years old. Deahl owned no slaves, but he lived with his widowed mother and four siblings, and she owned a slave. The percentage of soldiers from the planter class soared to close to 1 in 14 (7.1% in Lower and 6.8% in Upper South) in both regions when soldiers and their families were measured.

A majority of soldiers from the Lower South (50.3%) lived in slaveholding households, while 2 of every 5 (39.6%) in the Upper South did. In both cases, that compared favorably to the 24.9% of all slaveholding households in the South, according to the 1860 census. One in every 10 soldiers from the Lower South and almost 1 in every 11 in the Upper South resided in planter households. Among them was Private Dickert, of Alabama, who lived in the master's house and benefited from the 20 slaves on the plantation.[8]

Figure 6.6 indicates slaveholding by region.

To a great extent, slave ownership reflected the density of slaves to whites in soldiers' home counties. The median county ratio was 2.5 times greater among soldiers from the Lower South (88.1 slaves to every 100 whites) than for the Upper South (32.8). The average ratio was 105.6 slaves in the Lower South to 51.2 in the Lower South.[9]

These three categories of analysis—wealth, slaveholding, and slave density in the home county—suggest that different factors may have weighed more

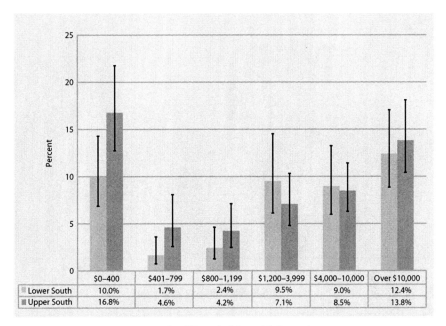

	$0–400	$401–799	$800–1,199	$1,200–3,999	$4,000–10,000	Over $10,000
Lower South	10.0%	1.7%	2.4%	9.5%	9.0%	12.4%
Upper South	16.8%	4.6%	4.2%	7.1%	8.5%	13.8%

FIGURE 6.5. Household wealth by region

heavily on the minds of men from the two regions when they joined the army. In the Lower South, slavery was a more dominant force in their lives, and it may have been a more powerful motivator to join the army. A large proportion owned slaves or resided in slaveholding households. Those who did not own slaves lived amid dense slave populations and observed firsthand the financial and social benefits of slaveholding, as well as the economic competition they might encounter if slaves were emancipated. In the Upper South, the line of Union landed invasion came directly through their home states. While many soldiers who resided there before the war possessed strong ties to slavery and doubtless viewed it as a reason to secede and ultimately fight for the Confederacy, defense of hearth and home may have been a stronger consideration. Their home states would be the battleground. Soldiers from the Upper South were furious over the threat and actual destruction to their homes, property, and loved ones. "If there is one degree of *hell* hotter than an other I think it will be retained for the Vandles who invade our homes, rob & destroy our property," a Virginian explained to his wife. "Our men seem to be desperate on the subject and will fight bravely every opertunity that is offered."[10]

Officers by region composed slightly skewed proportions in the sample, making up just below 1 in 11 (9.3%) in the Lower South and slightly less than 1

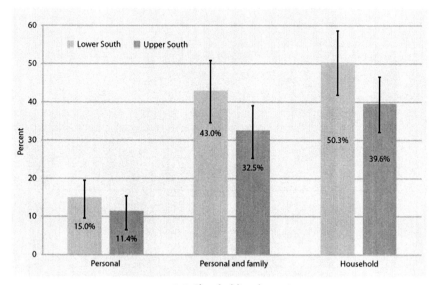

FIGURE 6.6. Slaveholding by region

in 14 (7.3%) in the Upper South. Although the higher level of wealth of enlisted men in the Lower South reflects the greater affluence of soldiers from that region, officers in the Upper South were richer than their Lower South counterparts. Officers from the Upper South boasted a combined median personal and family wealth of $3,000 and an average wealth of $18,148, compared to a median wealth of $2,750 and an average wealth of $8,893 for Lower South officers. Yet, interestingly, more than half (53.3%) of all officers or their families in the Lower South owned slaves. By contrast, slightly more than 4 in 9 (45.4%) officers or their immediate families in the Upper South were slaveholders. Among the enlisted population, men and their immediate families from the Lower South owned almost double the property of those from the Upper South. The combined median personal and family wealth for the Upper South was $850, in the low range of the middle class, and the average wealth was $6,340. Slightly less than 1 in 3 of those families (31.5%) owned slaves. In the Lower South, the median wealth for enlisted men and their families was $1,645, solidly in the middle class, and their average wealth exceeded that of their officers at $12,487. More than 2 of every 5 (41.8%) enlisted men or their immediate families in the Lower South owned slaves.[11]

Soldiers from both the Upper and the Lower South overwhelmingly joined the army in 1861 and 1862, but as the war entered its third and fourth years, geography emerged as a larger factor. Nearly 8 of every 9 soldiers (87.9%) who resided in the Lower South and served in Lee's army entered military service in 1861 or 1862, but only 1 in 8 (12.1%) joined during 1863 and 1864. By contrast, although nearly 7 of every 8 (85.9%) men from the Upper South joined up in the first two years of fighting, and nearly 1 in 7 (14.1%) swore the oath of service in 1863 and 1864. As the war dragged on, it became increasingly difficult for the Lower South to replenish its regiments with fresh manpower. As transportation broke down and areas in the Deep South became more threatened, authorities assigned new soldiers from that region to units closer to home.[12]

The number of conscripts from both regions reflected those changes, as well as sloppy record keeping. The sample for this study included only three men from the Lower South whose records specified that they were conscripts. Fourteen soldiers from the Upper South entered military service through conscription. Of those conscripts in the Lower South, not one of them deserted. Three of 14 in the Upper South abandoned the Confederate flag; interestingly, 2 of those 3 conscript-deserters came from well-to-do families.[13]

Although most conscripts were relatively poor, with more than 3 of every 5 (62.0%) worth less than $800, in a few instances they had wealthy backgrounds. Private Charles H. West, of Charleston, South Carolina, was conscripted in 1864. A father of five, the 33-year-old West owned eight slaves and was worth nearly $12,000 in 1860. West evidently believed in the Confederate cause but had physical problems. Not long after entering Lee's army, he was released due to his disability, yet he joined the Confederate navy, where he felt he could aid the war effort despite his incapacity. Among the conscripts from the Upper South, 3 of the 14 were worth more than $4,000. Private Hersey B. Parker, for example, came from a very wealthy family in Halifax, North Carolina. He served in the 16th Battalion North Carolina Cavalry before transferring to the 54th North Carolina Infantry.

Location also had a significant impact on AWOL and desertion rates. Based on the limited information that has survived, slightly less than 1 in 16 (6.5%) men from the Lower South were at one time AWOL, compared to 57.0% more (10.2%) among those who resided in the Upper South. The same regional distinctions held true for deserters. Troops from the Upper South had a much easier time escaping and heading home and did so in greater proportions. One in 6 (17.6%) men from the Upper South abandoned the Confederate cause, compared to 1 in 8 (13.1%) soldiers from the Lower South. According to the sample, only two soldiers from the Deep South deserted prior to September 1863, when military officials shifted part of Lee's army to northern Georgia. Stationed in Virginia, they had no hope of making it home unless they deserted while on furlough.

Once soldiers had a reasonable chance of reaching home, much larger numbers abandoned the ranks. Private Joseph Bratton was a case in point. A prewar farm laborer, the 22-year-old Bratton enlisted in the 2nd Mississippi Infantry in May 1861. At Gettysburg in July 1863, he was wounded and taken prisoner. Two and a half months later, Bratton was exchanged and sent home on furlough. Had he remained with the army, desertion to his home would not have been a viable option. Back in Mississippi, he went AWOL, joined another command, and eventually deserted for the remainder of the war.

Certainly both groups had the option of fleeing to Union lines, and a considerable number did so. But most deserters avoided that step until the late stages of the war. In many cases, the objective was to return home, and fleeing to the Union army brought them no closer to loved ones. When the Confederacy could no longer feed or clothe its troops satisfactorily, and the prospects of victory plummeted, destinations began to change. Rather than trying to make it home and run the risk of being caught as a deserter, it was easier to flee to Union lines. There Confederates avoided the harrows of more combat or severe punishment and received substantially more rations.

In both regions, deserters lacked the resources at home that their fellow soldiers who remained in the ranks had possessed in peacetime. The combined median personal and family wealth for deserters in the Upper South was $500, while nondeserters from that region held more than double that property, at $1,140. In the Lower South, the division between deserters and nondeserters was closer, but the value of property held by men who continued to rally around the flag was one-third higher. The combined median wealth of deserters from the Lower South was $1,380; for nondeserters, the figure was $1,840. Thus, in the Deep South real poverty may not have been the issue; rather, it may have been the comparative lack of wealth that led soldiers to loosen their allegiance to the Rebel cause and head home to look after loved ones.

While the financial distinctions between deserters and nondeserters were substantial (33.3%), the combined median wealth of deserters was still high enough to suggest that quite a number came from slaveholding families. In fact, in the Deep South 11.1% of all nonslaveholders deserted, compared to 10.4% of slaveholders. Among men from the Upper South, only 1 in 50 (2.0%) was a deserter and a member of a slaveholding family, while more than 1 in 7 (15.4%) was a deserter and came from a nonslaveholding family. Deserters were far less likely to live in slaveholding households, regardless of the region of residence. In the Lower South, less than 1 in every 11 (8.8%) men from slaveholding households deserted. More than 1 in 8 (12.8%) who resided in a

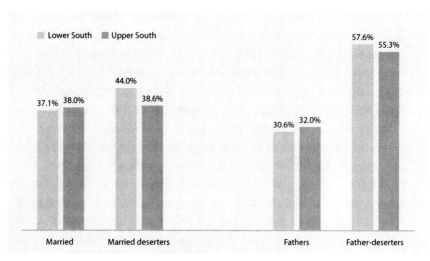

FIGURE 6.7. Marriage, fatherhood, and desertion by region

home without slaves deserted. In the Upper South, nearly 1 in every 4 (23.5%) soldiers in a house without slaves deserted, whereas less than 1 in 12 (8.2%) troops from slaveowning households deserted.[14]

More than simply wealth, marital status and children at home affected soldiers' decisions to desert the army. In the Lower South, married and single men deserted in roughly the same percentages, 10.9% of all married troops to 10.7% of those who were single. In the Upper South, marital status played a larger role: more than 1 in every 5 (20.3%) married men deserted, compared to 2 of every 13 (15.2%) who were single. Even more striking in both regions was the influence of children at home. Soldiers from the Lower South with children at home were 72% more likely to desert than those without children. In the Upper South, the influence of children at home was equally powerful. Fathers were 67% more likely to desert than childless soldiers.[15]

Figure 6.7 compares married soldiers and father-soldiers as deserters and nondeserters in the Upper and Lower South.

Proportionately, casualties were about equal, but injuries and fatalities fell harder on the Lower South. One in every 6 (17.1%) soldiers from the Lower South was killed in action, and 9 of every 20 (44.9%) were either killed or wounded. Georgian Henry S. Cooley was one of them. A resident of Antioch, Cooley had a wife and child and owned $2,600 worth of property, including two slaves. His father, who lived nearby, had $11,000 in property, including ten slaves. Cooley enlisted in the 21st Georgia Infantry in May 1862 and served well for more than two years before he was struck down at the Battle of Winchester in September 1864. More than 1 in 7 additional men from the Lower South died of disease, bringing the region's percentage of fatalities to 3 in 10. Among those who were not killed, wounded, or died of disease, 1 in 17 was captured and 1 in 17 was discharged for disease or disability. Thus, the total losses for the Lower South reached just below 3 of every 4 (72.5%) soldiers.

Among troops from the Upper South, slightly more than 1 in 12 (8.2%) lost their lives in combat and nearly 1 in 3 (33.2%) were killed or wounded. One in 12 men succumbed to disease. Including two men who were killed accidentally, the total death tally for the Upper South approached 1 in 5 (17.7%). More than 1 in 5 (20.6%) men from the Upper South who were neither killed, nor wounded, nor died of disease fell into Union hands. One in 14 more received a discharge for disability, bringing the total of soldiers killed, wounded, dead from disease, POWs before the surrender at Appomattox, or disabled to 69.3%.[16]

Figure 6.8 breaks down losses by region.

These casualty statistics indicate pronounced regional differences. Soldiers from the Lower South were nearly twice as likely to be killed in action, and approximately 37% were more likely to sustain battlefield wounds than their comrades from the Upper South. Moreover, men from the Lower South were more prone to die of disease. When it came to POWs, however, more than 1 in every 4 soldiers (26.1%) from the Upper South was seized by the enemy at least once prior to the surrender at Appomattox, whereas 1 in 9 (10.9%) men from the Lower South suffered the same fate.

Differences in the percentages of POWs between Upper and Lower South offer interesting insights into the changing nature of the war. By 1864, Union advances in other theaters compelled states in the Lower South to funnel their new recruits and conscripts to more local military commands. In the Upper South, the Union army controlled Kentucky and Tennessee, and Arkansas could not effectively contribute manpower to Lee's army. Virginia and North Carolina, then, were the viable sources of fresh troops, and as newcomers joined the army, they increased the actual number and percentage of men from those states. Thus, in the last 12 months of the war, the Army of Northern Virginia became more Virginian and North Carolinian in its composition. During the last year of fighting, Union forces under the overall direction of Lieutenant General Ulysses S. Grant attacked more vigorously than they had ever done before, collecting large numbers of Lee's infantrymen and artillerymen as prisoners. Nearly 4 of every 5 (78.3%) infantrymen who were captured during the conflict came from North Carolina and Virginia. Excluding those who surrendered at Appomattox, more than half (52.4%) of all North Carolina

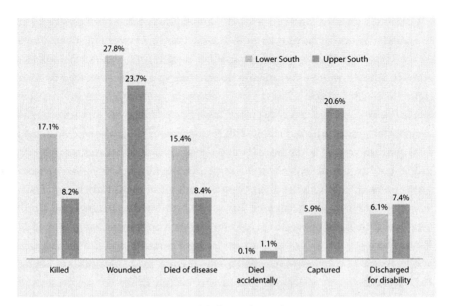

FIGURE 6.8. Losses by region

infantrymen and more than three-fourths (76.5%) of all Virginia foot soldiers captured during the war were taken from May 1864 to April 1865.

The cavalry, where the largest discrepancy between Upper and Lower South soldiers existed, suffered from more complicated factors. Of all horsemen from Lee's army who fell into Yankee hands before Appomattox, more than 7 of every 10 (71.4%) were Virginians. Only 1 in 9 (11.4%) cavalry prisoners came from the Lower South. By 1864, the overwhelming preponderance of Lee's mounted branch was Virginian. During that final year, Union cavalry-men were armed with repeating rifles, giving them a huge advantage in fire-power. They also had better mounts. Lee's quartermasters could barely feed the army's horses, while the Union provided up to ten times as much food for its animals. Against better mounts and vastly superior arms, Confederate cavalrymen were no match against Yankee horsemen. In the battles in the lower Shenandoah Valley in September and October 1864, in which Confed-erate forces suffered disastrous defeats, Lieutenant General Jubal Early had two cavalry divisions under his command, and every regiment except one was from Virginia.[17] Almost 3 of every 5 (58.3%) cavalrymen in Lee's army who was taken prisoner before the surrender at Appomattox fell to Federals once the campaign season opened in May 1864. Of those captives, nearly 4 of every 5 (78.6%) were Virginians.

Combined personal and family wealth among Lee's soldiers who were killed or wounded in action indicate a significant distinction between the two regions. In the Upper South, the combined median wealth for soldiers who suffered combat injuries was $1,700, nearly double the wealth of men who escaped injury in combat ($900). James Obey Gibson, a 19-year-old private from Lee County serving in the 25th Virginia Cavalry, was acting as a courier for his regimental commander at Fisher's Hill in September 1864 when he received a fatal gunshot wound in the head. Young Gibson had accumulated no property in life, but his parents were worth $15,555. In the Lower South, the statistics were reversed, although the distinction was not quite so overwhelming. Those who emerged from the battlefield unscathed possessed a personal and family wealth of $1,850, compared to $1,500 for troops who were killed or wounded. Private James A. McVicker of the 19th Georgia Infantry was shot in the knee at the Battle of Second Manassas in late August 1862. Doctors amputated his leg, but he never recovered. The 27-year-old McVicker left a wife, a child, and $1,200 worth of property. Interestingly, the average wealth in the Lower South was reversed: those injured in combat averaged $14,516, compared to $10,715 for the men who managed to emerge from battle safely.[18]

In both regions, death from disease fell on the poorer soldiers. In the Lower South, troops who fought off illnesses had almost double the combined personal and family wealth ($1,850) of those who succumbed to them ($950). In the less-affluent Upper South, the distinctions were even starker. Men who perished from illness were worth only $280, while those who survived had $1,000 worth of real and personal property. Among those who died was Private David Paris of Edneyville, North Carolina. Paris perished from camp illness within a few months of entering the service, leaving a wife, four children, and only $100 in total property.

This comparative approach offers some wonderful regional differences. But because the sample was not created with this approach in mind, the confidence levels are often fairly wide. In those instances the specific data is more inferential, and a comparative study of soldiers from the Upper and Lower South warrants closer examination by scholars.

CHAPTER SEVEN

Officers and Enlisted Men

The soldiers in his command regularly referred to a major as "'A. No. 1,'" re-
ported one of them to his sister, with "'A' standing for *Ass*." Other troops re-
sented their officers, too, especially early in the war when enlisted men were
unaccustomed to discipline and officers tried to impose it on them. Yet for
the most part, there was no great chasm between officers and enlisted men in
Lee's army.[1] Both elements came from the same communities. Although they
often had different experiences before the war, enough enlisted men traveled in the same economic and social spheres as the bulk of their officers, and
enough officers shared their background with the majority of enlisted men,
that distinctions were not so evident. Furthermore, the hardships and tragedies of war proved to be a great leveler, obliterating prewar differences.

Laws for the selection of officers rested with the various states, and most
of them required elections. The Confederate Congress was reluctant to tres-
pass on that prerogative, and President Davis concurred. "In the election and
appointment of officers for the Provisional Army," he conceded, "it was antic-
ipated that mistakes would be made and incompetent officers of all grades
introduced into the service." Yet, Davis explained, "In the absence of experience, and with no reliable guide for selection, executive appointments as well
as elections have been sometimes unfortunate."[2]

In the election of officers in 1861, soldiers tended to vote for men with prior
military experience or training, such as graduates of military academies and
schools, and persons of prominence in the community. As that initial year of
service began to expire, the Confederate administration and Congress, fear-
ing the dissolution of the army, made a big push to retain military strength.
They offered furloughs to those who reenlisted for two more years and other
benefits. Ultimately, as the spring campaign began, the slow reenlistment
rate convinced the government to act more aggressively. In April 1862, Congress passed a law with Davis's blessing that directed states to enroll all males
between 18 and 35 for conscription, except for those who had legal exemp-
tions. Draftees would serve a term of three years, unless the war ended sooner.

All one-year enlistees from 1861 would remain in the service for an additional two years.[3]

The mere consideration of a conscription bill in Congress sparked reenlistments. The men of 1861 feared that a draft would require them to serve three more years, so enlistment for two more years seemed like "the best of two evils." Others worried that if they went home and risked the draft, inevitably the government would take them; then they would be compelled to serve in some other unit composed of strangers. After a year in service, usually with friends and acquaintances from home, these men had forged powerful bonds of trust and confidence in the group, and the idea of standing in combat alongside outsiders was unappealing.

More than simply returning to their old unit and serving with long-standing comrades, quite a few soldiers perceived opportunity in the conscription law. With a draft and unit reconstitution, the door opened for individuals who sought commissions as officers. According to the law, reenlisted troops could select their own officers, which placed all original commission holders in jeopardy of losing their rank and created fresh possibilities for aspiring office-holders.

Many feared that the strong disciplinarians, the best trainers of troops, would lose out because they had alienated the men. According to historian Robert K. Krick, close to 1 in every 3 field officers failed to be reelected. While some competent colonels and majors (field-grade officers) lost their positions, the men retained most of the skilled commanders and promoted quality captains to fill vacancies. Usually aged or sickly field-grade officers, along with incompetent leaders, lost their posts in the election shuffle.[4]

A random sample of 17 regiments and batteries, which comprised approximately one-tenth of all the regiments and batteries in Virginia on 30 April 1862, determined that the men voted out of office just under 1 in 4 (23%). On the company level, soldiers most often elevated a junior lieutenant or a skilled noncommissioned officer to the position of lieutenant or captain. Seldom did a private sweep into a commissioned-officer slot.[5]

By and large, the election worked well. Veteran recruits had served long enough to know that they needed individuals with genuine leadership talent as their commissioned officers. Fresh elections offered opportunities for promising leaders to rise in rank and authority. Among those who resigned were the aged and the infirm who could not serve in the field; their prolonged absence overburdened everyone else. The election process eased them out of the army and enabled the Confederate government to replace them with individuals who were capable of performing their duties.

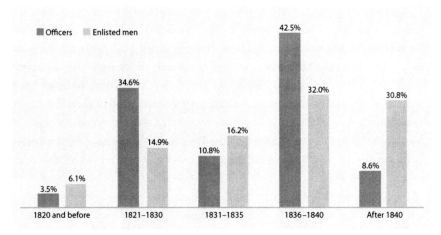

FIGURE 7.1. Year of birth of officers and enlisted men

Enlisted men got what they wanted: officers who cared for them and their needs. Officers who exhibited good judgment and formulated decisions fairly earned kudos and respect; those who disciplined men harshly and without genuine purpose, who ruled whimsically or with prejudice, generated animosity among the men and were turned out. Confederate soldiers came from a world of slaveholding and were exceedingly sensitive to the deprivation of rights. Officers who lorded it over the enlisted men lost their respect almost instantly.

After that round of new elections, the government required promotion strictly by seniority, with the enlisted men able to vote only to fill vacancies at the second lieutenant's rank. Lee found the seniority system restrictive, especially at the higher levels, but it was the law and he therefore had to obey it.[6]

Not surprisingly, officers tended to be a bit older than enlisted men. Among enlisted soldiers, the average year of birth was 1835.7 and the median birth year was 1838.0. For officers, the average was 1833.8 and the median was a full two years earlier at 1836.0. More than 1 of every 3 (34.6%) officers was born between 1821 and 1830, compared to 1 in 7 (14.9%) enlisted men. The years between 1836 to 1840 saw a huge increase in the birth of future officers, almost 4 of every 9 (42.5%), compared to fewer than 3 of 9 (32.0%) enlisted men. The greatest difference in the birth years of the two groups, though, occurred between 1841 to 1848, when more than 3 of every 10 (30.8%) enlisted men were born, compared to 1 in 12 (8.6%) officers. Fellow soldiers seldom entrusted young men with the responsibility of officership.[7]

Figure 7.1 tracks the year of birth of officers and enlisted men. Officers are defined as anyone who ever held the rank of lieutenant or higher.

Interestingly, officers were more likely to remain in their native state than enlisted men. Less than 1 in every 5 (18.1%) officers resided in a place other than his birth state, compared to more than 1 in every 4 (26.9%) enlisted men. This continuity may have strengthened the bonds of future officers in their home communities and eased their way to election as officers, while enlisted men, more mobile in their prewar lives, may not have established the stability necessary to win the trust of fellow soldiers as readily, especially early in the war. A majority (52.4%) of all officers in the sample resided in the Lower South before the war, while more than 5 of every 9 (55.7%) enlisted men lived in the Upper South.[8]

The percentage of officers and enlisted men who were married at the outbreak of the war was almost exactly the same. Less than 2 of every 5 officers (37.8%) and enlisted men (37.5%) had wives. Because officers were older, they were more likely to have children at home. Three of every 8 (37.2%) officers were fathers, while 3 of every 10 (30.7%) enlisted men had nonadult children. As one of four enlisted men in the sample who was a widower with children when he entered military service in 1863, John C. Bevil was an anomaly. Lieutenant Cyrus McLean Kerns was the only unwed officer in the sample with children. A poor laborer before the war, McLean rose from private to corporal to sergeant and finally second lieutenant in 12 months of service. His three children became orphans when he was killed on 28 June 1862 in the Seven Days' Battles.[9]

Officers tended to have more desirable prewar occupations than enlisted men. They were 3 times as likely to be professionals (15.2% compared to 5.2%) and twice as likely to hold white-collar jobs (8% compared to 3.8%). Only 1 in 12 (8.6%) officers had worked in unskilled positions. By contrast, enlisted men were 1.5 times as likely to be unskilled (13.6% compared to 8.6%) and slightly more likely to be farmers (54.1% compared to 48.7%), skilled workers (9.4% compared to 8.0%), or students (14.0% compared to 11.6%) before the war.[10]

Figure 7.2 compares the prewar occupations of officers and enlisted men.

With superior occupations, officers on the whole were wealthier than their enlisted comrades. Officers boasted an average personal wealth of $6,322 and a median wealth of $800, compared to an average enlisted man's personal wealth of $1,299 and a median wealth of $0. Seven of every 9 (76.6%) enlisted men possessed total assets of less than $400, while just below half of all officers (48.2%) did so. More than 1 in every 5 officers were worth more than $10,000, compared to 1 in every 25 (3.8%) enlisted men.[11]

Figure 7.3 displays the personal wealth of officers and enlisted men.

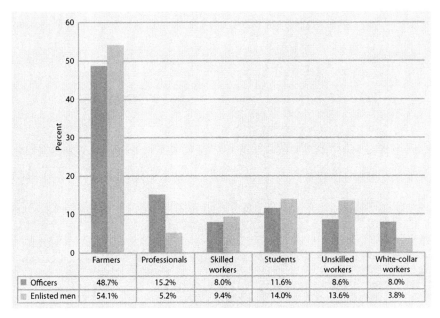

	Farmers	Professionals	Skilled workers	Students	Unskilled workers	White-collar workers
▓ Officers	48.7%	15.2%	8.0%	11.6%	8.6%	8.0%
▒ Enlisted men	54.1%	5.2%	9.4%	14.0%	13.6%	3.8%

FIGURE 7.2. Occupation of officers and enlisted men

When family wealth was factored into the equation, the financial situation changed significantly. The median total wealth of enlisted men leaped to $1,200, and the average wealth rose to $7,949. Officers had a combined median wealth of $3,000 and an average wealth of $14,917. By economic class, 4 of 9 (43.8%) enlisted men fell into the poor category, compared to 1 in 5 (19.4%) officers. A third (33.3%) of all officers qualified for the middle class, compared to only 2 of 9 (21.9%) enlisted men. Nearly half (47.3%) of the officers and more than a third (34.5%) of enlisted men possessed personal or family wealth that placed them in the upper class.

Four of every 11 (37.3%) enlisted men were worth under $400, yet almost 1 in 5 (19.0%) had a combined wealth greater than $10,000, and just below 1 in 6 (15.4%) had between $4,000 and $10,000 in total assets. By contrast, 4 of every 11 (36.8%) officers and their families with whom they lived were worth more than $10,000 and another 1 in 10 (10.5%) claimed assets of between $4,000 and $10,000. Interestingly, 1 in 5 (19.4%) officers and their immediate families had $400 or less in total accumulated wealth, indicating that as the war extended and casualties mounted, soldiers elected good combat troops to second lieutenant vacancies, not necessarily men from well-to-do families. One in 4 (24.7%) enlisted men and more than 2 in 5 (42.5%) officers resided in households with more than $10,000 in total wealth.[12]

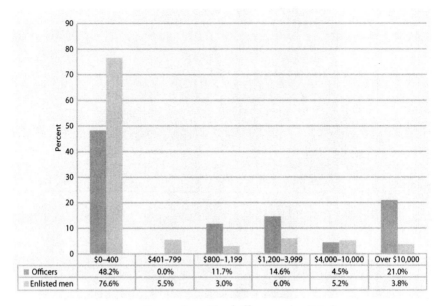

	$0–400	$401–799	$800–1,199	$1,200–3,999	$4,000–10,000	Over $10,000
Officers	48.2%	0.0%	11.7%	14.6%	4.5%	21.0%
Enlisted men	76.6%	5.5%	3.0%	6.0%	5.2%	3.8%

FIGURE 7.3. Personal wealth of officers and enlisted men

Figure 7.4 indicates the combined personal and family wealth of officers and enlisted men.

Slave ownership again reflected the superior occupations and greater wealth of officers. One in 9 (10.8%) enlisted men personally owned slaves, while 3 of 7 (37.2%) officers retained bondsmen and bondswomen. By organizing soldiers into groups of slaveholders and nonslaveholders, we can see that 1 in every 20 enlisted men owned 1 or 2 slaves, and another 1 in 20 owned 3 to 19 slaves. One in 200 (0.5%) enlisted men owning 20 or more slaves achieved the status of the planter class. Officers claimed far more extensive personal ownership of chattel slaves. One in 10 (10.2%) officers had 1 or 2 slaves, and nearly 1 in 6 (15.6%) owned between 3 and 10 slaves. Almost another 1 in 12 (7.9%) claimed possession of 11 to 19 bondsmen and bondswomen, and 1 in 29 (3.5%) with 20 or more slaves belonged to the planter class.

Figure 7.5 breaks down slave ownership by officers and enlisted men.

Once families with whom officers and men resided in 1860 are factored into the equation, slave ownership increases dramatically. Nearly 3 of every 7 (36.1%) enlisted men or their immediate family members owned slaves, while nearly half of all officers (49.5%) did. Two surprising aspects of slave owner-ship were that more than one-quarter (25.4%) of all officers or their families with whom they lived had three to ten slaves, double the ratio of enlisted men,

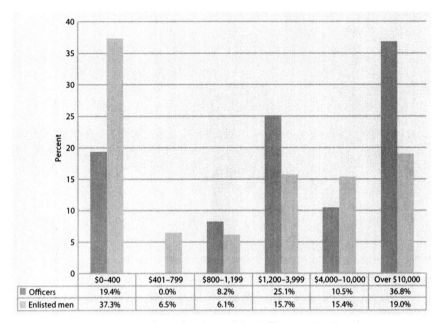

	$0–400	$401–799	$800–1,199	$1,200–3,999	$4,000–10,000	Over $10,000
Officers	19.4%	0.0%	8.2%	25.1%	10.5%	36.8%
Enlisted men	37.3%	6.5%	6.1%	15.7%	15.4%	19.0%

FIGURE 7.4. Personal and family wealth of officers and enlisted men

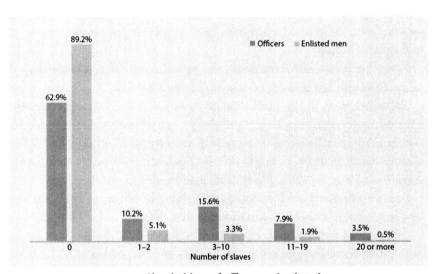

FIGURE 7.5. Slaveholding of officers and enlisted men

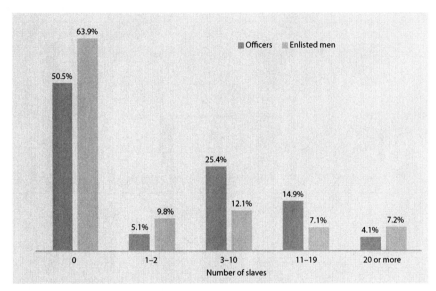

FIGURE 7.6. Personal and family slaveholding of officers and enlisted men

and that 1 in every 15 (7.2%) enlisted men or their families came from the planter class, a percentage that nearly doubled that of officers (4.1%). Thus, while a significantly higher proportion of officers or their immediate families owned slaves, enlisted men and their families had far greater representation in the planter class.[13]

Figure 7.6 breaks down the combined personal and family slaveholding of officers and enlisted men by the number of slaves owned.

The attachment to the institution of slavery was even stronger for both enlisted men and officers. Nearly 4 of every 9 (42.7%) enlisted men resided in slaveholding households, while more than 3 of every 5 officers (62.8%) did so. Greater than 1 in every 3 (34.3%) officers lived in homes with 3 to 10 slaves, and almost 1 in every 10 (9.5%) enlisted men resided in planter households.[14]

Figure 7.7 breaks down household slaveholding of officers and enlisted men by the number of slaves they and their families owned.

Officers and enlisted men came from counties with similar percentages of the slave-to-white population. The median county percentage for enlisted men was 59.0% and the mean was 75.6%. For officers, the median was a bit lower at 42.5%, but the average hit 76.7%. Among both enlisted men (36.5%) and officers (40.7%) roughly the same percentage came from counties with low slave-to-white ratios, that is, less than 1 black for every 3 whites. More than 3 of every 5 (63.5%) enlisted men resided in counties where the percentage varied from between 33.1% and 250% blacks to whites; about 5 of every

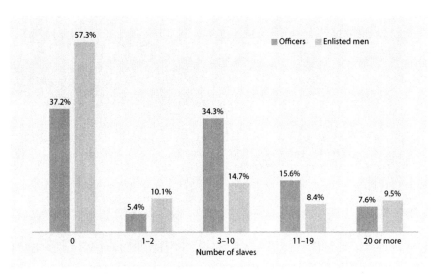

FIGURE 7.7. Household slaveholding of officers and enlisted men

9 (54.9%) officers also hailed from counties in that range. Fewer than 1 in 50 (1.8%) enlisted men and 1 in 25 (4.1%) officers resided in counties with ratios greater than 250 slaves to 100 whites, areas with extremely dense slave populations.[15]

Figure 7.8 contains slave-to-white ratios in the home county of officers and enlisted men.

Neither age nor wealth nor slaveholding determined who would become officers. The single most powerful factor was year of enlistment. Except for two assistant surgeons in the sample who entered in 1863 and 1864, every other person who held a commission in Lee's army enlisted in 1861 or 1862. More than 3 of every 4 (75.7%) officers joined the army in 1861, and another 17.6% entered in 1862. A soldier had to earn credibility with his comrades before they would elect him for a vacant second lieutenancy. By contrast, just less than 5 of every 9 (54.4%) enlisted men entered the service in 1861 and another 3 of 10 (31.0%) signed up in 1862.[16]

Figure 7.9 tracks the year officers and enlisted men entered Lee's army.

Not surprisingly, no conscripts in the sample were elevated to the rank of commissioned officer. According to service records, only 1 in every 33 enlisted men (3.1%) joined the service as conscripts, and 1 in every 250 entered as substitutes. More than half (52.9%) of all conscripts and their families if they resided with them were worth $400 or less. One in every 9 (11.8%) conscripts came from families worth more than $10,000. Slightly more than 2 of 9 (23.5%) conscripts or their families owned slaves, a much smaller number

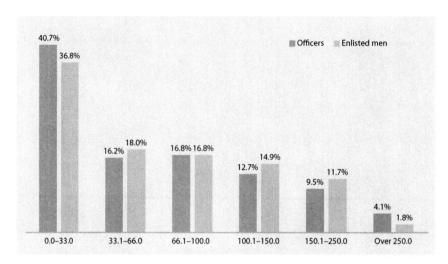

FIGURE 7.8. Slave-to-white ratio in home county of officers and enlisted men

than the 36.1% of all enlisted men who did. The combined median wealth was $950, some $250 less than what nonconscript enlisted men and their families were worth.

Enlisted men dominated those who left the ranks without authorization either temporarily or permanently. One in every 33 (3.4%) officers at one time was AWOL, while 1 in every 11 (9.0%) enlisted men took "French leave," as soldiers called AWOL. Among deserters, defined by the Confederate War Department as individuals who left the army with no intention of returning, 1 in 75 (1.6%) officers deserted his post. Lieutenant Samuel Langley was one of the two officers in the sample who deserted. A prewar student from a wealthy, slaveholding family, Langley began the war as an enlisted man. He suffered a leg wound in June 1864 and deserted four months later, never to return. By contrast, 1 in every 6 (15.7%) enlisted men deserted the ranks. Predictably, enlisted soldiers from poor families tended to desert in considerably larger numbers. They had the loosest bonds with their home communities, and the hardships of war fell on their families most heavily. Close to 1 in 5 (19.0%) men whose combined personal and family wealth totaled less than $400 deserted the army; another 1 in 6 (17.0%) with a combined wealth between $400 and $799 also left for good.

The most striking statistic about deserters emerged from the middle economic bracket, soldiers whose wealth when combined with their families ranged from $800 to $3,999. Three of every 10 (30.9%) enlisted soldiers who had a personal and family wealth from $800 to $1,199 deserted, as did almost

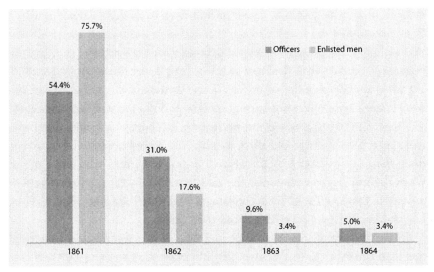

FIGURE 7.9. Year of entry of officers and enlisted men

1 in 5 (18.3%) who had total assets ranging from $1,200 to $3,999. Throughout Lee's army, nearly 2 of every 9 enlisted men in the middle class deserted.[17]

Approximately 1 in every 4 (24.8%) enlisted men had children at home, yet 3 of every 7 (36.7%) men who deserted had children at home. Among deserters with children at home and whose wealth could be ascertained from census records, 5 of every 9 were in the poorest financial category—less than $400. Two of every 5 deserters were worth between $400 and $799, so that a majority (52.3%) of poor deserters had children at home. Nearly 4 of every 9 (43.8%) enlisted men who, with their families, were worth between $800 and $1,199 left behind children when they entered the army. The percentage of deserters with children at home declined in the upper middle and lower wealthy categories, but more than 2 of every 3 deserters from the richest group, with total assets over $10,000, had children at home. Children at home were such an overriding factor among enlisted men that 1 in 7 such father-deserters came from families worth more than $10,000.[18]

Among all deserters who were enlisted men, only 1 in 13 (8.0%) personally owned slaves, and slightly less than 2 of every 9 (21.4%) or their families owned slaves. One in 9 (11.3%) enlisted men who never deserted owned slaves, and slightly less than 2 of 5 (38.8%) nondeserting enlisted men or their families held title to bondsmen and bondswomen. The families of the two officers who deserted owned slaves.

Both of these officers were minors (under 21) when the war erupted. Among enlisted men, 1 in 17 (6.6%) deserters was born before 1821. Roughly 1 in 5 deserters entered the world between 1821 and 1830 and another 1 in 5 between 1831 and 1835. The proportion leaped to more than 3 in every 10 (31.5%) in the years 1836 to 1840, then declined to 2 in 9 (21.7%) for those born after 1840. Yet when we compare the desertions in the context of the percentage of soldiers in Lee's army who were born in specific periods, the story becomes quite different. The largest group of enlisted men with children at home, those who were born between 1821 and 1830, also had the highest number of deserters, more than 1 in 5 (20.5%). Approximately 1 in every 9 men who was a minor when the war began abandoned the ranks (11.6%), by far the lowest rate of desertion. Of the 171 soldiers in the sample who were born after 1840, not one had children at home according to the 1860 census.

Within the sample, those who at one time held a commission composed less than 1 of every 12 (8.1%) men. Slightly more than 2 of 5 (40.8%) officers served as an enlisted man at one time. One in every 40 (2.5%) held the rank of second lieutenant; 1 in 50 (2%) was commissioned a first lieutenant; slightly more than 1 in 40 (2.7%) held the rank of captain; 1 in 200 (0.5%) was a major; 1 in 1,333 (0.075%) held the rank of lieutenant colonel; and 1 in 366 (0.27%) was a colonel. Among enlisted men, 7 of every 9 (77.8%) always maintained the rank of private. One in 21 rose to corporal, and nearly 1 in 11 (9.3%) donned the sergeant's chevron.

Approximately 1 in every 4 (24.8%) officers was killed in action, a stunning statistic, whereas 1 in every 9 (10.7%) enlisted man lost his life in battle. An additional 2 in every 7 (26.8%) officers who were not killed in combat were wounded in action at least once. More than one in 4 (25.3%) enlisted men who lived through battle nevertheless had one or more injuries. All told, more than half (51.5%) of all officers were either killed in action or wounded once, and 4 of every 11 (36%) enlisted men suffered similar battlefield casualties.[19]

Figure 7.10 indicates the percentage of officers and enlisted men who were killed in action or wounded at least once.

Combat wounds and fatalities were spread throughout various wealth groups. Among enlisted men, slightly less than 1 in 3 (31.5%) of those whose personal and family assets totaled below $400 and nearly 4 of every 9 (42.3%) of those whose combined personal and family wealth ranged between $400 and $799 were killed or wounded. Statistics dipped among those enlisted men in the middle brackets: 2 of every 7 (26.6%) who claimed personal and family wealth between $800 and $1,199 and 1 in 3 (32.9%) with combined assets between $1,200 and $3,999 were killed or wounded. The wealthiest enlisted men sustained the heaviest losses in combat. Slightly more than 4 of every

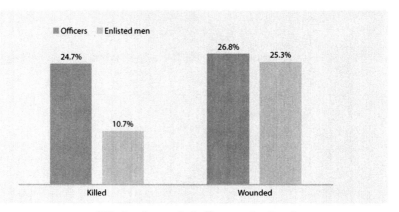

FIGURE 7.10. Killed and wounded officers and enlisted men

11 (36.5%) with combined wealth between $4,000 and $10,000 were either killed or wounded once, and more than half (51.2%) of the most affluent group of enlisted men, those whose personal and family wealth totaled more than $10,000, sustained at least one combat injury.

Strangely enough, among officers the wealthiest group suffered the fewest battlefield casualties (37.0%), but that statistic was skewed by rich assistant surgeons and surgeons. Among those whose personal and family wealth ranged between $4,000 and $10,000, nearly 8 of every 9 (85.2%) were killed or wounded at least once. At least half of all other wealth groups for officers were combat casualties, with the poorest element, between $0 and $400, enduring the smallest percentage of combat injuries at exactly 50.0%.

No officers in the sample died of disease, indicating both the huge combat losses and a healthier lifestyle before the war and in camp. By contrast, 1 in every 8 (12.7%) enlisted men perished from an illness; these individuals had a median personal and family wealth of $800. More than 4 of every 9 (45.3%) enlisted men who succumbed to illness had a combined personal and family wealth of $400 or less, yet more than 1 in every 4 (26.3%) claimed combined assets of at least $4,000, with 1 in 7 (14.4%) worth more than $10,000. Clearly, wealth alone did not shield enlisted men from the ravages of disease.[20]

Another 1 in 7 (14.2%) enlisted men who escaped death from combat or disease or who avoided serious injury was taken prisoner prior to the surrender at Appomattox. Of the officers who were neither killed, wounded, nor died of disease, approximately 1 in 7 (15.0%) became POWs. An additional 1 in 160 (0.6%) enlisted men lost their lives in various accidents, and 1 in 20 (4.9%) were discharged for disabilities other than wounds. Among officers, 1 in 33 (3.4%) were "retired" from the service because of an incapacity to serve.

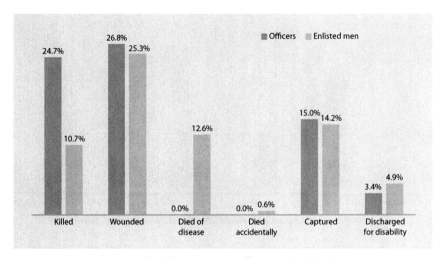

FIGURE 7.11. Total losses among officers and enlisted men

Two of every 3 (66.5%) officers were killed, wounded, or captured at least once. In total, slightly more than 2 of every 3 (67.1%) enlisted men were killed, wounded, imprisoned by the Federals, died of disease, or discharged for disability. If we remove deserters for the war from our calculations, we can see that almost 3 of every 4 (74.3%) enlisted men died or were wounded, captured, or discharged.

Figure 7.11 breaks down total losses of officers and enlisted men.[21]

Tensions between officers and enlisted men existed almost exclusively on a personal level. Some privates and noncommissioned officers disliked or were disdainful of individuals who held commissions, but there was no blanket animosity between the two groups. Too many officers had served as enlisted men before they received their commissions, and in most cases officers were elected to that post by their own soldiers. There were enough enlisted men from wealthy, slaveholding families and enough (1 in 5) officers from modest backgrounds to ensure shared prewar histories. Soldiers could not help noticing that 1 in every 4 officers was killed in action and more than half were either killed or wounded once. The death rate in combat was 2.25 times higher for officers than for enlisted men, and the chances of receiving at least one wound was 1.11 times greater for officers. Officers shared virtually all the same hardships, made the same sacrifices, and encountered worse on the battlefield, facts not lost on enlisted soldiers.

CHAPTER EIGHT

Year of Enlistment

In the aftermath of John Brown's bizarre scheme to end slavery by seizing the U.S. Arsenal in Harpers Ferry, Virginia, in October 1859 and distributing weapons to runaway slaves, Southern states recruited old militia units back to strength, created new ones, and even formed volunteer units that could serve beyond state boundaries. Recruits offered their services as part of the Virginia forces, and even before the commonwealth officially seceded from the Union, Confederate president Jefferson Davis directed manpower from other states to rush to its aid. This was the first wave of volunteers in 1861.

Some went to Virginia as entire regiments. Once there, companies banded to form regiments, and regiments, arriving either whole or in fragments, united to create brigades. Volunteers rallied around the banner, some armed with quality rifled muskets but others bringing with them bird guns, pistols, and knives. But a shortage of quality weapons and accoutrements, as well as an inability to master the art of logistics, discouraged many enthusiastic Rebels from entering the army.

Later that summer and into the fall, largely due to the great Confederate success in the Battle of First Manassas, a second wave of volunteers organized companies and regiments for service in Virginia. By the time that flood of volunteers ceased, nearly half (49.3%) the sample of men who served in the Army of Northern Virginia had joined the Confederate army.

That winter, Confederate authorities worried about the future of national defense. Most of the men who had volunteered in 1861 had signed up for only a year, and political and military officials feared the army might disband just as the spring campaign season arrived. The government offered various inducements to extend their tours of service, but soldiers hesitated. Some felt they had done their duty; it was time someone else stepped up to assume responsibility for the Confederate nation's defense. Others were tired of military life — the novelty had surely worn off; they wanted to go home, handle family affairs, consult with loved ones about the decision. Then perhaps they would return to the army. Still others wanted to see how many of their comrades would reenlist before they took the plunge.

National security could not wait. In April 1862, the Confederate Congress passed and Davis signed into law the Conscription Act. All those who entered the army in 1861 would have to extend their service by two years. As compensation, they would receive a furlough to return home as circumstances permitted, and they could elect new officers or keep their old ones if they liked. Soldiers who were dissatisfied with their organization could switch to another branch of service or join a new regiment as long as they remained in the Confederate army. By the summer, the Confederacy would then begin drafting men between the ages of 18 and 35 to bring troop strength up to 6% of the white population of each state. Davis willingly agreed to defer conscription to give states a chance to fill up their ranks with inducements and avoid the stigma of military service as a "draftee." By late summer, the Confederacy began to conscript soldiers in earnest. One in every 3 men (33%) in the sample joined the army in 1862.

Over the next two years, the Confederacy used the carrot and stick to continue raising troops. Some volunteered rather than dishonor the family name by being drafted. Quite a number of others were young men, coming of age, who eagerly offered their services to the Confederacy. One in every 9 (11.2%) of the sample entered military service for the first time in 1863, a rate that trickled to 1 in 16 (6.5%) in 1864. Only a handful of men volunteered in 1865, so few that none made the sample.[1]

The age of soldiers by year of entry into military service varied significantly over the course of four years. The volunteers of 1861 had an average age of 25 when they entered the service, and the median age was 23. The following year, 1862, enlistees averaged a half-year older, and the median year of birth fell back to 1837, indicating a slightly older population. For those who entered military service in 1863, ages tended to polarize between more extremes. The average year of birth declined to 1834.6, yet the median increased to 22 years of age (1939.0) when the war broke out. By 1864, large numbers of young and old men entered the army. The median birth year jumped to 1841.0, and the average climbed to 1837.2.

By grouping birth years, however, more interesting patterns emerge. Soldiers who were born between 1799 and 1820 constituted between 1 in 20 (5.1%) and 1 in 23 (4.4%) enlistees in 1861 and 1862. In 1863 they made up 1 in every 7 (13.7%) men who joined; the next year they composed 1 in every 8 (12.1%). In addition, men who were between 31 and 40 when the war broke out comprised 3 of every 11 (over 27%) new soldiers during those last two

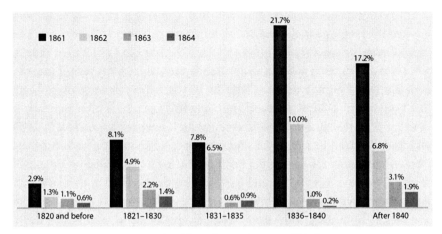

FIGURE 8.1. Year of entry by year of birth

years. Thus, in 1863 and 1864, 2 of every 5 (41.0% and 39.6% respectively) men who entered the army were 33 years of age or older. In those same years, 1863 and 1864, almost 2 of every 5 (38.6% and 38.4%) new soldiers came at the other end of the age bracket, those who were born between 1841 and 1848. A majority of the men who rushed to arms in 1861 and 1862 were between 21 and 30 years of age when fighting broke out. During the last two years of active recruitment, this age group accounted for 1 in every 5 (20.4% in 1863 and 21.9% in 1864) soldiers.[2]

Figure 8.1 is a breakdown of year of entry into military service by age.

To a large degree, geographic mobility reflected the age of soldiers when they entered the service. Only 1 in every 11 (8.8%) men who joined the army in 1864 resided in a state other than the one in which they were born. By contrast, almost 3 of every 10 volunteers in 1861 had left their birth state for homes elsewhere. The anomaly was 1863, when nearly one-third (32.8%) had migrated to a new state. Perhaps the high percentage of older soldiers—more than 2 of every 5 (41.0%) were at least 33 years of age—may have been a telling factor in the 1863 migration rates.

The proportion of troops entering the army from the Upper South versus the Lower South remained relatively constant over the four years, except for 1863. In that year, the share of men from the Upper South rose from a little below 5 in 9 to 13 in 20 (64.8%), or close to 6 in 9. This was the last year when a rather substantial number of soldiers entered the army for the first time, when the Confederacy still had a fairly sizable population for conscription, and when the men it took for Lee's army tended to reside in that theater of war.

Prewar occupations reflected both the high percentage of young males who entered the army late in the war and government policies to fill the ranks. The ratio of students went from 1 in 8 (12.5%) in 1861 and 1 in 10 (9.9%) in 1862 to 3 in 11 (26.8%) in 1863 and 3 in 10 (30.2%) in 1864. By the last year of the war, comparatively few men were available for service except those coming of age. The proportion of farmers leaped from one-half (49.2%) in 1861 to nearly 2 of every 3 (65.7%) in 1862. The following year, it fell back to one-half (49.5%) and then declined to just under 2 in every 5 (39.2%) in 1864, reflecting the need to keep more farmers in the fields producing food. Skilled workers held steady at nearly 1 in 10 (9.9% and 9.3%) during the first two years of the war. As wartime needs became clearer, the ratio of skilled workers fell to less than 1 in 26 (3.8%) in 1863, since the government preferred to keep skilled workers at home producing materials to supply the war effort and the needs of civilians. The next year, however, the ratio of skilled workers soared to 1 in 10 (10%). The Confederacy began inducting skilled workers through the draft and employing them at their trade for the direct benefit of the army. Interestingly, white-collar nonprofessionals made up only 1 in every 25 soldiers in Lee's army. These jobs were usually held by young males on a professional apprentice track, such as bank or merchant-store clerks. Virtually all of them enlisted in 1861 or 1862.[3]

Figure 8.2 breaks down year of entry into the army by prewar occupation.

Soldiers' year of entry into Lee's army according to their marital and parental status represented interesting trends. In 1861, less than 3 in every 11 (27.9%) volunteers were married. Single men, society's most expendable and the ones generally with the fewest commitments, rushed off to war in the *rage militaire*. The next year saw a pronounced shift, as a majority (54.0%) of those who entered the army left wives at home. Thus in the initial waves of recruitment the Confederacy had tapped motivated single men to serve, and in the second year married men stepped forward. In 1863, marital status returned to a more balanced ratio of 3 single for every 2 married men, one that most closely resembled figures for the entire war. In 1864, however, as the manpower pipeline began to dry up and the army mustered in a larger proportion of skilled workers and fewer men under age 29, slightly more than half (51.6%) of the men were single.

Statistics on soldiers with children at home tended to follow marital patterns. In 1861, less than 1 in every 4 (23.8%) volunteers left children behind. Those who entered the army in 1862 or 1864 were most likely to have children. In both years, more than 2 of every 5 (42.4% and 40.7% respectively) men who entered the army left children back home at least temporarily fatherless.[4]

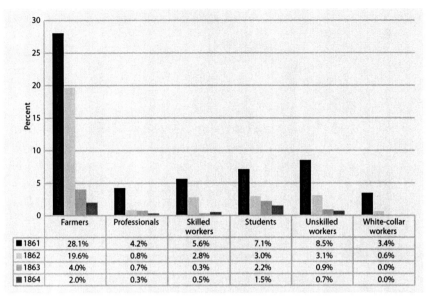

	Farmers	Professionals	Skilled workers	Students	Unskilled workers	White-collar workers
■1861	28.1%	4.2%	5.6%	7.1%	8.5%	3.4%
1862	19.6%	0.8%	2.8%	3.0%	3.1%	0.6%
1863	4.0%	0.7%	0.3%	2.2%	0.9%	0.0%
■1864	2.0%	0.3%	0.5%	1.5%	0.7%	0.0%

FIGURE 8.2. Year of entry by occupation

Figure 8.3 breaks down year of entry into the army by marital and parental status.

Age and marital status offered valuable indicators of personal wealth. Only in 1862, when a majority of new soldiers were married, did troops have a median personal wealth above $0, and in that year it was only $30. The average personal wealth ranged from a low of $1,254 in 1861 to a high of $2,891 in 1864. Not surprisingly, given that their numbers represented a high percentage of single men, the volunteers of 1861 were among the army's poorest soldiers, with more than 7 of every 9 (78.5%) worth between $0 and $400. One in 10 was middle class (9.9%), worth between $800 and $3,999. Barely 1 in 17 (5.9%) was valued at $4,000 or more. With such a high percentage of married volunteers, the men of 1862 had more assets in the middle (13.5%) and upper range (14.0%). The last two years of the conflict saw greater extremes, reflecting age of the soldiers. In 1863, more than 3 of every 4 troops were worth $400 or less and more than 1 in 6 (17.4%) were worth at least $4,000. In 1864, some 13 of every 20 (63.7%) were poor, while almost 3 of every 10 (29.2%) were rich, reflecting the preponderance of soldiers between 29 and 45. In 1863 and 1864, between 1 in 18 (1863) and 1 in 14 (1864) were of the middle economic class.[5]

Figure 8.4 tracks year of entry into the army by personal wealth.

When we combined the personal and family wealth of those troops who resided with close relations, poverty declined and a real middle economic

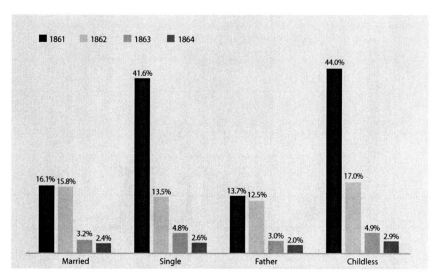

FIGURE 8.3. Year of entry by marital and parental status

class emerged. The median personal and family wealth ranged from $1,200 for volunteers in 1861 to $3,860 for men who entered the army for the first time in 1864. Soldiers of 1862 boasted the highest average wealth at $11,237, while the recruits of 1861 had the lowest at $7,049. Among the volunteers of 1861, close to 4 of every 9 (42.8%) had total assets under $800, the highest ratio of poor troops and families according to year of enlistment. At the same time, just fewer than 1 in 4 (23.2%) was in the middle economic class. The 1863 year group had the lowest percentage in the middle class at 21.9, while 1864 had the highest at 23.6. A staggering 3 of every 7 (37.9%) men who joined the army in 1863 and nearly 4 in 9 (43.4%) in 1864 possessed a combined wealth of $4,000 or more. This reflected the large number of young men who were coming of age and still lived at home, as well as men between the ages of 40 and 45, many of them already established in society, who in mid-July 1863 were suddenly subject to the draft.[6]

Figure 8.5 displays the year of entry into Lee's army by economic class for personal and family wealth.

Slave ownership followed along comparable lines with Southern wealth. Only 1 in 10 (9.5%) volunteers in 1861 owned bondsmen and bondswomen. Since more than 2 of every 3 (67.3%) enlistees in 1861 were born after 1835, and more than 7 of every 10 (72.1%) were unmarried, this figure does not appear unusual. The following year, 1862, with more married and well-to-do men entering the army, greater than 1 in every 6 (18.2%) soldiers held slaves

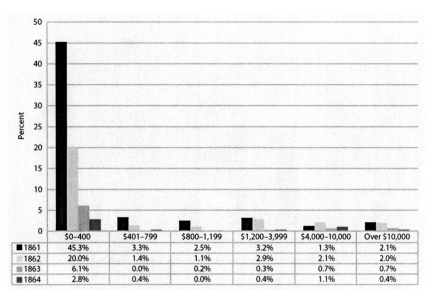

	$0–400	$401–799	$800–1,199	$1,200–3,999	$4,000–10,000	Over $10,000
■ 1861	45.3%	3.3%	2.5%	3.2%	1.3%	2.1%
1862	20.0%	1.4%	1.1%	2.9%	2.1%	2.0%
■ 1863	6.1%	0.0%	0.2%	0.3%	0.7%	0.7%
■ 1864	2.8%	0.4%	0.0%	0.4%	1.1%	0.4%

FIGURE 8.4. Year of entry by personal wealth

personally. That ratio declined in 1863 to less than 1 in 7 (13.7%), but with older, more established men joining the army in 1864, the ratio jumped to more than 2 in 9 (23.1%).[7]

When personal slaveholding combined with those slaves owned by family members with whom the soldier resided, numbers changed but the patterns remained similar. Once again, servicemen in 1862 or their families had the highest proportion of slave ownership at just below 4 in every 9 (42.1%), followed by the 1864 year group and their families at 2 in 5 (40.7%). Men who joined the army in 1863 had the lowest rate of combined personal and family slave ownership at slightly above 3 in 10 (31.0%), followed by the recruits of 1861 at 7 in 20 (35.3%). The 1863 year group had by far the fewest soldiers or families with only one or two slaves at 1 in 100 (1.0%), yet it also had the highest proportion of soldiers from the planter class at 1 in 10 (10.2%).

Soldiers from 1863 came from the lowest proportion of slaveholding households at 3 of every 7 (38.5%). Almost half (47.6%) of all volunteers and conscripts in 1862 resided in slaveholding households, the highest among the four years. Soldiers of both 1861 (43.6%) and 1864 (44.0%) averaged approximately 4 in every 9 from slaveowning households.[8]

Figure 8.6 breaks down year of entry into the army by personal, combined personal and family, and household slave ownership.

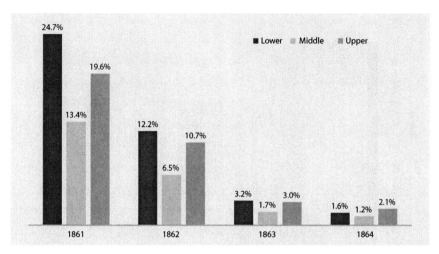

FIGURE 8.5. Year of entry by economic class

Most interestingly, the men who entered the army in 1864 had by far the lowest ratio of soldiers who came from planter families at 1 in every 60 (1.7%) —almost four times lower than the next lowest year group, 1861, which had 6.3%. The termination of the Twenty (later Fifteen) Negro Law, as it was called, which had allowed families with 20 or more slaves to keep an adult white male at home, had no significant impact on recruitment, because so many able-bodied white males of military age from planter families were already in uniform. In 1864, 1 in every 30 (3.3%) came from planter households, a rate 2.8 times lower than the next lowest year group, the volunteers of 1861. Thus, the elimination of the slave exemption had no real impact on numbers entering military service from planter households, either.

While soldiers in the 1861 and 1863 year groups resided in counties with comparatively low averages of slave-to-white ratios—72.0% of the 1861 group and 74.1% of the 1863 group lived in areas with a white majority—a surprising 3 of every 4 (74.5%) soldiers of 1862 did so as well, even though the 1862 group came from the highest percentage of personal and family slaveowning and slaveholding households. The soldiery of 1864, with strong ties to slave-owning, claimed almost 5 of every 9 (53.3%) troops from counties with a black majority.

In the dash to arms in the first year of war, 9 of every 10 (89.0%) volunteers chose to serve in the infantry, and more men went into the artillery (6.9%) than the cavalry (4.5%). In 1862, more enlistees gravitated to the cavalry. The harsh reality of infantry service and a conscious movement to increase the number of cavalry regiments—a shortage of cavalry at First Manassas in July

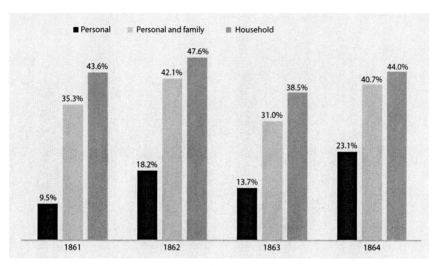

FIGURE 8.6. Year of entry by slaveholding

1861 had severely impaired Confederate pursuit after the victory—resulted that year in the assignment of more than 1 in 6 recruits (17.7%) to cavalry units. The new wave of artillerymen at 7.3% remained roughly the same as previously, but the proportion of infantrymen declined to 3 of every 4 (75.1%). The swashbuckling media image of cavalrymen, particularly under Major General J. E. B. Stuart, as well as the perception of its ease of duties compared with the demands of the infantry and the artillery produced a flood of men in the mounted branch in 1863 and 1864. In 1863, slightly more than 3 in 10 (30.7%) joined the cavalry, and despite declining fortunes and huge losses of infantrymen in 1864, nearly 2 in 9 (21.4%) entered the army as horsemen that year. Almost 1 in every 8 (11.9%) new soldiers in 1864 joined the artillery, while the infantry rebounded slightly from a low of 63.9% in 1863 to 2 of every 3 (66.6%) the following year.[9]

Figure 8.7 traces year of entry into the army by branch of service.

Virtually all officers entered the Army of Northern Virginia during the first two years of the war. In 1861, 1 in every 9 (10.8%) volunteers became a commissioned officer, a group that constituted close to 3 of every 4 (72.7%) officers in Lee's army. In 1862, 1 in 20 (5.1%) men was commissioned. Overall, they composed over 19 of every 20 (95.4%) officers under Lee's command. In the sample, only two more men received a commission—one in each of the next two years—for the rest of the war; both were assistant surgeons.[10]

According to existing records, nearly all of the soldiers in the sample entered military service through enlistment. A solitary soldier in the sample joined the

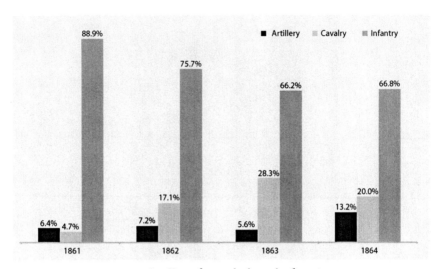

FIGURE 8.7. Year of entry by branch of service

army as a substitute. Crawford Talley, a prewar painter with a wife and child at home, enrolled in the 4th Virginia in June 1862 as a substitute for J. R. K. Bentley. Within days Talley was captured. Two months later, he was exchanged, but by December Talley had deserted, never to return.

Only in 1863 did a substantial proportion come from the draft. In that year, close to 1 in every 7 (13.4%) soldiers was conscripted. In 1862, one in every 33 (3.0%) was drafted, and in 1864, 1 in 39 (2.6%) entered against their will.

Figure 8.8 displays the percentage of conscripts in Lee's army by year of entry.

Philip Brady of New Orleans, an Irishman by birth and a married father of one child, served in the 1st Louisiana Infantry from April 1861 (before the Confederate Congress established conscription) until July 1862, when he was discharged from military service for being overage. After the government expanded the draft age, Brady was conscripted in January 1864 and assigned to the 2nd Company of the Richmond Howitzers. He served faithfully until he was captured in April 1865.

In addition to Brady, conscripts tended to come from the poorer segments of society. In 1862, 9 of every 20 (44.8%) conscripts had total combined assets (personal and immediate families) of $400 or less; the next year, more than half (51.3%) the conscripts and their families fit into that economic category. Five of 9 (55.2%) conscripts had combined personal and family wealth of under $800, while 9 in 20 boasted total assets between $4,000 and $10,000. According to the sample, two conscripts, one who entered the army in 1863

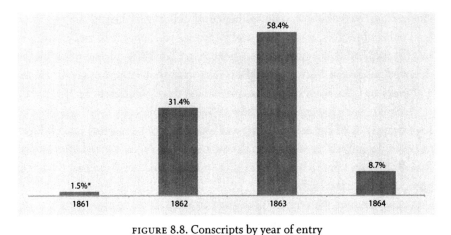

FIGURE 8.8. Conscripts by year of entry
*The percentage for 1861 came before the Confederate Congress established conscription.

and the other in 1864, possessed personal and family wealth over $10,000. In 1862, one-third (33.3%) of the conscripts came from slaveholding families. That ratio dipped to 1 in 9 (11.1%) in 1863. The sole conscript of 1864, Private Charles H. West of the 27th South Carolina Infantry, owned eight slaves and had personal wealth valued at almost $12,000. At the time of his conscription West was a 33-year-old father of five.

Soldiers who entered the army in the first two years of the war were much more likely to go absent without leave than their later comrades. One in 10 (9.6%) volunteers of 1861 went AWOL, and that statistic remained roughly the same at 9.8% the following year. The proportion of men who went AWOL declined to 1 in 40 (2.5%) in the 1863 year group, and among the soldiers of 1864 it slipped to 1 in every 101 (0.9%) men.[11]

On the surface, desertion rates by the year of entry into military service followed a reasonable pattern, except for one year. Slightly more than 1 in every 7 (14.9%) enlistees in 1861 deserted at least once during the course of the war, an average of 3.7% per year of service. That ratio of deserters held fairly steady at 1 in 7 (13.7%) among the soldiers of 1862, but the annual percentage of desertions per year escalated to 4.6. For the men of 1863, desertions soared to a little below 3 in every 10 (28.9%), with an annual percentage of 14.5. The 1864 year group abandoned the ranks permanently at 8.1%, a very high level that was indicative of the hard combat service, severe shortages, and a faltering war effort, but it paled in comparison with the rates for soldiers from the previous year.[12]

What affected desertion rates among the year groups more than any other single factor was the powerful influence of children at home. Among those who enlisted in 1861, fewer than 2 of 7 (27.2%) were married, and less than 1 in 4 (23.8%) had children at home. Almost 1 in 5 (18.8%) soldiers with children deserted, while 1 in 8 (12.5%) childless men deserted. Fathers made up almost 3 of every 10 (29.2%) of those who abandoned the Confederate army.

The next year's group, that of 1862, reflected its majority marriage rate and high frequency of fatherhood. Three of every 8 (37%) deserters had children at home. Examined another way, almost 1 in 6 (16.1%) of those fathers abandoned the flag. One in every 8 (12.5%) childless soldiers from the 1862 year group fled from the ranks.

Among the men who entered the army in 1863, almost 4 of every 9 (42.9%) deserters had children at home, even though fewer than 2 of every 5 (39.6%) married before the war and only 3 of 8 (37.9%) had children. Interestingly, 1 in 7 (15.2%) men who stayed in the ranks was a father.

Of those who entered Lee's army in 1864, 2 of 3 deserters had children at home, while 2 of every 5 (40.7%) in the entire year group had children. Among the men who joined the army in 1864 and had no children at home, only 1 in every 30 (3.3%) deserted the army.[13]

The economic level of deserters by year of entry into the army varied widely. Among the volunteers in 1861, almost 4 of every 9 (42.9%) deserters came from families that were worth between $0 and $400. Another 1 in 5 (20.8%) deserters possessed family wealth between $1,200 and $3,999. The lowest percentages of deserters were from the two wealthiest groups. One in 13 soldiers (7.9%) who abandoned the ranks had a family valued at between $4,000 and $10,000, and 1 in 15 (6.9%) who did so had families worth over $10,000. Among soldiers who joined the army in 1862, almost half (48.4%) of all deserters had personal and family wealth between $0 and $400, and 3 of 5 (59%) were valued at less than $800. Fewer than 1 in 6 (15.5%) deserters was from a family valued at $4,000 or more. Among deserters in the 1863 year group, 4 in 9 (43.7%) came from the poorest element, yet more than 3 of 10 (31.2%) possessed personal and family wealth of $4,000 or more. In 1864, almost 4 of every 5 deserters were in the poorest group, below $400 in personal and family worth, and slightly more than 1 in 5 (21.5%) deserters came from combined wealth between $4,000 and $10,000.[14]

Figure 8.9 tracks the economic class of deserters by their year of entry into the army. Economic class was based on combined personal and family wealth—if soldiers lived with their families.

Soldiers who came from slaveholding families were much less likely to desert. In fact, men from nonslaveowning families in 1861 were more than 7

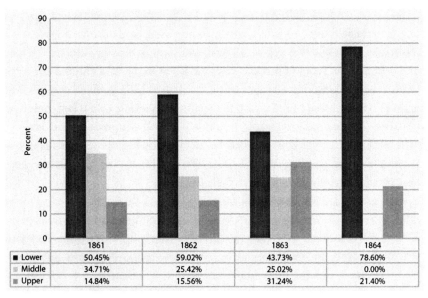

	1861	1862	1863	1864
■ Lower	50.45%	59.02%	43.73%	78.60%
Middle	34.71%	25.42%	25.02%	0.00%
■ Upper	14.84%	15.56%	31.24%	21.40%

FIGURE 8.9. Economic class of deserters by year of entry

times as likely to desert as those from slaveowning families. In 1862, that figure slipped to more than 4.4 times as likely to desert. In 1863, soldiers from
families with no bondsmen or bondswomen were more than 4.1 times as likely
to desert. Among the men who entered the army in 1864, those without slaves
in their families were twice as likely to abandon the flag.[15]

Not surprisingly, casualties fell disproportionately on soldiers who joined
the army in the first two years of the war. Two of every 3 (67.7%) troops killed
in action were among the volunteers of 1861, and 1 in every 4 (24.1%) who lost
their lives in battle entered military service in 1862. Despite the heavy combat
in 1863 and 1864, soldiers who entered Lee's army during those two years were
far less likely to be killed on the battlefield. Only 1 in every 29 (3.5%) soldiers
who gave their lives in combat joined Lee's army in 1863, and 1 in 22 (4.5%)
entered in 1864. The continual, intense fighting in the 1864 campaign most
likely preyed on the raw troops, causing the 1864 year group to suffer greater
fatalities in combat than the men who had joined a year earlier. Moreover, the
unusually high desertion rate of the 1863 year group kept many soldiers off the
battlefield.[16]

The statistics for wounded soldiers were fairly similar. More than 5 of every
9 (56.3%) men wounded at least once volunteered for army service in 1861,
and another 4 of 11 (35.3%) joined the following year. Less than 1 in 6 (6.3%)
was from the 1863 year group, and a mere 1 in 50 (2.0%) entered in 1864.

Yet when we look at killed and wounded as a total percentage of the year in which these troops joined the army, some differences become apparent. Of those who were killed in action, a consistent pattern emerges among the men in the first three years of service. About 4.7% of those who entered the army in 1863 were killed; the kill rate among the men of 1862 doubled to 9.5%; and of those who enlisted in 1861, with the lengthiest service, 14.2% lost their lives in battle. The anomaly, however, was that of those who entered the army in 1864, 1 in 9 (11.1%) died in combat. No doubt, this high proportion could be attributed to the grinding campaigns in 1864 and the lack of battlefield experience, which cost the 1864 soldiers their lives.

Proportions altered somewhat among wounded in action. Nearly 3 in 10 (28.8%) 1861 volunteers sustained wounds. That number swelled to almost 1 in 3 (32.6%) for those who signed up in 1862. Heavy fighting during their first year in the army and their lack of training may have been significant factors in those losses. For the men who entered in 1863, about 1 in 6 (17.2%) was wounded, and 1 soldier in 9 — exactly the same percentage as those who were killed in action — in the 1864 year group suffered wounds.

Figure 8.10 shows the percentage of men killed and wounded by year of entry into Lee's army.[17]

When we combine those who were wounded at least once and those who were killed in action, the results are more predictable. Based on this calculation, 2 of every 5 (40.0%) volunteers in 1861 were killed or wounded at least once. For those who entered military service the next year, the ratio remained virtually the same (39.3%). Soldiers who joined the army in 1863 were killed or wounded at a rate slightly greater than 1 in 5 (21.9%). The men of 1864 lost more than 2 in 9 (22.3%) peers on the battlefield.

An examination of combat injuries and fatalities indicates a clustering effect. Soldiers who entered the army in 1861 and 1862 had almost identical percentages. Heavy combat service over the years took its toll on 2 of every 5 men from those years. A combination of comparatively limited fighting in 1861 and heavy fighting for inexperienced and lightly trained men in 1862 led to the convergence. Among the recruits of 1863 and 1864, a similar clustering around 2 of 9 troops occurred. Once again, soldiers who entered military service in 1863 unquestionably experienced harsh combat, but the men who joined up in 1864 were thrust into battle immediately and had no hiatus or time to acclimate to battlefront conditions.

Figure 8.11 depicts the percentage of men wounded at least once or killed in action by year of entry into military service.[18]

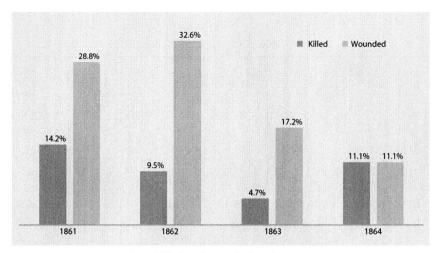

FIGURE 8.10. Killed and wounded within year of entry

Wealthier men from the first two recruitment years had the highest percentages of casualties. In the 1861 year group, 2 of every 5 (39.5%) soldiers with combined personal and family assets of $4,000 to $10,000 were killed or wounded, and almost half (48.2%) of all men with combined assets exceeding $10,000 experienced the same losses. In 1862, 3 of every 11 (28.0%) in the $4,000 to $10,000 category and almost 4 of 9 (42.9%) in the above $10,000 group were either wounded at least once or killed in action. The number of killed and wounded in the economic categories for 1863 and 1864 were too small to make any reliable claims, but in both years the fate of soldiers in the two wealthiest categories suggests a more confused portrait. For the men of 1863, only 12.6% of all soldiers who were killed and wounded came from families worth $4,000 or more, whereas 27.9% of the 1864 year group met the same fate.[19]

Similar statistics emerged from an examination of personal and family slaveholding and of killed and wounded in battle. More than half (53.3%) of the soldiers from slaveholding families who volunteered in 1861 were killed or wounded, compared to a third (33.2%) from nonslaveholding families. The next year, the difference closed to 41.6% slaveholders to 39.8% men with no slaves. Among men who joined in 1863, just below 1 in 6 (15.4%) soldiers from slaveholding families were killed and wounded; 1 in 3 (32.7%) nonslaveholders suffered the same fate. With the draft age bumped back to 45, a greater percentage of older, more financially comfortable men entered the army. Many of them fell to illness or lacked the combat aggressiveness of their younger

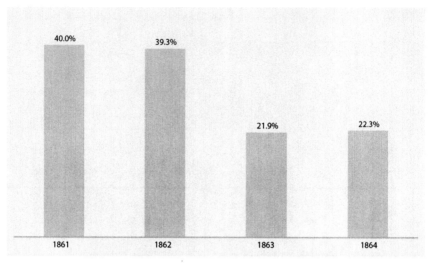

FIGURE 8.11. Wounded at least once or killed by year of entry

comrades and escaped the battlefield unscathed physically. In 1864, with only four slaveholders in the entire sample, the percentage of soldiers from non-slaveholding families who were killed or wounded exceeded those from slave-owners' families, 30.6% versus 14.9%.[20]

Although tales of woe over illness early in the war were widespread and accurate, death from sickness actually affected the 1862 and 1863 year groups more than the other two groups. Troops who volunteered in 1861 succumbed to disease at the rate of 1 in 10 (9.6%). That rate accelerated to 1 in 7 (14.2%) in 1862 and to a tragic 1 in 5 (21.1%) in 1863. Perhaps due more to the collapse of effective record keeping and the soaring casualties than to hearty constitutions, only 1 in 100 (0.94%) men who joined the army in 1864 fell to illness. In 1861, the poorest class of soldiers (worth less than $400) died from disease at the rate of more than 1 in 7 (15.3%), followed by soldiers who came from families worth $800 to $1,199 also at 1 in 7 (14.5%). Among the men from 1862, the poorest once again suffered badly, losing a little less than 1 in 6 (16.0%), yet middle-class soldiers endured the greatest percentage of fatalities. Slightly less than 3 in 10 (28%) men from families worth between $800 and $1,199 and more than 1 in 6 (17.3%) whose families enjoyed prosperity between $1,200 and $3,999 succumbed to disease. Statistics for 1863 and 1864 were too limited for a reliable conclusion, but in 1863 the middle class and the lower half of the upper class demonstrated the highest percentage of fatalities from disease. For those who entered the army in 1864, only one soldier in the sample who

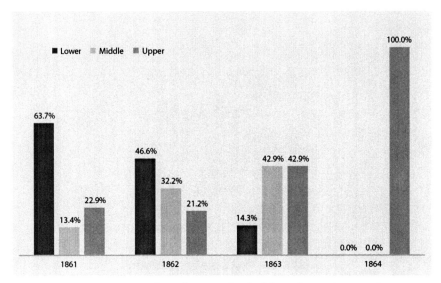

FIGURE 8.12. Economic class of troops who died from disease by year of entry

died of disease was located in the census records. Private James O. Rothwell, who had just turned 18 years of age, enlisted in the Albemarle Everette Artillery. The son of a slaveholding father, Rothwell lost his life to chronic diarrhea on 20 September 1864.[21]

Figure 8.12 traces the economic class of soldiers who died from disease by year of entry into Lee's army.

Rothwell defied the trend. Among those who entered the army in 1861, 1862, and 1863, soldiers from nonslaveholding families died at a higher rate from disease than those from slaveowning families.

In total casualties—killed, died of disease, died accidentally, wounded, captured by the enemy, or discharged for disability—the burden quite naturally fell disproportionately on those who served the longest. More than 7 of every 10 (70.6%) volunteers in 1861 endured at least one of these afflictions. Those who joined the fighting in 1862 suffered casualties at an even higher rate: almost 3 in every 4 (72.2%). Many of the men of 1862 were immediately thrust into some of the most disastrous campaigns of the war, with little training or physical or psychological hardening to help them confront and cope with the hardships of combat and army life. The troops who arrived in 1863 lost 5 of every 9 (54.1%) comrades. Had so many men in that year group not deserted, the percentage of losses would most certainly have been considerably higher. The surprising statistic, though, was the proportion of losses among the men

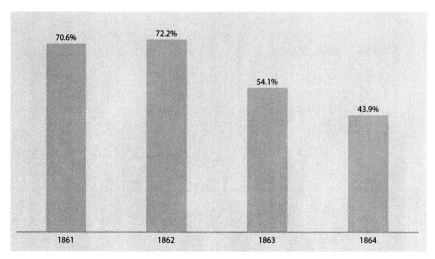

FIGURE 8.13. Total losses by year of entry

who entered the ranks for the first time in 1864. In one year or less of service, 4 of every 9 (43.9%) of them were lost to the Confederate army.[22]

Figure 8.13 compares the total losses in Lee's army by year of entry.

Despite some subtle shifts in age, marital status, and fatherhood, the backgrounds of soldiers by year of enlistment exhibited unusual consistency. Only in areas in which longer military service resulted in greater risks and more likely elevation in rank did significant distinctions appear by year group.

CHAPTER NINE

Age

Prosecessionist "Fire-Eater" Edmund Ruffin was 67 years old when his beloved Virginia joined the Confederate States of America. He served briefly, but the hardships of military service compelled him to leave the army. John T. Bivins of Milledgeville also enlisted and was forced to leave. Bivins had run off to war at age 14. His father secured his army release from the commander in chief, Jefferson Davis, imploring the president to allow young Bivins to grow up before he performed honorable service for his country. Most soldiers, though, resembled Private James D. Gilliam of the Lynchburg Artillery. A 22-year-old unskilled laborer, Gilliam lived with his widowed mother and six siblings when he enthusiastically answered the initial call to arms in April 1861.

Only 1 in 18 (5.9%) of all the men who served in Lee's army was older than 40 in 1861. Roughly 1 in 6 (16.6%) was between 31 and 40, and about the same ratio (15.8%) applied to those between 26 and 30 when the war broke out. One-third (32.9%) of all soldiers were between 21 and 25, and nearly 1 in 5 (19.4%) spanned the ages 18 through 20. One in 10 (9.5%) was a minor—17 and under—when the war began. (The year of birth of the soldiers in Lee's army is tracked in Chapter 1, Figure 1.1.)

Generally, older soldiers were more likely to move to a new state than younger ones. Nearly 2 of every 5 (38.1%) men over age 40 settled in a new state at least once. That ratio declined steadily through the age group 21 to 25, but among those from 18 to 20, it jumped back up to more than 1 in 4, an apparent anomaly. Soldiers under 18 in 1861 seldom moved to a new state (14.3%).

Among the various occupations, the oldest troops had the highest percentage of farmers. Two of every 3 (66.1%) men over the age of 40 cultivated the soil for a living. The oldest men also dominated the professional class at a rate of 1 in 7 (15.1%). Skilled workers tended to cluster in the middle-age brackets. One in every 5 (19.6%) men born between 1831 and 1835 had a skill, as did more than 1 in 8 (12.9%) soldiers between the ages of 31 and 40. Younger men, particularly those who were barely of majority age in 1861, had yet to learn a trade and defined themselves as unskilled. One in 6 (13.5%) soldiers who were

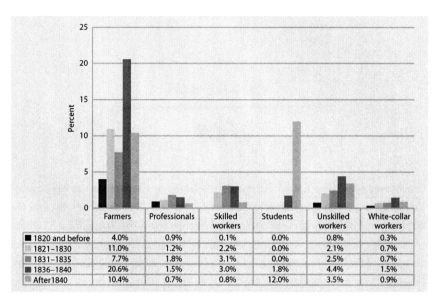

	Farmers	Professionals	Skilled workers	Students	Unskilled workers	White-collar workers
■ 1820 and before	4.0%	0.9%	0.1%	0.0%	0.8%	0.3%
1821–1830	11.0%	1.2%	2.2%	0.0%	2.1%	0.7%
1831–1835	7.7%	1.8%	3.1%	0.0%	2.5%	0.7%
■ 1836–1840	20.6%	1.5%	3.0%	1.8%	4.4%	1.5%
After 1840	10.4%	0.7%	0.8%	12.0%	3.5%	0.9%

FIGURE 9.1. Occupation by year of birth

18 to 20 years old fit this category. Most of the younger soldiers were still students when takers collected data for the 1860 census. Nearly 1 in 3 (31.2%) young adults between 18 and 20 and 2 of every 3 (67.1%) youths under 18 in 1861 were still in school, indicating by and large a well-educated soldiery.

Figure 9.1 displays prewar occupations by year of birth.

Nearly all older men were married before the war. This was true of almost 19 of every 20 (93.6%) soldiers over age 40 and 4 of 5 (80.1%) between 31 and 40. The ratio of married to single slipped to 3 of 5 (61.7%) for soldiers between 26 and 30. The overwhelming majority of those under 26 were single. Nearly 3 of every 4 (73.6%) men between 21 and 25 and 99.7% of those between 18 and 20 were single. The average year of birth for married men was 1829.2; for single men it was 1839.3. The median year of birth for married men was 1831, and for single soldiers it was 1840.

Parenthood mirrored marital status and age. Older soldiers more frequently had children at home, while younger men did not. According to the 1860 census, more than 3 of every 4 (76.2%) soldiers over the age of 40 had children living in their homes and troops between 31 and 40 had essentially the same ratio of 3 of 4 (75.0%). The proportion declined to 5 in 9 (54.7%) for soldiers who were 26 to 30, but then it fell off drastically. One in 6 (17.2%) men between 21 and 25 left children behind when they went off to war, and none of the younger soldiers claimed offspring.[1]

For the most part, as one would anticipate, personal wealth increased with

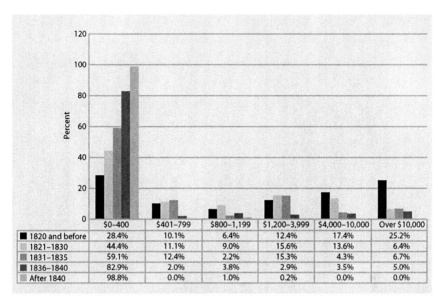

	$0–400	$401–799	$800–1,199	$1,200–3,999	$4,000–10,000	Over $10,000
■ 1820 and before	28.4%	10.1%	6.4%	12.4%	17.4%	25.2%
1821–1830	44.4%	11.1%	9.0%	15.6%	13.6%	6.4%
■ 1831–1835	59.1%	12.4%	2.2%	15.3%	4.3%	6.7%
■ 1836–1840	82.9%	2.0%	3.8%	2.9%	3.5%	5.0%
After 1840	98.8%	0.0%	1.0%	0.2%	0.0%	0.0%

FIGURE 9.2. Personal wealth by year of birth

age. Soldiers over age 40 had an average personal estate of $7,480 and a median net worth of $1,700. Those numbers declined to an average of $2,620 and a median of $600 for men who were born between 1821 and 1830. By the age group born between 1831 and 1835, median wealth had fallen to only $200. None of the other age brackets had a median wealth above $0. Average wealth also fell steadily until it reached $0 for troops who were born after 1843. More than 1 in 4 (25.2%) soldiers who were over 40 in 1861 possessed more than $10,000 in total assets, and more than 1 in 6 (17.4%) had a total new worth of $4,000 to $10,000. Nearly 4 of every 9 (42.7%) personally were in the wealthy class. The older group also included the smallest percentage of soldiers with less than $800 at 3 of every 8 (38.4%).

Among other age brackets, the percentage of men with personal wealth from $0 to $400 increased from 4 in every 9 (44.4%) for men born between 1821 and 1830 to every soldier who was under 18 in 1861. One in 5 troops in the 1821–30 bracket possessed total personal wealth of $4,000 or more. Men between the ages of 26 and 30 in 1861 comprised the largest middle class at more than 1 in 6 (17.5%).

Figure 9.2 gives the percentage of soldiers' personal wealth by their year of birth.

Once personal and family wealth, if a soldier lived with family, are combined, the statistics change dramatically. The oldest soldiers no longer have

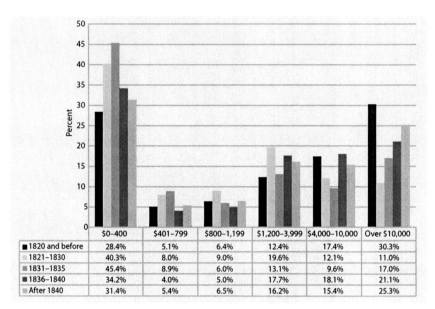

	$0–400	$401–799	$800–1,199	$1,200–3,999	$4,000–10,000	Over $10,000
■ 1820 and before	28.4%	5.1%	6.4%	12.4%	17.4%	30.3%
1821–1830	40.3%	8.0%	9.0%	19.6%	12.1%	11.0%
▨ 1831–1835	45.4%	8.9%	6.0%	13.1%	9.6%	17.0%
■ 1836–1840	34.2%	4.0%	5.0%	17.7%	18.1%	21.1%
▨ After 1840	31.4%	5.4%	6.5%	16.2%	15.4%	25.3%

FIGURE 9.3. Personal and family wealth by year of birth

the highest combined median wealth; the youngest troops do. Many of the
younger soldiers had parents as old, if not older, than the soldiers in the oldest age bracket, reflecting the notion that in general the older men grew the
more wealth they accumulated. Ultimately, age would negatively influence
their ability to earn high incomes and their total worth would decline, but that
would have affected very few young soldiers. The median wealth for men over
40 was $2,900, an extremely comfortable sum, but it paled in comparison
with soldiers who were minors when the war broke out. Their parents possessed enough assets for a median of $3,869. Men between 21 and 25 ($1,694)
and between 18 and 20 ($1,350) also came from families with high median
wealth. It was the soldiers from 26 to 40 who struggled. Men born between
1831 and 1835 had a combined personal and family median wealth of only $650,
and those born between 1821 and 1830 accounted for a median wealth of $850.
Because the youngest soldiers lived with their parents, they composed the
smallest fraction of troops with $400 or less in total assets at barely 1 in 5
(21.1%).[2]

Figure 9.3 shows the percentage of combined personal and family wealth by
year of birth.

Within households, wealth increased in every age group except the oldest,
where it remained the same. The median wealth of soldiers between the ages
of 31 and 40 rose from a combined personal and family wealth of $850 to

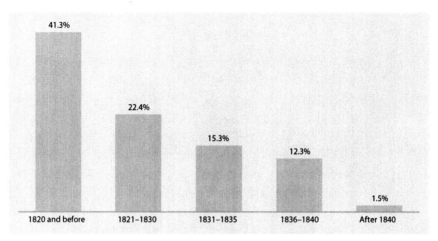

FIGURE 9.4. Personal slaveholding by year of birth

a household wealth of $1,295. Men between 26 and 30 increased their personal and family wealth from $650 to $900, which placed their lifestyle in the middle class. For troops between 21 and 25, median household wealth doubled, rising from $1,694 to $3,750 compared to personal and family wealth. Among men from 18 to 20, household wealth was 85% greater; even among the youngest it jumped another 13%.[3]

More than 2 of every 5 (41.3%) soldiers over 40 personally owned slaves. That dwindled steadily to 2 of 11 (22.4%) for troops between 31 and 40 and 1 in 7 (15.3%) for those between 25 and 30. One in every 8 (12.3%) men born between 1836 and 1840 had slaves, but only 2 soldiers in the sample under age 21 personally owned any slaves.[4]

Figure 9.4 contains the percentage of personal slaveowners by year of birth.

If we add family slaves to the equation, a more uneven portrait emerges. A majority of those soldiers under the age of 18 or their families had slaves (50.1%), as well as more than 9 of every 20 (46.3%) men over the age of 40. Two of every 5 (40.9%) soldiers from 18 to 25 or their families also owned slaves. Yet the percentage of men between 26 and 40 who possessed slaves was well below the average. Three in 10 (30.4%) born between 1831 and 1835 and 1 in 4 (25.0%) born from 1821 to 1830, or the family members with whom they resided, owned slaves. This imbalance carried over to slaveowning households, where close to half or more of the soldiers in each age group resided in a slaveowning household, except for troops between the ages of 26 and 40. Only 3 of every 8 (37.5%) men between 26 and 30 and 1 in every 3 (32.9%) between 31 to 40 resided in households with slaves.[5]

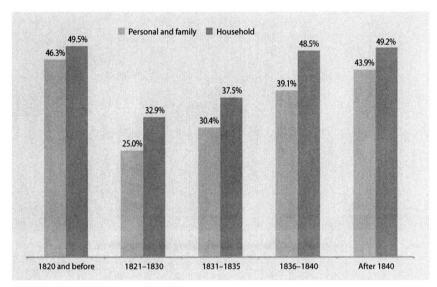

FIGURE 9.5. Personal and family, and household slaveholding by year of birth

Figure 9.5 shows the percentage of combined personal and family and household slaveholding by year of birth.

Although older soldiers were more likely to move to a new state, more than 5 of 9 (56.8%) remained in the Upper South. Young men between 18 and 25 in 1861 also lived predominantly in the Upper South. Only those under age 18 (56.7%) and between 26 and 30 (53.8%) had a majority come from the Lower South. Troops in the three youngest age brackets and those in the oldest resided in communities with the densest slave populations. Men over 40 had an average black-to-white ratio in their county of 4 to 5 (81.2%), while soldiers under 18 in 1861 lived in counties with 17 blacks to 20 whites (85.3%). Soldiers between 21 and 25 had more than a 4-to-5 ratio (82.5%), and those between 18 and 20 came from counties that averaged a 3-to-4 ratio (74.5%).[6]

Older and very young soldiers largely entered the Army of Northern Virginia later in the war, while those between 18 and 25 volunteered heavily that first year. Among soldiers over 40, nearly 3 in 10 (28.5%) joined the army in 1863 or 1864, even though only 17.8% of all soldiers in Lee's army entered in those two years. Men between 31 and 40 also swore the oath to serve in the Confederate army late in the war at a rate 19.7% higher than the army's soldiers as a whole. In 1862, men between 26 and 30 joined the army in far greater numbers—2 of every 5 (41.4%)—than those in any other age group. Some 2 of every 3 (66.0%) soldiers who served in Lee's army from ages 18 to 25

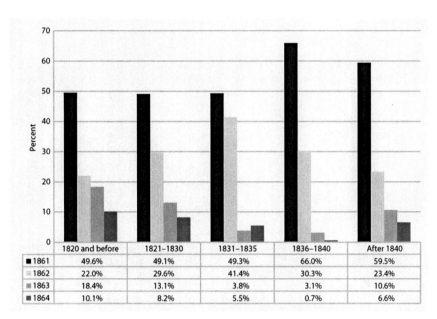

	1820 and before	1821–1830	1831–1835	1836–1840	After 1840
■ 1861	49.6%	49.1%	49.3%	66.0%	59.5%
1862	22.0%	29.6%	41.4%	30.3%	23.4%
▨ 1863	18.4%	13.1%	3.8%	3.1%	10.6%
■ 1864	10.1%	8.2%	5.5%	0.7%	6.6%

FIGURE 9.6. Age at entry by year of birth

enlisted when the war began. Three of 7 (37.3%) troops under 18 in 1861 joined the army in 1863 or 1864.[7]

Figure 9.6 traces age at entry into the army by year of birth.

The vast majority of men who were conscripted, nearly 2 of every 3 (64.7%), were between the ages of 26 and 40. An overwhelming number of soldiers who spanned those years were married—80.1% of 31- to 40-year-olds and 61.7% of 26- to 30-year olds—in an army where only 36.8% of all troops were actually married. They were also likely to have children at home, 75.0% for 31- to 40-year olds and 54.7% of 26- to 30-year-olds in an army where only 31.2% had children at home. Men with wives and children had different obligations and priorities than did single men, and they were much more likely to hesitate to enlist for fear that their family's well-being would suffer. The only soldiers in the sample who paid for substitutes were between 31 and 40 years of age in 1861.[8]

Age influenced soldiers in determining which branch of service to enter. Younger soldiers, caught up in the glamour of the cavalry, joined the mounted arm. Soldiers over 30 disproportionately entered the cavalry, too, but for very different reasons. The infantry and the artillery were more taxing physically. Older men preferred to ride rather than walk. Except for those who were minors when the war began, all other age groups entered the infantry at a rate

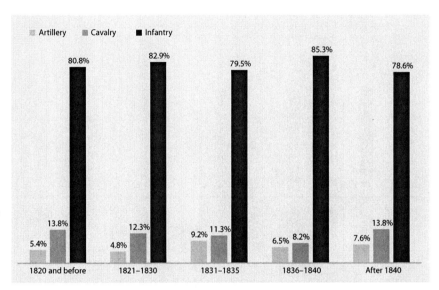

FIGURE 9.7. Branch of service by year of birth

of 4 of every 5 or slightly higher, commensurate with the 81.8% that infantry constituted in Lee's army. Those under age 18 in 1861 and men between 26 and 30 in the same year were the only groups to join the artillery at disproportionately high levels. The youngest men entered the conflict later and, armed with knowledge of its consequences, may have shied away from the infantry, where losses were staggering. Men between 25 and 30 had by far the highest percentage of skilled workers (19.6%, with an armywide average of 9.2%) among them, and a disproportionate number of skilled workers most likely found the artillery appealing for reasons of technology, necessary skill, and teamwork.[9]

Figure 9.7 tracks the selection of branch of service by year of birth.

Only two birth year groups had a higher percentage of officers than Lee's army generally. Even though officers comprised less than 1 in every 12 (8.1%) men who served, soldiers between the ages of 31 and 40 more than doubled that rate with better than 1 in 6 (17.8%) earning commissions. A slightly higher proportion of soldiers between the ages of 21 and 25 (11.1%) could also be found in the officer's ranks. None of the troops in the sample who were minors at the time of the war earned commissions, and only 1 in 26 (3.8%) between 18 and 20 in 1861 ever received commissions as officers.[10]

In Lee's army, soldiers between 18 and 25 were twice as likely to go absent without leave as those in other age brackets. This may have reflected a lack of self-discipline in that group. One in 8 (12.1%) troops between 21 and 25 and 1

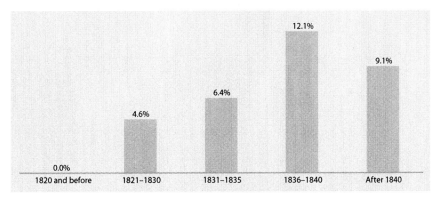

FIGURE 9.8. AWOL by year of birth

in 9 (10.9%) between 18 and 20 were AWOL at least once. Only men between 26 and 30 came close to that record, at less than 1 in 16 (6.4%).[11]

Figure 9.8 provides the rate of AWOL by soldiers' year of birth.

Older soldiers were more likely to desert than younger troops. Men over 40 abandoned the army at the rate of 17.9%; those between 31 and 40, at the rate of 17%; and those between 26 and 30, at the rate of 16.3%. The overwhelming majority of them had wives and children at home — powerful inducements to desert. For the three age brackets of soldiers who were 30 and older, married rates varied from 61.7% to 93.6% and parents with children at home ranged from 54.7% to 76.2%. Younger soldiers, especially those who were very young when the war began, often served fewer years and therefore did not endure as many long-term hardships; thus they had fewer opportunities or service-related reasons to desert. Although men between the ages of 18 and 25 enlisted in great numbers in 1861 and 1862, a bit more than a quarter (26.4%) of those between 21 and 25 had wives and only 2 in 1,000 (0.2%) between 18 and 20 were married. One in every 6 (17.2%) between 21 and 25 and none in the sample between 18 and 20 had children; they deserted at the rate of roughly 1 in 8 (13.5% and 13.2% respectively).

Figure 9.9 shows desertion rates by year of birth.

Soldiers between ages 18 and 25 had by far the highest rate of those killed in action. One in every 6 (16.6%) between 21 and 25 and more than 3 in every 17 (17.9%) between 18 and 20 lost their lives in combat. Troops between 21 and 25 accounted for a stunning 42.3%, just under 4 of every 9, of all soldiers in Lee's army who were killed in battle. Men between 18 and 20 totaled another 3 in every 10 (29.1%). Not surprisingly, both groups had the highest percentage of men who served in the infantry.

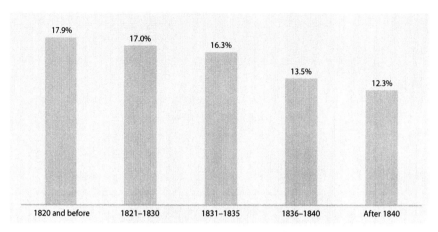

FIGURE 9.9. Desertion by year of birth

Only the oldest age group, over 40, predominantly escaped without combat injuries. One in 16 (6.4%) was killed, and not one in the sample was wounded. That was nearly five times below the second lowest rate of killed or wounded, men between 31 and 40 (31.0%). Nearly half (48.5%) of all men between 21 and 25 were wounded at least once or killed in action, and approximately 2 of every 5 suffered a similar fate in age groups 26 to 30 (38.9%) and 18 to 20 (41.1%). Even the youngest soldiers—those under age 18 in 1861, most of whom had to wait a year or more before they could serve—were victims of the battlefield at a rate of almost 1 in every 3 (31.7%).[12]

Figure 9.10 presents the percentage of soldiers killed in action or wounded at least once by year of birth.

Clearly, the hardships of everyday military service took the greatest toll on men who were over 40 years of age. More than 1 of 4 (26.1%) soldiers who were in that age group in 1861 died of disease. For those between 31 and 40, the rate fell to 1 in 9 (11.3%)—largely because 17.0% deserted and 21.3% of that age group entered the army in 1863 or 1864. The next age bracket, between 26 and 30, lost 13.8%, or just under 1 in 7 men, to illness, but over 9 of every 10 (90.7%) of them had joined the army in 1861 or 1862. The percentage of soldiers who perished from disease declined steadily with decreasing age; men 20 and under succumbed at a rate of less than 7.0%.[13]

Interestingly, older soldiers were much more likely to fall from illness than from lead. The great killers of younger soldiers were battlefields, not field camps or winter quarters. The transition from higher fatalities due to disease to combat occurred among soldiers in the 26 to 30 age bracket.

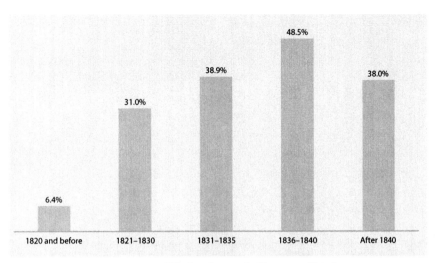

FIGURE 9.10. Killed and wounded by year of birth

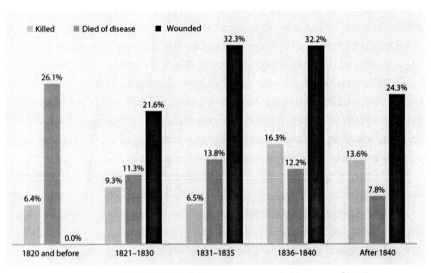

FIGURE 9.11. Killed, died of disease, or wounded by year of birth

Figure 9.11 indicates the percentage of deaths by combat or disease and of soldiers wounded—all by birth year.

Total battlefield casualties—killed, wounded, or captured—indicated heavy losses for each age group except those over 40. Among those over 40, less than 1 in 5 (18.8%) was a casualty of combat. For soldiers 40 and younger, the battle-

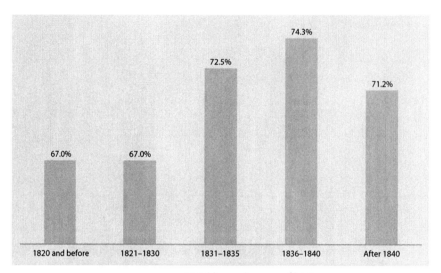

FIGURE 9.12. Total losses by year of birth

field proved devastating and almost indiscriminate. Those between 31 and 40 ranked second in the least number of casualties, but they still fell victim to combat at the rate of 4 of every 9 (44.0%). For men born between 1841 and 1843, more than 3 of every 5 (61.8%) were killed, wounded, or captured.

All told, the cost of the war for Lee's army proved surprisingly consistent. Other than soldiers under age 18 in 1861—who still suffered almost 5 of 9 men (54.7%) killed, wounded, captured, died of disease, or discharged for disability—the losses in each of the other age brackets ranged from 67.0% of those over 30 to almost 3 of every 4 (73.2%) men between 21 and 25.

Figure 9.12 displays the army's total losses—killed, wounded, death from disease or accidents, captured, or discharged for a disability—by year of birth.

As the evidence demonstrates, war was predominantly a young man's endeavor. Many soldiers in their thirties and forties found the camp hardships, campaigning, and absence from loved ones to be overwhelming. They simply had too many obligations at home and lacked the physical stamina to endure the demands of active field service in Lee's army.

CHAPTER TEN

Marriage and Fatherhood

Marriage and parenthood played vital roles in military service, affecting many aspects of the army experience. They influenced when soldiers entered the army, how they did so, when they left, and even what risks they bore. For those who were married, especially those with children, marriage imposed burdens of worry beyond those of most single men. Like young soldiers and their parents, many married men had never spent a night apart from their bride until they entered the army. "On my couch when deep sleep has fallen on others," confessed a Georgian to his wife, "I often shed tears at the cruel separation that divides me from my loved ones." Soldiers pined over being away while their children learned to walk, talk, and grow up without them. Many were absent for the birth of a child. They worried about the well-being of their wives and children, concerned about enemy invaders, food shortages, steady income, and recalcitrant slaves. Yet marriage and parenthood offered soldiers stability and continuity. In most cases, a married soldier or a soldier-father had not only parents and siblings but also a wife and the broader community of in-laws on whom he could rely for help. He also had a life to return to after the war, whereas many single troops had no such guaranteed, established world at war's end.[1]

According to the 1860 census, 3 of every 8 (37.5%) soldiers in the sample were married, and 5 of every 8 (62.5%) were single. By the time they entered military service, a slightly higher percentage were most likely married. The 1860 census also tells us that a bit more than 3 in 10 (31.2%) men had children at home. By the time they entered the army that proportion would have increased slightly as well. Only 1 in every 104 (0.96%) single men had left offspring in their home. Slightly less than 1 in 5 married men had no children.

Figure 10.1 indicates the marital and parental status of soldiers in Lee's army.

The median birth year for married soldiers was 1830.0, with an average of 1829.2. Single soldiers had a median birth year that was ten years later, 1840.0, and on average they were 10.1 years younger. Troops who left behind

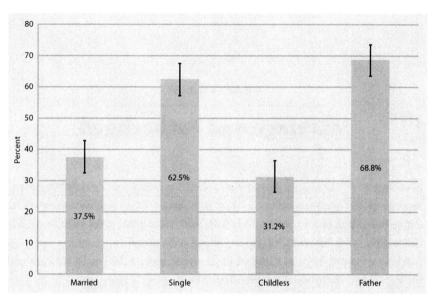

FIGURE 10.1. Marital and parental status

children also had a median birth year of 1830.0 but averaged even older at 1828.6. To a great extent, ages varied only slightly between married soldiers who were childless and wedded men with children. Understandably, the huge gaps occurred with younger soldiers. Nine of every 20 single soldiers were born after 1840, compared to 1% of all married men. No soldiers born after 1840 in the sample were fathers; more than 2 of every 5 (42%) troops who had no children were under 21 when the fighting began.

Figure 10.2 charts soldiers' marital and parental status by year of birth.[2]

On prewar occupations, clear patterns between married and single troops emerged, and those same patterns were reflected in parenthood as well. Two of every 3 (66.8%) married soldiers earned a living by tilling the soil, compared to 9 of 20 single men (45%). A higher percentage of husbands held professional (7.0% compared to 5.6%) or skilled (13.2% compared to 6.9%) positions. Single soldiers dominated the student (22.4% compared to 0.0%) and white-collar (6.1% compared to 1.0%) categories, and they had a slight edge in unskilled labor, just under 1 in 7 (14.0%) to just under 1 in 8 (12.1%). Similar distinctions existed between those who were fathers and those who were childless. A higher percentage of fathers held positions as farmers, professionals, and skilled workers. Those without children were often students, white-collar workers, or unskilled toilers.

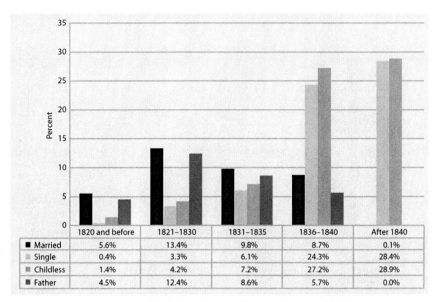

	1820 and before	1821–1830	1831–1835	1836–1840	After 1840
■ Married	5.6%	13.4%	9.8%	8.7%	0.1%
Single	0.4%	3.3%	6.1%	24.3%	28.4%
▨ Childless	1.4%	4.2%	7.2%	27.2%	28.9%
■ Father	4.5%	12.4%	8.6%	5.7%	0.0%

FIGURE 10.2. Marital and parental status by year of birth

Figure 10.3 breaks down soldiers' prewar occupations by marital and parental status. Percentages for each pair of categories equal 100%.

Before the war, married soldiers were slightly more likely to have resided in a state that was not their place of birth. Approximately 3 of 11 (26.9%) married troops had moved to a new state, compared to 1 in 4 (24.9%) single troops. Moreover, 2 of 7 (28.3%) fathers lived somewhere other than their birth state, while 1 in 4 (25.1%) childless soldiers did. Roughly 5 of every 9 married (54.1%) and single (55.1%) men lived in the Upper South. Fathers were a bit more likely to reside in the Lower South, 32.0% compared to 30.6%, but, again, the difference was not that significant. Both married soldiers and fathers resided in counties with precisely the same median slave-to-white ratio of 41.1 to 100.0, with married troops having a slight edge in the average ratio of 72.6 to 66.4. By contrast, single troops had a median ratio of 60.6 and an average of 78.3. The median ratio for childless soldiers was 59.1, with an average of 79.9.[3]

Single soldiers were much more likely to reside in urban areas. With all the married soldiers who made a living as farmers, it is not surprising that only 1 in 27 (3.7%) came from urban areas, compared to 1 in 17 (6.1%) single soldiers. Fathers had a slightly greater presence in urban areas than married soldiers generally—1 in 23 (4.3%), whereas 1 in 18 (5.6%) who were childless hailed from cities.

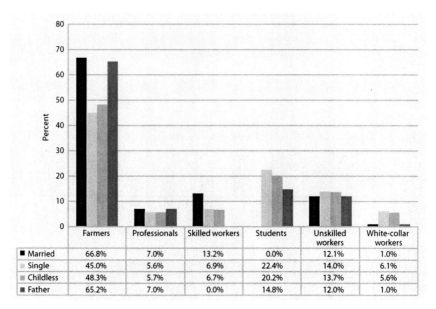

	Farmers	Professionals	Skilled workers	Students	Unskilled workers	White-collar workers
■ Married	66.8%	7.0%	13.2%	0.0%	12.1%	1.0%
Single	45.0%	5.6%	6.9%	22.4%	14.0%	6.1%
Childless	48.3%	5.7%	6.7%	20.2%	13.7%	5.6%
■ Father	65.2%	7.0%	0.0%	14.8%	12.0%	1.0%

FIGURE 10.3. Occupation by marital and parental status

In a reflection of their ages, soldiers in wedlock and those with offspring accumulated more wealth than single and childless troops. Married soldiers had a median personal wealth of $365, and soldier-fathers ranked even higher at $500. Eight of every 9 (88.3%) single soldiers accumulated personal wealth of $400 or less, compared to half (50.3%) of all married men. Almost half (48.6%) of all fathers and 17 of 20 (85.6%) childless troops owned less than $401 in property. Over 1 in 5 (21.0%) fathers had personal wealth of $4,000 or more, and more than 1 in 9 (11.4%) boasted personal wealth greater than $10,000. Among married men, 1 in 5 (20.3%) had personal estates valued at $4,000 or more and 1 in 10 (10.0%) surpassed $10,000 in total wealth. Only 4.5% of all single soldiers were worth $4,000 or more, and childless troops slightly exceeded that statistic at 5.5%.[4]

Figure 10.4 breaks down soldiers' personal wealth by their marital and parental status. Percentages in each category for married and single equal 100, as do those of fathers and men without children.

Once the riches of parents and other family members with whom soldiers resided were added to the equation, the preponderance of wealth shifted in the opposite direction. Even though husbands comprised 3 of every 8 (37.5%) troops in Lee's army, they made up 4 of every 9 (44.0%) soldiers in the lower class. At 35.0% percent, they were slightly underrepresented in the middle class, and they were further underrepresented (29.8%) in the upper class.

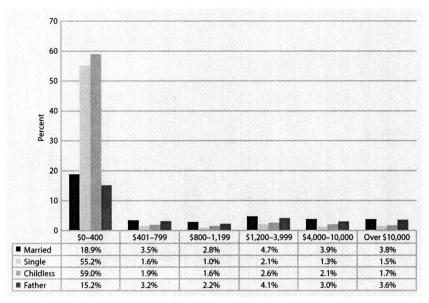

	$0–400	$401–799	$800–1,199	$1,200–3,999	$4,000–10,000	Over $10,000
■ Married	18.9%	3.5%	2.8%	4.7%	3.9%	3.8%
Single	55.2%	1.6%	1.0%	2.1%	1.3%	1.5%
▨ Childless	59.0%	1.9%	1.6%	2.6%	2.1%	1.7%
■ Father	15.2%	3.2%	2.2%	4.1%	3.0%	3.6%

FIGURE 10.4. Personal wealth by marital and parental status

Single soldiers possessed a combined median wealth of $2,000, compared to $725 for married men. Three of every 10 (30.8%) single men had combined personal and family wealth of less than $400, while nearly 4 in 9 (43.2%) married men did so. Two of 7 (28.4%) married men possessed combined property valued at $4,000 or more, yet 2 of every 5 (40.1%) single men fell into that opulent category.

Figure 10.5 depicts combined personal and family wealth by marital status.

Soldier-fathers, too, were substantially overrepresented in the lower class. Slightly more than 3 in 10 (31.2%) soldiers in Lee's army were parents, yet nearly 4 in 10 (39.4%) had personal and family wealth below $800. Fathers approximated their army proportions in the middle class (29.9%) but fell well below army percentages in the upper class (22.4%).[5]

Those without children boasted a median wealth of $1,800, while fathers claimed only $700 worth of combined riches. Four in 9 (44.2%) parents and slightly more than 3 in 10 (32%) soldiers without children had a combined wealth under $401. One in 4 (25.5%) fathers boasted a combined wealth of $4,000 or more, whereas 2 in 5 (40.0%) childless men did.

Figure 10.6 indicates personal and family wealth by parental status.

With total household wealth, the gap grew even larger. The median household wealth of married soldiers crept up to $900, barely in the middle class. For single men, it totaled $4,397, moving into the upper class. In fact, 52.0% of

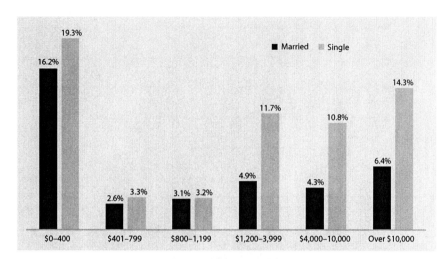

FIGURE 10.5. Personal and family wealth by marital status

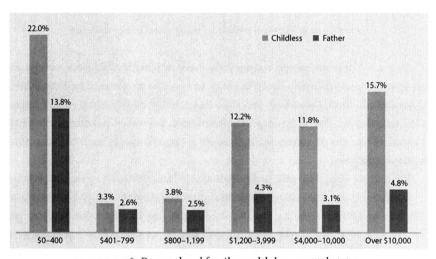

FIGURE 10.6. Personal and family wealth by parental status

all single soldiers resided in households worth $4,000 or more, and less than 2 of 9 (21.4%) lived in households worth under $400. For soldiers with children, median household wealth rose to $850, a pale comparison with the $3,500 figure for childless troops. An astounding 42.0% of all soldier-parents resided in households with $400 or less in total value, compared to 19.8% of men without children. Three in 10 (30.1%) childless troops lived in households that were worth over $10,000, whereas fewer than 2 of 11 (17.6%) soldiers with children did so.[6]

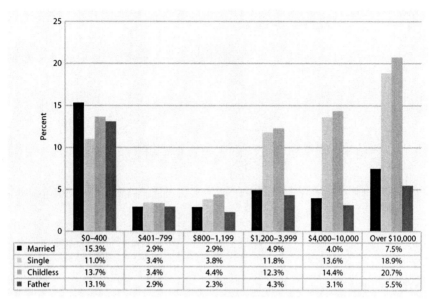

	$0–400	$401–799	$800–1,199	$1,200–3,999	$4,000–10,000	Over $10,000
■ Married	15.3%	2.9%	2.9%	4.9%	4.0%	7.5%
Single	11.0%	3.4%	3.8%	11.8%	13.6%	18.9%
Childless	13.7%	3.4%	4.4%	12.3%	14.4%	20.7%
■ Father	13.1%	2.9%	2.3%	4.3%	3.1%	5.5%

FIGURE 10.7. Household wealth by marital and parental status

Figure 10.7 shows total household wealth by marital and parental status. Percentages for married and single troops equal 100, as do those for fathers and men with no children.

Patterns of slave ownership mimicked wealth. Single (6.2%) and childless (6.8%) soldiers were 4.0 times as unlikely to own slaves personally as their married and parenting comrades. Yet single (1.4 times) and childless (1.5 times) soldiers were far more likely to come from families that owned slaves; they were also far more likely to live in slaveholding households (1.6 and 1.7 times respectively). Single troops were 2.5 times as likely to live with their planter families, and childless troops were 4.0 times as likely to do so. In fact, more than half of all single (52.1%) and childless (50.7%) soldiers came from slaveowning households.[7]

In Figure 10.8 personal, personal and family, and household slave ownership is broken down by marital and parental status. The combined percentages of marital status and fatherhood equal the combined percentages within Lee's army.

In the first year of war, during the *rage militaire*, single men enlisted at a rate two and a half times greater (72.1% compared to 27.9%) than married men. They were the minutemen of their day, the individuals with fewer and less critical personal commitments. By 1862, circumstances had changed. The pressing need for manpower demanded that married men join the ranks as

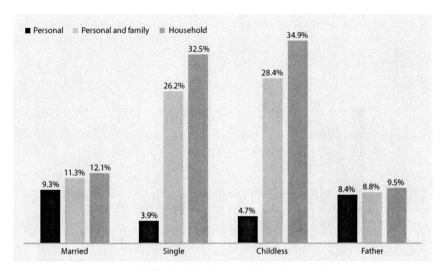

FIGURE 10.8. Slaveholding by marital and parental status

well. "Those who stick by their wives now under the pretense of devotion to them won['] t do," cavalry general J. E. B. Stuart wrote his wife. "Be not deceived wifey, those who stay at home now are forgetful of their highest duty to their wives and children and in fact to themselves & obey the single impulse of present ease, present security." In the second year of the conflict, 5 of 9 (54.0%) soldiers who joined the Army of Northern Virginia were married. In 1863, once again single soldiers dominated the ranks of newcomers at 3 of every 5 (60.4%), and the following year their entry dipped to just above half (51.6%).[8]

Fathers turned out in even lower numbers that first year. Only 23.8% of all volunteers in 1861 were fathers, a ratio of more than 3 childless soldiers for every father. Even though a majority of troops who joined the army in 1862 were married, fewer than 4 in every 9 (42.4%) that year left behind children. In 1863 and 1864, the ratio remained fairly steady at 3 childless soldiers for every 2 dads (37.9% in 1863 and 40.1% in 1864).[9]

Figure 10.9 tracks the years soldiers entered Lee's army according to marital and parental status. Both the single/married and father/nonfather categories equal 100%.

Married men were slightly overrepresented in the infantry, constituting nearly 2 of every 5 (39.3%) troops in that branch. They were slightly underrepresented in the cavalry (32.4%), which required the wealth to provide one's own horse, and at 1 in 4 (24.2%) they were heavily underrepresented in the artillery. Soldier-fathers mirrored married troops. They comprised a dispro-

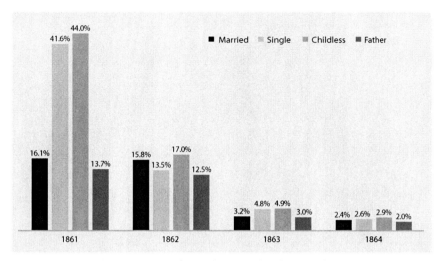

FIGURE 10.9. Year of entry by marital and parental status

portionate share in the infantry (32.8%) and made up only 1 in every 6 (17.1%) artillerymen, some 83.0% below their overall percentage in the army. In the mounted branch, fathers were underrepresented by about 11.0%.[10]

Figure 10.10 indicates the branch of service chosen by the soldiers in Lee's army according to their marital and parental status. Both single/married and father/nonfather categories equal 100%.

Interestingly, married men had their proportionate share of commissions. One in 12 (8.6%) soldiers in the sample were officers, and 1 in 12 (8.7%) married men held a commission. Fathers, however, were overrepresented in the officer corps by nearly 20%. The age of fathers and the responsibilities of parenthood may have made them better suited to look after the well-being of fellow soldiers.[11]

Despite Stuart's words to his wife, marriage and parenthood were influential factors in discouraging men from enlisting in the army. Although married men made up less than 1 in every 3 soldiers in Lee's army, more than 2 of 3 (68.2%) conscripts had wives at home. Moreover, although just less than 1 in 5 married men had no children at home, every married conscript did. The lone substitute in the sample also had children at home. Thus, more than marriage per se, the realities of caring for a wife and children were central considerations for many men who did not enter the army voluntarily.[12]

Once they were in the army, husbands and fathers were slightly less likely to absent themselves without authorization. In both instances, married troops went AWOL slightly less often (2.5%) than their 37.5% representation in Lee's

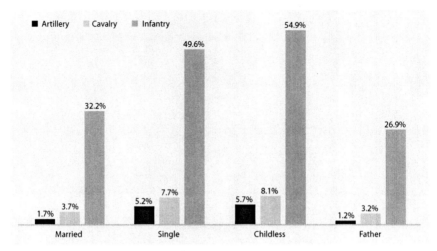

FIGURE 10.10. Branch of service by marital and parental status

army would suggest, and soldier-fathers went 4.7% less than in keeping with their proportion (31.2%). But husbands and fathers were more likely to desert. Soldiers who left a wife at home were 30.9% more apt to desert than single men, and those with children were a whopping 80.3% more likely than childless troops. Concern for children at home thus proved to be an extremely powerful factor in desertion rates.[13]

Figure 10.11 provides the percentage of men who deserted by marital and parental status. In each instance, the percentage is based on 100% in that category.

Deserters certainly made up higher proportions among the married poor and lower middle class. One in every 5 (20.6%) married soldiers with under $400 in total property, 15.6% of them with $400 to $799, and 24.4% of them with $800 to $1,199 abandoned the ranks with no intention of ever returning. Among soldier-fathers, 1 in 4 (24.7%) of the poorest troops, 15.4% of the upper poor, and 30.1% of the lower middle class deserted. Wealth, too, was unquestionably an influential factor in limiting desertion among husbands and fathers. Both husbands (11.4%) and fathers (15.4%) who lived in slaveholding families were underrepresented in desertion figures.[14]

On the surface, it appeared that in the course of their service husbands and fathers incurred fewer risks. Married men suffered approximately 3 of every 10 (29.3%) combat deaths, although they constituted 3 of every 8 (37.5%) men in the army. Fatherhood indicated similar distinctions. Although 31.2% of the army consisted of dads, 24.1% of all men who were killed in action had children at home. Yet when we factor in those who were wounded, the differences

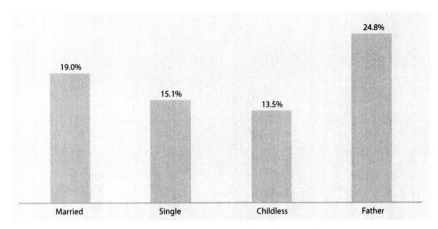

FIGURE 10.11. Desertion by marital and parental status

diminish significantly. Seven of every 20 (34.7%) married men and nearly 3 of 10 (29.1%) fathers were killed or wounded, differences that were statistically insignificant from their proportions in the army. During their military service, husbands and fathers were less likely to become a prisoner of war. Two in 9 (22.3%) married men fell into Union hands before Appomattox, compared to more than 1 in 4 (26.7%) single troops. Among soldier-fathers, the statistics were closer, but men without children were more likely to be captured by the enemy (25.7% compared to 23.6%).[15]

Figure 10.12 presents a breakdown of combat casualties based on marital status and parenthood.

Although married men made up 3 in every 8 soldiers in Lee's army, they constituted nearly 5 of every 9 men who died of disease. Soldier-fathers perished disproportionately due to disease, but their statistics pale in comparison with those of married men. Three of every 8 deaths from disease deprived children of a father, but that was 18.0% above their percentage in the general army population. Among soldier-husbands, deaths from disease were 45.2% greater proportionately. Statistics clearly indicate that age was a powerful factor in deaths due to disease, and married men and fathers tended to be older. This unusual gap between married men and fathers may have simply been a measuring problem. Some older husband-soldiers may also have been fathers, but none of their children still lived at home. They would register in the census as childless, when in fact they were parents of grown children.[16]

All told, just under 1 in 10 (10.2%) husbands were killed in action or by some other means and 1 in 6 (16.5%) died of disease. Thus, more than 1 in 4 (26.7%) married men gave their lives for the Confederate cause. Nearly 1 in 4 (24.1%)

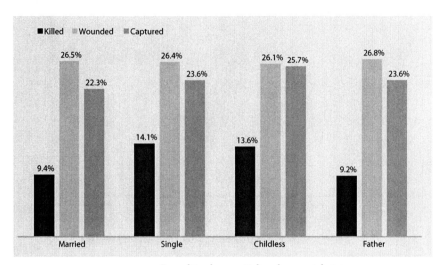

FIGURE 10.12. Casualties by marital and parental status

more were wounded, and an additional 1 in 4 (25.0%) fell into enemy hands and became POWs prior to the surrender at Appomattox. And finally, almost 1 in 5 more were discharged or left the service due to age or disability. In total, 72.9% of all soldier-husbands were killed, died of accidents or disease, were wounded or captured, or left the service due to some infirmity.

Almost as many single soldiers died. One in 7 (14.7%) were killed in action or by accident, and an additional 1 in 12 (8.3%) succumbed to disease. Thus, just under 1 in 4 (23.0%) single men gave their lives for the Confederacy. More than 1 in 4 (26.4%) who did not die were wounded, and more than 1 in 8 (13.3%) who did not fall in battle became a POW. Another 1 in 27 (3.7%) left the service on account of disability. The total for single soldiers who were killed, wounded, died, taken prisoner, or discharged for disability was 2 of every 3 (66.3%), a staggering figure, but by comparison only 91% of the number for married men.[17]

In a comparison of fathers with childless soldiers, the statistics flip. One in 10 (10.2%) fathers died in battle or from accident, and another 1 in 8 (13.6%) fell to disease. Taken together, slightly less than 1 in 4 (23.8%) gave their lives in the war. One in 5 (20.1%) who did not die were wounded, and an additional 1 in 8 (14.0%) were captured. One in 14 (7.3%) fathers left the service due to age or infirmity. All told, 13 of 20 (65.2%) fathers were killed, died of disease, wounded, captured, or discharged for disability.

Childless soldiers in Lee's army suffered more casualties. One in 7 (14.1%) was killed or died accidentally, and almost 1 in 9 (10.6%) perished from dis-

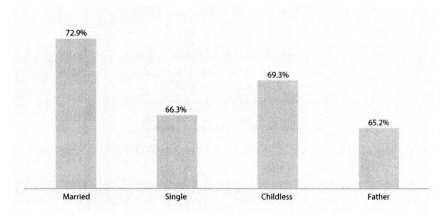

FIGURE 10.13. Total losses by marital and parental status

ease, bringing the death toll of troops without children to 1 in 4 (24.7%). In addition to those who sacrificed their lives, 1 in 4 (25.2%) sustained at least one wound, and 1 in 7 (14.1%) more were taken prisoner. One in 20 left the service due to age or medical condition. The total losses among men without children amounted to 7 in every 10 (69.3%). That tally indicates that losses among fathers were only 94.0% as great as those among men without children.[18]

Figure 10.13 shows total individual losses — killed, wounded, died of disease, POW, or discharged for disability out of 100% in each category — by marital and parental status.

Statistics on husbands and fathers verses the unwed and the childless provide a mixed portrait. Although soldiers who were married, especially those with children, were more likely to desert the Confederate flag, they do not appear to have dodged their military obligations, hardships, and dangers while in uniform. Their conduct does not indicate any inferior commitment to the Confederate cause. Rather, it simply suggests that duties to a wife and children at home sometimes trumped military obligations.

CHAPTER ELEVEN

Economic Class

Even though social and cultural factors play a significant role in the determination of class structure, for this study I have applied fundamental financial guidelines to determine class: combined personal and, if a soldier lived with his immediate family, family wealth. The calculation consisted of the addition of real property to personal property according to 1860 census records. The lower class constituted those soldiers with a combined personal and, if relevant, family wealth of $0 to $799; the middle class ranged from combined assets of $800 to $3,999; and the upper class consisted of men with combined property of $4,000 or more.

Although guidelines for the lower, middle, and upper classes are fairly subjective, they are based on my knowledge of the data and the time period in consultation with other leading scholars in the field. In discussions with Dr. James McPherson, we agreed on the $800 demarcation of total wealth for the lower end of the middle bracket, although we both believe that a smaller amount of wealth would qualify for a skilled worker in an urban area. Even though urban and town real estate might be more expensive than farmland, a skilled worker would need to own very little of it, compared to a farmer. A skilled worker worth $800 would probably live much better than a farmer whose total worth reached $800. The top end of the middle bracket was set liberally at $3,999, which in many cases would enable someone to own up to three slaves. Dr. Gary Gallagher, who also reviewed the statistics, has suggested that $3,999 might be too high. It may very well be overly high, but after extensive consideration I decided to leave it.

A huge census database called the Integrated Public Use Microdata Series (IPUMS) enabled me to compare my sample of Lee's army with a sample of 1% of all households in the United States in 1860. In the entire country, the breakdown by economic class for families (a single person living alone constitutes a family) in 1860 was 50.5% for lower-class families, 30.1% for middle-class families, and 19.4% for upper-class families. Statistics from states that contributed soldiers to Lee's army, however, offered a more accurate compari-

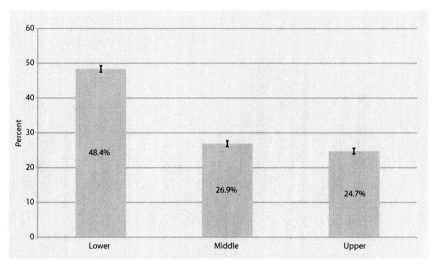

FIGURE 11.1. Economic class of families in the states represented in Lee's army

son. In my states, the IPUMS sample includes 70,985 families and has a margin for error of less than 1%. Soldiers in my sample spanned years of birth from 1799 to 1848. I therefore generated an IPUMS sample of families with males between those birth years and produced statistics that are fairly similar to the overall IPUMS sample of states represented in Lee's army.

Figure 11.1 gives a breakdown by economic class of families with males who were born between 1799 and 1848 in the states that contributed soldiers to Lee's army.

In the sample of Lee's army, 4 of every 10 (41.7%) men—and their families if the soldiers lived with them—were in the lower class, with $799 or less in total wealth. Two of every 9 (22.8%) qualified for the middle class, with assets between $800 and $3,999, and 4 of 11 (35.5%) were in the upper class, with $4,000 or more. Compared to the states from which these soldiers came, wealthy soldiers were overrepresented. In the states where soldiers in the sample resided before the war, nearly one-half (48.4%) were poor, slightly more than one-quarter (26.9%) were in the middle range, and one-quarter (24.7%) were wealthy. By comparison, my sample for Lee's army indicates that soldiers and their families were wealthier than the residents of their states. The statistical differences, moreover, were outside the margin for error for the lower and upper classes, indicating that the differences were statistically valid.[1]

Figure 11.2 compares the Army of Northern Virginia to the states from which Lee drew his men by economic class.

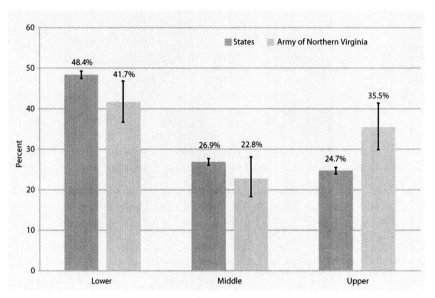

FIGURE 11.2. Composition of states and army by economic class

Among soldiers in Lee's army, a peculiar phenomenon existed: the younger the soldier, the more personal and family wealth he registered in the 1860 census. Because younger soldiers often lived with their parents, who were much closer to maximizing their earning potential, many younger soldiers had smaller personal wealth but much greater combined personal and family wealth than their comrades. Those with a total wealth of $799 or less had a median birth year of 1837.0 and an average birth year of 1834.9. Middle-class soldiers had a median birth year one year later, 1838.0, and averaged more than half a year younger at 1835.6. The youngest were the richest. The median birth year for those with personal and family wealth of $4,000 or more was also 1838.0, but the average birth year was 1836.4. Nearly half (47.0%) of all soldiers who were born between 1844 and 1848 fit into the upper class. At the opposite end of the spectrum, almost the same ratio (47.7%) of men who were born in 1820 or earlier were also among the wealthy class. Those in the largest poor groups were between 26 and 30 and 31 and 40 when the fighting began. Troops between 26 and 40 years of age were almost always out from under their parents' roof and in most cases had not yet achieved their ultimate level of economic success.[2]

Figure 11.3 breaks down soldiers' economic status according to their year of birth.

Poorer soldiers were also more likely to have migrated to a different state

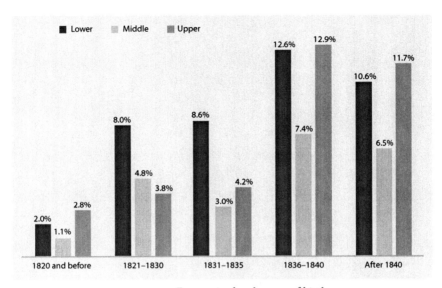

FIGURE 11.3. Economic class by year of birth

from the one in which they were born. One-third (33.5%) of the lower class had moved to a new state in search of opportunity, and slightly over 3 in 10 (30.7%) of the middle class did so as well. But only 1 in 7 (14.5%) upper-class soldiers had sought a start elsewhere. They were either well ensconced in their birth state or saw an opportunity for success there and ultimately found it.[3]

Figure 11.4 shows the percentage of soldiers in Lee's army who in 1860 resided in a state other than their birth state.

Marital status according to economic class buttressed the age factor. Less than 5 of every 9 (54.5%) soldiers in the lower class were single, whereas nearly 2 of every 3 (65.0%) in the middle class and over 7 of 10 (70.2%) in the upper class were single. Married men, particularly in their late twenties and thirties, were more likely to struggle financially, while single men were prone to remain in their parents' home and benefit from their own labor as well as their parents' or siblings' accumulated wealth.[4]

Figure 11.5 shows marital status according to economic class, with married and single soldiers in each class totaling 100%.

The percentage of soldiers with children at home declined by economic class as well. Four of every 10 (39.4%) men from the lower class left children behind when they entered military service, while 3 of 10 (29.9%) middle-class soldiers and only 2 of 11 (22.4%) upper-class troops claimed offspring. With so many young soldiers from wealthy families, it is reasonable that they would have the smallest percentage of marriages. Yet the number of soldiers with

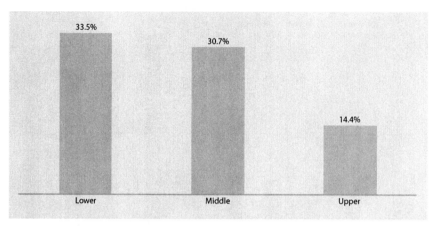

FIGURE 11.4. Migration to a new state by economic class

children flowed in the opposite direction. Poor troops averaged the fewest number of children at home at 2.5%, whereas those from the middle class averaged 3.5% and the upper class, 3.6%.[5]

Prewar occupations by class reflected typical patterns for the wealthy. Soldiers from the upper class (3.8%) were nearly three times as likely as those from the middle class (1.3%) and almost four times as likely as those from the lower class (1.0%) to be professionals. Wealthy class troops also held more white-collar jobs — 2.3%, compared to 1.0% for the middle class and 0.8% for the poor class. Soldier-sons of rich parents understandably dominated the list of prewar students, since maintaining a teenager or young adult in school or college was a luxury. Approximately 13.8% of all soldiers were students before the war, and 8.6% of those — 62.3% of all prewar students — were from the upper class. Among the wealthy class, nearly 1 in 4 (24.1%) men was still in school in 1860, and close to 5 in 9 (53.6%) identified themselves as farmers or planters.

Lower-class soldiers dominated skilled and unskilled occupations. One in 11 (9.2%) men in Lee's army was skilled, and 71.7% of them fell into the poor group. The same was true of unskilled workers. More than 1 in 8 (13.2%) troops were classified as unskilled, and 83.3% of that total had combined assets of $800 or less. In fact, 3 of every 11 (26.7%) poor soldiers were unskilled. Yet the lower class had the most farmers at 19.5% of Lee's entire army. These poor troops thus had little presence among professionals, white-collar employees, and students: only 5.9% of them were students, and less than 1 in 40 (2.4%) held professional or white-collar jobs. Doubtless, many troops in the lower

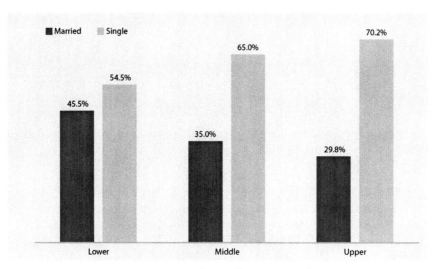

FIGURE 11.5. Marital status by economic class

economic class were just beginning their careers and had yet to accumulate much income, but their prospects for considerable earnings were strong.

While the infrequency of students, professionals, and white-collar persons and the frequency of unskilled workers were to be expected, the number of poor farmers and especially skilled workers was surprising. Only 1 in every 20 (4.8%) soldiers in the sample was both head of household and tenant farmer, which means that 8.9% of all farmers fit into that category. Therefore, close to 1 in 9 (10.6%) farmers was not a tenant yet possessed less than $800 in total assets. Even though skilled workers would not have needed large amounts of land to practice their trade, it would seem on the surface that demand for their expertise would have enabled them to amass greater riches than they did. Certainly age would have been a factor. More than 2 of 5 (41.6%) skilled workers were less than 26 years old in 1861 and had yet to accumulate much wealth. Nonetheless, competition from skilled slaves and capable whites must have held down the wages of skilled workers.[6]

The middle class represented the most balanced economic bracket. It ranked second in every occupation except farming, constituting only 15% of all growers. Nonetheless, because the middle class was so small in Lee's army, nearly 2 of every 3 (65.7%) men in it were farmers.[7]

Figure 11.6 indicates soldiers' percentage of each economic category and their occupations.

Understandably, none of the lower-class soldiers personally owned slaves.

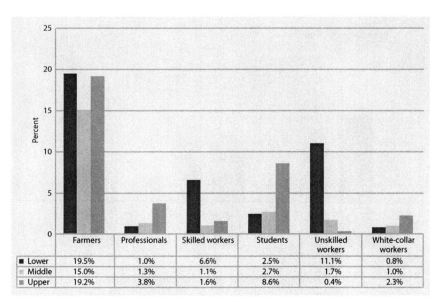

	Farmers	Professionals	Skilled workers	Students	Unskilled workers	White-collar workers
■ Lower	19.5%	1.0%	6.6%	2.5%	11.1%	0.8%
Middle	15.0%	1.3%	1.1%	2.7%	1.7%	1.0%
■ Upper	19.2%	3.8%	1.6%	8.6%	0.4%	2.3%

FIGURE 11.6. Occupation by economic class

In the middle class, approximately 1 in 12 (8.3%) did so, and in the upper class the ratio was more than 3 in 10 (31.4%). By incorporating the slaves owned by soldiers' immediate families if they all lived together, we find that the percentage of slaveholders increases dramatically. With this calculation, 2 in 11 (22.2%) middle-class soldiers and 9 in 10 (90.5%) upper-class troops either owned slaves themselves or their immediate families did. These statistics lend credence to claims of a linkage between wealth and slaveholding. Nearly all of the middle-class soldiers in Lee's army from slaveholding families had one or two slaves, while affluent troops often owned a considerable number of bondsmen and bondswomen. More than 1 in 7 (14.6%) well-to-do soldiers owned one or two slaves, but almost 4 in 11 (35.5%) possessed 3 to 10. More than 1 in 5 (21%) owned between 10 and 19 slaves, and nearly 1 in 5 (19.5%) qualified as members of the planter class.[8]

In statistics on household slaveowning by economic class, ties to the peculiar institution become even more powerful. More than 1 of every 8 (13.0%) soldiers from a poor family lived in a household with slaves. That ratio rose to just under 3 of 10 (29.3%) men from the middle class, then leaped to over 10 of 11 (91.1%) troops from the upper class.[9]

Figure 11.7 has basic information on slaveholding by economic class. The graph is based on the percentage of each population that either personally owned slaves or their family did.

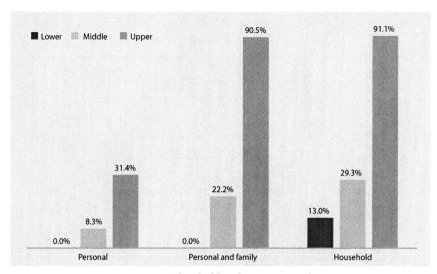

FIGURE 11.7. Slaveholding by economic class

By and large, the wealthier his family, the more likely a soldier resided in a county with a higher ratio of blacks to whites. Troops from the lower economic class lived in counties where the median ratio was 2 blacks to every 5 whites, with an average of just under 2 of every 3 (63.8%). The middle-class troops inched up to a median closer to 1 to 2 (47.4%), with an average up to 7 to 9 (77.2%). The wealthy soldiers came from dense slave-to-white counties, with a median ratio of more than 3 to 4 (76.1%) and an average of 8 to 9 (88.6%).

Far more poor soldiers came from the Upper South, with a ratio of more than 3 of every 5 (63.2%). Yet a bare majority (50.3%) of the affluent troops also came from the Upper South. That constituted a slight overrepresentation of wealthy residents of the Deep South (49.7%, with 45.0% of the sample residing there), but it also indicates the more bifurcated nature of economic life in the Upper South for men in Lee's army. The Lower South was home to a majority of soldiers in the middle class, with 52.5%.

Figure 11.8 compares the three economic classes of soldiers in the Upper versus the Lower South. The combined percentage in each economic class equals its percentage of Lee's army as a whole.

Soldiers who joined the artillery tended toward economic extremes, while the infantry exhibited the greatest balance among the three economic classes. Approximately one-half (49.6%) of all artillerymen were poor, yet nearly 4 in 11 (34.9%) came from the upper class. Less than 1 in 7 (15.5%) artillerymen were from the middle class. Among infantrymen, fewer than 4 in 9 (42.3%)

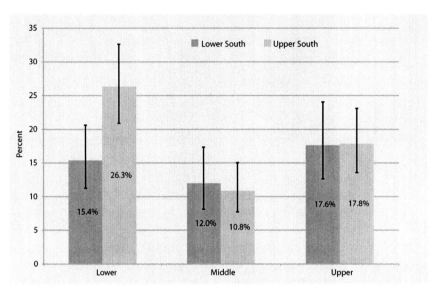

FIGURE 11.8. Economic class by region

were poor, and more than one-third (33.9%) were rich. Just under 1 in every 4 (23.7%) musket toters fit into the middle class. The cavalry boasted the highest ratio of affluent soldiers, with more than 9 of every 20 (46.8%) from the upper class. Because horsemen required mounts, it also had the lowest ratio of poor soldiers, just below 1 in 3 (32.4%). Only 1 in 5 (20.9%) cavalrymen came from a middle-class home.[10]

Figure 11.9 indicates the economic status of the three branches of service, with each branch equaling its percentage in the army.

Economic class had little impact on year of enlistment. Almost 3 of every 5 (59.2%) poor soldiers enlisted in 1861, demonstrating both their passion for military service and the competitiveness of military pay compared to their civilian earnings. Wealthy troops had the lowest ratio of first-year enlistments at 5 of 9 (55.3%) men, but they also had the highest rate of enlistment in 1862 at more than 3 of 10 (30.2%). All three economic classes ranged in the 80th percentile of service in 1861 or 1862. The highest percentage of men who entered in 1864 came from the upper class, but they were largely soldiers coming of age and composed only 2.1% of all troops who served in Lee's army.

The overwhelming percentage of soldiers from every economic class served solely as enlisted men. Slightly more than 19 of every 20 (96%) poor men and 8 of 9 (88.6%) soldiers from rich families joined and remained in the ranks throughout the war. In proportion to the numbers in their class, a higher percentage of the middle class received commissions as officers than any other

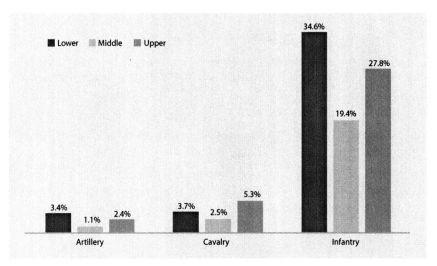

FIGURE 11.9. Economic class by branch of service

group. One in every 8 (12.5%) commanded troops in Lee's army. One in 9 (11.4%) wealthy soldiers and 1 in 25 (4.0%) poor men led troops as commissioned officers. Yet because of the disparity of men from each class, actual representation within the officer corps was very different. One in every 5 (19.3%) officers came from the lower class, 1 in 3 (33.3%) were from the middle class, and close to half (47.3%) entered the army with upper-class backgrounds. Not surprisingly, just fewer than 4 of 9 (43.8%) enlisted men possessed riches below $800. Two of every 9 (21.9%) had middle class upbringings or earned that economic status, and more than 1 in every 3 (34.4%) enlisted men came from wealth.[11]

Figure 11.10 breaks down the economic class of officers and enlisted men in Lee's army. The percentages for officers and enlisted men mirror their makeup in the sample.

Like so many other areas of investigation, the frequency of conscription varied by wealth. Nine of every 20 (45.7%) conscripts came from the lower economic class. More than 3 of 10 (31.1%) came from the middle class, and more than 2 of 9 (23.3%) were well-to-do sons from affluent families of the upper class.[12]

The same was true of soldiers who were absent without leave. One in every 10 (11.1%) poor troops absented himself temporarily without authorization. Among men of the middle class, that ratio declined to 1 in 8 (8.6%). Well-to-do troops were the least likely to take "French leave"; 1 in 20 (5.1%) did so.

Although poorer soldiers had the least to fight for and were the least inte-

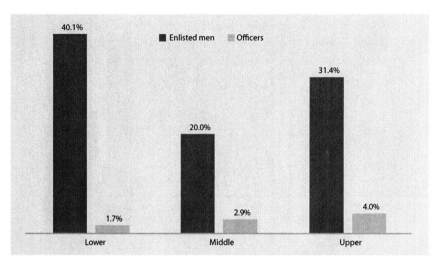

FIGURE 11.10. Economic class of officers and enlisted men

grated into Confederate society, they did not have the highest desertion rate among the three classes. That dubious honor fell to middle-class soldiers, of whom nearly 1 in 5 (19.1%) fled Lee's army. Middle-class troops had accumulated a fair amount of wealth. Many had created a comfortable lifestyle for themselves and their families, one they could not sustain in military service on army pay. Poor soldiers deserted at a slightly lower rate—just less than 3 in 16 (18.1%). Troops from the wealthy class deserted most infrequently. With the most at risk in the war, only about 1 in 16 (7.2%) abandoned their comrades.[13]

Children, however, altered the equation. Among poor deserters, more were fathers than not, and 23.3% of all poor soldiers with children deserted. Among middle-class men, that rate fell to 18.7%. Wealthy fathers had the lowest desertion record at 14.3%.

Figure 11.11 reveals the percentage of deserters from Lee's army according to economic class and parental status.

Combat fatalities and injuries fell unevenly on the economic classes. The poor suffered the highest percentage of men killed in action at 13.4%, followed closely by the well-to-do at 12.7%. The proportion of men killed from both economic classes exceeded the percentage of men in Lee's army from each class. The upper and lower classes lost slightly more than 1 in 8; based on the margin for error, the difference between the two classes was statistically insignificant. Middle-class troops enjoyed the lowest death-by-combat rate at less than 1 in 11 (9.3%). By combining those who were wounded at least once with those who were killed, the balance shifted toward the rich. Four of every

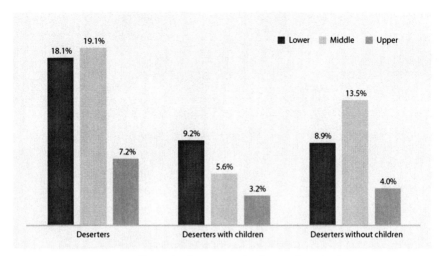

FIGURE 11.11. Desertion by economic class and parental status

9 (44.4%) soldiers with personal and family property valued at $4,000 or more were killed or wounded. Slightly fewer than 4 of 11 (35.8%) poor soldiers were wounded at least once or killed—24% less than their wealthy comrades. The middle class lost 34.5% killed and wounded. That was 28.7% below the upper class, but in real terms—because of the small size of the middle class—it was half the actual percentage of killed and wounded compared to rich soldiers, 7.9% to 15.8% in Lee's army. Killed and wounded among poor troops constituted 14.9% of the army.[14]

Figure 11.12 shows the percentage of soldiers who were killed and wounded in action (no repeat victims) by economic class. The bars are based on 100% for each economic class.

A combination of poor sanitary practices, a lack of prewar exposure to illnesses, a lifetime of inferior diets, and an inability to supplement diets when foodstuffs were available earlier in the war most likely caused poor soldiers to die of disease at a higher rate than troops from the two other economic classes. Close to 1 in every 7 (13.5%) soldiers from the lower class perished from illness. In actual numbers, these deaths comprised nearly half (48.6%) of all fatalities from illness in Lee's army for the entire war. More than 1 in 8 (12.7%) middle-class soldiers succumbed to illness, a rate that declined to 1 in 12 (8.6%) for wealthy soldiers. Better education and an awareness of proper sanitation, combined with a more balanced diet before and early in the war, may have helped these men through their first year of military service, when so many other soldiers lost their lives to disease. Although medical care was

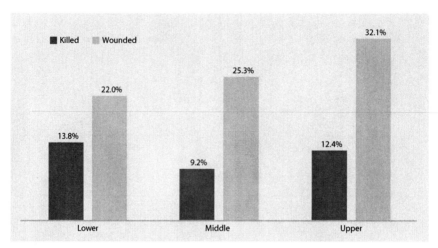

FIGURE 11.12. Killed and wounded by economic class

poor for everyone, some wealthier soldiers may have benefited initially from more personal attention from nurses, who performed the single most important function to preserve the life of the sick: they kept patients clean.

Another influence may have been the previous experience of soldiers from urban areas, where they were more likely to have been exposed to various illnesses. One in every 18 (5.6%) wealthy soldiers lived in one of the top 100 cities in the United States in 1860. Soldiers who resided in urban areas almost always caught childhood diseases and other afflictions, such as measles, mumps, chicken pox, small pox, and typhoid fever. By fighting off these illnesses earlier in life, men from urban areas could be expected to have developed a resistance to them and were less likely to die from such maladies while serving in the army. Yet urban exposure evidently did not make that much difference. The lower class had the second highest prewar urban population at 5.5%, with the middle class the least urbanized at 3.9%.

Close to 3 of 11 (26.5%) soldiers from the lower economic class lost their lives in the war. The middle class sacrificed under 3 in 11 (26.0%) of its sons for the Confederate cause as well, with the wealthy dying at just below 1 in 5 (19.3%). By adding those who were wounded in action at least once, prisoners of war before Appomattox, and soldiers discharged for disability, the middle class suffered the worst by far. More than 3 of every 4 (76.2%) soldiers in that economic category were killed, wounded, prisoners of war, died of disease, or were discharged for some disability. Men from the upper class came next with 7 of 10 (69.7%) wartime victims. The lower class suffered horribly, but in comparison its men endured the least among the economic groups with

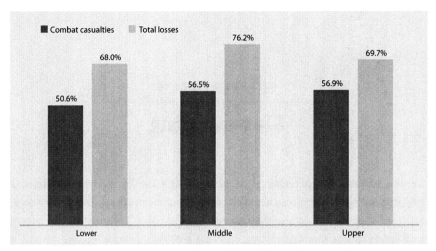

FIGURE 11.13. Combat casualties and total losses by economic class

slightly more than 2 of 3 (68%) losses. Troops from the upper class registered the highest rate of casualties in the field (killed in action, wounded in action, or captured) at 56.9%, followed by soldiers from the middle class at 56.5% and the lower class at 50.6%. Upper-class soldiers ranked second in combat fatalities; they were by far the most wounded in action and had the fewest men who surrendered to the enemy.

Figure 11.13 provides the percentage of combat casualties and total losses (killed, wounded, died of disease, captured by Union forces, or discharged for some disability) for each economic class.

The experiences of Lee's army challenges the notion of a rich man's war and a poor man's fight. Compared to the states and the age groups from which the army recruited, wealthy soldiers were significantly overrepresented and poor soldiers were underrepresented. The reason rests in a simple case of demographics. Wealthier families in those states had more children per family than middle-class or poor families. The median wealth for families with one to four members was $275, with an average wealth of $4,067. For families with five to nine members, the median wealth was $1,000, with an average of $6,311. For families with ten or more members, the median wealth increased to $2,000 and the average jumped to $8,280. Thus, affluent families had more offspring who could and did serve in the army.[15]

CHAPTER TWELVE

Slaveholding

On the surface, the percentage of personal and family slaveowners tells us much about their background and little of their motivations. But if we accept the idea that individuals owned slaves because they believed in the merits and legitimacy of the institution, and that individuals seceded and fought at least in part to protect family, friends, property, and a way of life that they believed was threatened, then Confederate soldiers' personal attachment to slavery was a powerful motivation in their military service. It was a building block upon which they forged a sense of mission and a spirit of camaraderie

In Lee's army, a clear majority, 62.8%, neither owned slaves personally nor did their family with whom they resided. Thus, slightly more than 3 in every 8 (37.2%) soldiers or their immediate families were slaveholders. According to the U.S. Census for 1860, 1 in every 4 *households*, not families, owned slaves. The family ratio was more than 50% higher than households in the seceding states as a whole. In Lee's army, 4 of every 9 (44.4%) soldiers lived in slave-owning households before the war, which was 77% greater than in Southern households as a whole. Other soldiers worked for slaveowners, had clients and customers who were slaveowners, had family members with whom they did not reside who were slaveholders, or had other strong bonds to the peculiar institution. When we weigh the fact that Southern states seceded from the Union to protect slavery — one need merely look at the official justifications for secession that a number of the states provided — slavery was an extremely powerful force in the lives of men in Lee's army.[1]

Figure 12.1 shows the percentage of personal and immediate family slave-holders versus nonslaveholders in Lee's army.

Among those who came from slaveholding families, larger slaveowners were overrepresented. One in every 10 (9.4%) men in the Army of Northern Virginia or their immediate families owned 1 or 2 slaves. More than 1 in 8 (13.2%) had between 3 and 10 bondsmen and bondswomen. One in every 13 (7.7%) had 11 to 19 slaves, and 1 in 14 (6.9%) owned 20 or more slaves and qualified for the planter class.

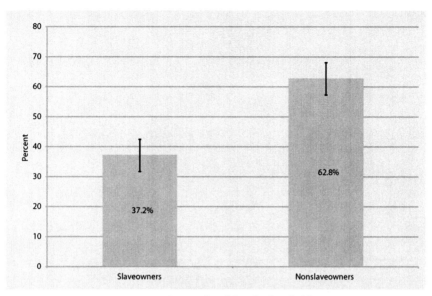

FIGURE 12.1. Personal and family slaveholding

Figure 12.2 provides a tabulation of the number of slaves held by soldiers in Lee's army or their immediate families.

Soldiers who did not own slaves tended to be older than their slaveholding comrades. Nonslaveholders had a median birth year of 1837.0, compared to 1838.0 for slaveholders, and those without slaves averaged close to one year older, 1835.1 to 1836.4. The median birth year for soldiers who either personally or their families were large slaveholders was 1839.0. This youth reflected the fact that 2 of every 3 large slaveowning soldiers lived with their families before the war, rather than owning those slaves themselves. The average age varied from 1835.7 for those who owned from 11 to 19 slaves to 1837.5 for the owners of 3 to 10 slaves. Soldiers from families who did not own slaves represented a smaller percentage of younger people, those who were 25 or younger in 1861. Slightly more than 4 of 7 (57.7%) were born after 1835. Among slaveholding families, the percentage of soldiers born after 1835 ranged from a low of 61.8% in the planter class to 68.6% for those owning 3 to 10 slaves.[2]

Figure 12.3 breaks down slaveholding and nonslaveholding by year of birth. The percentages add up to equal the percentages of slaveowners and non-slaveowners in Lee's army.

Mobility was much greater among soldiers and their families who owned no slaves than it was among slaveholding families. Nonslaveholding families were 2.5 times more likely to move to a new state. One in every 3 (33.6%) nonslave-

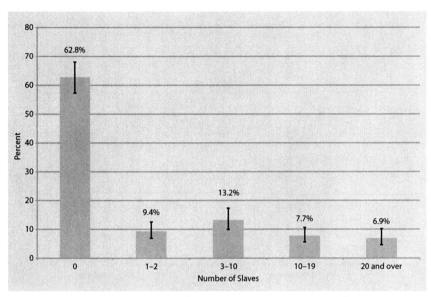

FIGURE 12.2. Personal and family slaveholding by number of slaves

holders resided in a state that differed from their birth state, while only 1 in 7 (13.6%) slaveholding families did. In fact, the more slaves a soldier or his family owned, the less likely he resided away from his birth state. Planter families were the least likely to emigrate, with only 1 in every 18 (5.5%) doing so. Those who owned one or two slaves were three times more likely (16.8%) to move.[3]

Prewar occupations of the men in Lee's army varied considerably, based on slave ownership and the number of slaves the soldiers and their families possessed. In most cases, slightly more than half were farmers, whether they owned slaves or not. Two-thirds (66.7%) of those who owned 1 or 2 slaves were farmers, the highest percentage in any category. The lowest proportion of farmers and their families, more than 4 of every 9 (46.5%), owned 3 to 10 slaves. Soldiers from slaveholding families had double the rate of white-collar workers and professionals than nonslaveholders. One in every 24 (4.4%) non-slaveholders held professional positions, compared to 1 in 11 (8.9%) slaveholding professionals. The ratio of slaveholding professionals rose to almost 1 in 6 (15.7%) in families that owned 3 to 10 slaves, then it slipped to 1 in 24 (4.3%) among planter families—nothing extraordinary since most owners of 20 or more slaves were farmers. Not surprisingly, 1 in every 5 (20.0%) nonslaveholders was unskilled, whereas unskilled slaveowners, at 1 in every 56 (1.8%), were rare. Usually, they were the children of slaveholders and had yet to carve out a more lucrative career for themselves. Students offered the most lopsided

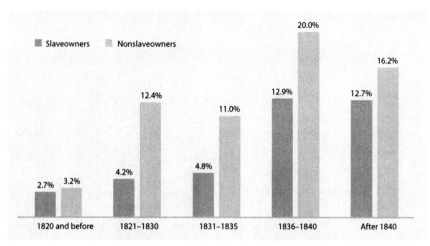

FIGURE 12.3. Slaveholding by year of birth

representation in favor of slave ownership. Future soldiers in school in 1860 constituted only 1 of every 16 (7.4%) in nonslaveholding families. In small slaveholding families, 2 of every 3 (66.7%) soldiers worked the fields alongside the slaves, and only 1 in 12 (8.1%) kept their sons in school. In families with 3 or more slaves, the ratio of students jumped to 1 in 4, and in families with more than 11 slaves, it climbed to 1 in 3 or greater. All told, 1 in every 4 (24.3%) soldiers from slaveholding families was a student before the war.[4]

Figure 12.4 indicates slave ownership by occupation. The total percentages of slaveholders and nonslaveholders equal their percentages in Lee's army.

Because approximately twice as many soldiers came from slaveholding families as opposed to owning slaves themselves, a large number of men still lived with family members and most of them were single. As a result, nonslaveholders were married at disproportionately higher rates than slaveholders or soldiers from families that owned slaves. In Lee's army, 7 of every 10 (70.0%) slaveholders or men from slaveholding families were single; 4 of every 7 (58.1%) nonslaveholders were single. Among those from the planter class, only 1 in 5 (19.6%) troops was married, reflecting the fact that they still lived at home in 1861.[5]

With a high singles rate, less than 1 in every 4 (23.7%) soldiers who owned slaves or whose families owned them had children at home. By contrast, 3 of every 8 (35.7%) nonslaveholders left children behind when they joined the army. Yet the demographics are very interesting. Among those who had children, the average number of children increased with the rise in the number of slaves they owned, except for the planter class. Nonslaveholders with children

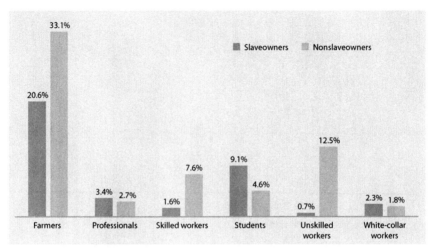

FIGURE 12.4. Slaveholding by occupation

averaged 3.17; those with 1 or 2 slaves, 3.29; and owners of 3 to 10 slaves, 3.78. Those with children at home, or their families, who owned 11 to 19 bondsmen and bondswomen, averaged 4.03 children. Members of the planter class had only 2.00 children. Most likely, the more slaves a person owned, the more children he tended to have. The aberration among the planter class number may have been the result of the small representation of planters (6.9%) in the sample or the age of the soldiers' parents. An examination of the 1850 census records for planter-sons who still lived at home in 1860 indicated an average of 5 (5.3) children in the family. By 1860, some siblings had grown up and left the house or attended school away from home.[6]

Figure 12.5 traces the average percentage of children by the number of slaves owned by soldiers or their families.

In Southern society, slavery and economic class intertwined so tightly that the linkage between slaveholding and wealth was powerful. Soldiers or their families that owned slaves were on the whole much richer than those who did not. For personal soldier-slaveowners, the median wealth reached $8,000, with the average soaring to nearly $11,000; for nonslaveowners, the median was $0 and the average was $350. The combined personal and family median wealth for slaveowners was $11,460, with an average combined wealth of $21,332. Nonslaveowners and their families had a meager combined median wealth of only $220 and a combined average wealth of $963. None of the slave-owners or their families was from the lower economic class, worth $800 or less. Only 2 of 11 (22.2%) slaveowners and their families fit into the middle class, and 9 of 11 had a combined wealth of $4,000 or more. In the middle

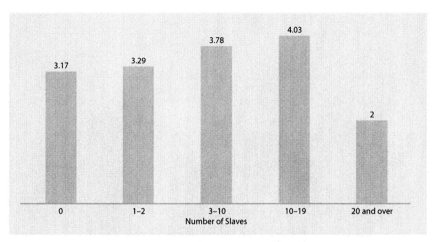

FIGURE 12.5. Slaveholding by percentage of children at home

class, by a 7-to-1 margin over the next category, slaveowners and their families owned 1 or 2 slaves. Nearly 1 in every 5 (19.5%) owners in the wealthiest category possessed 20 or more slaves.[7]

Figure 12.6 compares slaveholding and nonslaveholding by economic class.

Slightly more than 1 in every 8 (13.0%) soldiers owned at least one slave. Another one-quarter (24.2%) of their families with whom they resided had slaves. Only 1 in 14 (7.2%) lived in another family's household with chattel, but neither he nor his family owned any.[8]

Although 5 of every 9 (55.0%) men in Lee's army resided in the Upper South before the war, soldiers who were slaveholders or from slaveholding families in the Lower South had much more representation and influence. Almost 4 of every 9 (43.0%) men or their families from the Lower South possessed slaves. In the Upper South, fewer than 1 in 3 (32.5%) either personally owned slaves or their families with whom they lived owned them.

Soldiers and their families who owned slaves more often lived in areas with dense slave populations. Slaveholding soldiers in Lee's army and their families resided in counties that averaged one slave for every white person (99 to 100) with a median ratio of 87.6 to 100.0. Nonslaveholders, on the other hand, tended to live in predominantly white areas, with an average of 66 slaves to 100 whites and a median black-to-white ratio of 42.5%. Four of every 9 (45.0%) nonslaveholders lived in counties with very small black population areas, 33 to 100 or less; only 2 of every 9 (23.0%) slaveholders resided in these areas.[9]

Although soldier-slaveholders and men from slaveowning families had

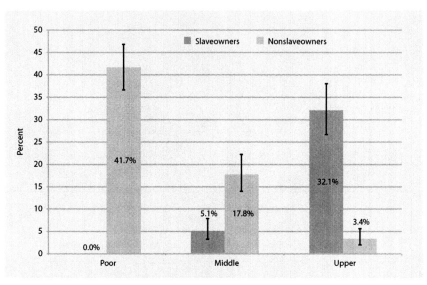

FIGURE 12.6. Slaveholding by economic class

strong representation in each of the three branches of service, far more gravitated to the cavalry. Four of every 9 (44.6%) horsemen had a personal or family investment in bondsmen and bondswomen. Soldiers from slaveowning families tended to be wealthier since a cavalryman had to provide his own mount. Thus, the richer, slaveholding Confederates were overrepresented in the mounted branch. Infantry attracted the fewest slaveholding soldiers. Just under 3 in every 8 (36.1%) foot soldiers or their families had slaves. Artillerymen ranked in the middle with 3 of 8 (38.0%) personal or family slaveholders.[10]

Nearly 3 of every 10 soldiers in the army were infantrymen who owned, or their families owned, slaves. Cavalrymen with direct ownership ties to slavery amounted to 1 in every 20 (5.0%) men in Lee's army, and artillerymen with immediate slave connections composed 1 in 38 (2.6%).

Whether slaveholders or not, soldiers entered the service overwhelmingly in the first two years of the war. Three of every 5 nonslaveowners (59.5%) and 5 of every 9 (54.7%) slaveowners or soldiers from slaveholding families enlisted in 1861, and nearly 8 of 9 nonslaveowners (86.6%) and slaveowners or men from slaveowning families (88.0%) had joined by 1862.[11]

Figure 12.7 shows the percentage of slaveowners and nonslaveowners by year of entry into Lee's army.

Confederates with ownership ties to slave property were nearly twice as likely to be officers as enlisted men. Approximately 1 in 9 (11.4%) slaveowners or men from slaveholding families became officers at one point in the war,

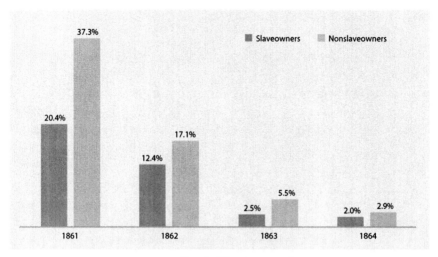

FIGURE 12.7. Slaveholding by year of entry

while just under 1 in 14 (6.9%) men without any personal or family ownership of slaves received commissions. Interestingly, almost 9 of every 10 (88.6%) soldiers who owned slaves or whose families did served the entire war as enlisted men. More than 9 of every 10 (93.1%) men without any slave ownership connection were enlisted men for the duration as well. There was no stigma for slaveholders serving as enlisted men.[12]

Not surprisingly, soldiers who did not own slaves had a greater penchant for leaving the army without authorization. About 1 in 11 (9.4%) was absent without leave at least once, compared to 1 in 16 (6.7%) soldiers who owned, or their families owned, slaves.[13]

Moreover, nonslaveholders were much more likely to desert. Greater than 1 in every 6 (18.1%) nonslaveholding soldiers — or their families — deserted from the army. Less than half that figure, approximately 1 in 12 (8.4%) soldiers who owned slaves — or their families did — deserted the ranks. Generally, the fewer slaves a soldier or his family owned, the more likely he was to desert. Men with one or two slaves deserted at only a slightly smaller frequency (16.8%) than nonslaveholders. One in 99 soldiers (1.1%) who personally owned or came from families that owned 9 to 19 slaves fled the ranks, and 1 in 24 (4.3%) of the planter class deserted. Among nonslaveholders, almost 2 in every 9 (21.8%) fathers deserted, while parents who owned slaves or lived with family members who did had a desertion rate of less than 1 in 6 (15.4%).[14]

Figure 12.8 gives the percentage of deserters by slaveholding status.

Wealth played an interesting role in desertion for slaveholders and nonslave-

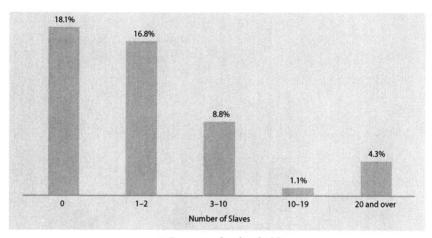

FIGURE 12.8. Desertion by slaveholding status

holders alike. Poor and middle-class soldiers without slaves personally or in their immediate families deserted at high rates, with middle-class troops leaving the army at a greater proportion. Among men with no direct connection to slavery, 18.0% of the lower class and 19.6% of the middle class deserted. Of the middle-class soldiers who were connected to slavery, 17.8% deserted. Clearly, quite a number of troops in the middle economic range sought to shield their remaining wealth by heading home. Those slaveholding soldiers with a combined personal and family wealth of between $1,200 and $3,999 deserted at an astonishing rate of almost 1 in every 5 (19.0%), yet more than 1 in 7 (14.8%) of their nonslaveholding counterparts also deserted. It is possible that soldiers or their families in that elevated economic bracket were just beginning to achieve success in their own eyes. With too much to lose by remaining in the ranks, they left the army to protect their hard-earned property.[15]

Soldiers with and without personal or family ties to slavery were killed in action at roughly the same ratio, 1 in 8 (12.0%). The two groups with the highest percentage of killed in action were those who owned, or their immediate family owned, 3 to 10 slaves (15.6%) and 10 to 19 slaves (17.4%).

Figure 12.9 indicates the percentage of soldiers in Lee's army who were killed or wounded based on how many slaves they or their immediate families owned. The total percentage equals the percentage of personal and family slaveholders for the army as a whole.[16]

No doubt, nonslaveholding soldiers in Lee's army suffered disastrously. One man in the sample (0.5%) without ties to slavery was missing in action. In addition to the 11.9% killed in combat, some 21.9%—slightly less than 2 in 9

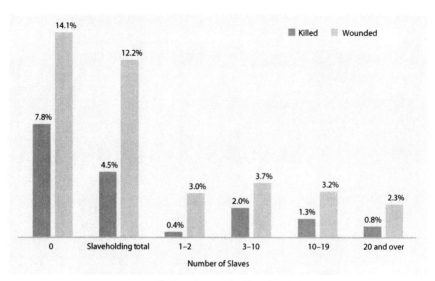

FIGURE 12.9. Killed and wounded by slaveholding status

— of these soldiers who survived were wounded. Combined with the killed and missing in action, 34.0% were killed or wounded. Another 14.7% who did not endure a battlefield injury or fatality became prisoners of war before the final surrender. Thus, slightly under half (48.7%) of the men who, with their immediate families, had no direct connection with slavery were battlefield casualties. Despite these heavy combat losses, slaveholders in uniform or men from slaveholding families suffered worse. In addition to the 1 in 8 (12.0%) slave-connected men who were killed in action, another one-third (31.3%) were wounded at least once. Nine of every 20 (43.3%) soldiers with immediate ties to slave ownership, then, were wounded at least once or killed in action, 27.4% higher than their fellow troops who had no slaves. Another 1 in 7 (13.2%) men with property ties to slavery who had never been injured in combat was captured prior to the surrender at Appomattox. Taken together, nearly 3 of every 5 (56.5%) soldiers with slave ownership in their personal or immediate family were combat casualties at least once, a total rate that was 16.1% higher than that of their comrades who had no slaves.[17]

Figure 12.10 compares the percentage of slaveholders and nonslaveholders who were killed, wounded, or captured prior to the surrender at Appomattox.

Death fell heavily on both groups. More than 1 in 8 (13.0%) soldiers without an immediate connection to slave ownership perished from disease, compared to more than 1 in 9 (9.2%) men who owned slaves or their families

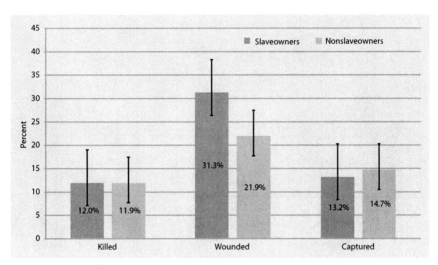

FIGURE 12.10. Combat casualties by slaveholding status

did. The same wealth that enabled soldiers or their families to procure slaves also provided slaveholding men with other financial benefits, such as better prewar diets, superior educations, and certain comforts, especially food and clothing to supplement the standard army issue. These advantages enabled wealthier soldiers to take better care of themselves and follow guidelines for appropriate sanitation, thereby helping to protect them from disease. Nevertheless, 2 in 9 (21.9%) soldiers with ties to bondage, as well as more than 1 in 4 (25.5%) troops without a slavery connection, lost their lives in the war.[18]

Warfare and military service imposed steep physical consequences on all soldiers, though men or their immediate families who owned slaves suffered more. Nearly 3 in every 4 (72.4%) men tied directly to slavery were killed in action, died of illness or injury, were wounded, captured before the surrender at Appomattox, or discharged for physical disability. Among troops with no personal or immediate family slave ownership, 2 of every 3 (67.8%) endured the same fate.

Figure 12.11 displays the total losses—including killed, wounded, captured, died of disease, died accidentally, or discharged for disability—for slaveholders and nonslaveholders in Lee's army.

As various Confederate states clearly explained in their justification of secession, they left the Union to preserve the institution of slavery. Although attempts by the Northern states to restore the Union required an invasion of those seceding states and Confederates rushed to arms to protect their homes

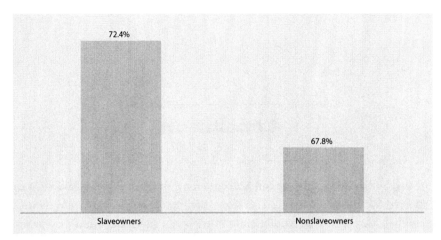

FIGURE 12.11. Total losses by slaveholding status

and homeland, among the issues central in their thoughts was the mission of safeguarding their right to own bondsmen and bondswomen. Soldiers who owned slaves—or lived with family members who did—turned out in great numbers to fight on behalf of their newly created nation. They incurred higher casualties, deserted less frequently, and suffered more for their slaveholding Confederacy than the troops who did not own slaves and were otherwise unconnected to the peculiar institution.

Conclusion

In September 1862, 58-year-old Baltimorean Elizabeth Phoebe Key Howard cheered for close to five hours as men from Stonewall Jackson's old division marched past her. "The Confederate army was a sight that almost overcame me," she admitted to her husband. Howard had seen plenty of Federal troops, but these men were completely different. "Dirty, (I must say it) bronzed by exposure—marked by hardship & suffering—badly clad from want—yet with a look of firm patient and cheerful endurance and unflinching courage and determination." They were unlike any people she had ever seen. "I caught myself wondering what race of men they were." To her mind, "They looked to me not made of flesh and blood but stone and iron."[1]

Seven months later, a surgeon could not restrain his admiration for the soldiers in Lee's army. To his children he wrote:

> Am I in truth in the midst of these actors in those immortal deeds—
> are these men who surround me the illustrious heroes whose names will
> be handed to remote posterity as having braved and done all that men
> should brave and do to achieve their liberties? . . . It is indeed a gratifica-
> tion to look upon their upright and proud faces, and I often wish Harry
> and even Lockert [his children] that I might take them by the hand and
> lead them through these ranks and point out to them the men of whom
> it will be said in after times "These were giants in those days."

Unlike his Rebel compatriots, Mexican War veteran William Pitt Ballinger was not quite so wordy, but in eight words he summarized these and other sentiments when he exclaimed in his diary after yet another Confederate victory, "What a glorious army that of Lee is."[2]

The birth years of soldiers in the sample for this study ranged from 1799 to 1848. The median age in 1861 was 23, and the average was a bit older at 25. Cavalry tended to attract extremes in age, young and old, men who did not wish to walk and those who were caught up in the thrill of swashbuckling tales of J. E. B. Stuart's horsemen. The artillery drew the youngest average age.

Northern-born Confederates were the oldest, with a median age of 29 in 1861; foreign-born troops were four years younger, and Southern-born soldiers reflected the age of the army in general. The median age of troops from the Upper South was one year older than those from the Lower, or Deep, South. Not surprisingly, officers averaged two years older than enlisted men.

Nearly half of all soldiers in Lee's army were born in Virginia or North Carolina. Foreigners by birth constituted 3.4% of the sample, and Northern-born men were slightly more numerous at 4.0%. North Carolina was the seat of birth for the largest percentage of infantrymen, followed well behind by Virginia and Georgia. Five of every 9 cavalrymen claimed the Old Dominion as their birthplace, as did a slight majority of artillerymen.

Like their place of birth, nearly half of all soldiers in Lee's army claimed Virginia or North Carolina as their prewar state of residence. One in every 4 infantrymen came from North Carolina, followed well behind by Virginia and Georgia. More than 3 of every 5 horsemen and over 5 of 9 artillerymen hailed from Virginia. Almost 3 of every 4 men lived in the same state in which they were born, indicating some migration. The only Upper South state with regiments in Lee's army that joined the Union after the 1790s was Arkansas. Thus, the Lower South was the region of expansion, and almost 1 in every 3 soldiers from there was born in a different state. Poorer soldiers, men with fewer attachments in search of a better life, were more likely to have moved to a new state than wealthy men. That same pattern was exhibited by slaveowners, who were less likely to migrate than nonslaveholders. State boundaries, however, were not as rigid as one might expect. Approximately 2.3% of all soldiers enlisted in a state unit that was not their prewar state of residence.

Compared to the counties in states from which Lee's army tapped its manpower, soldiers in the sample lived in counties that averaged a 16.6% higher slave-to-white ratio. In those counties nonslaveholders were more likely to have family and friends who owned bondsmen and bondswomen, and they were more likely to do business with slaveholders. These issues would most likely have strengthened their ties to the institution of slavery. Soldiers in all three branches of military service lived in states with a higher slave-to-white average than their home states. The home counties of officers and enlisted men had almost identical slave-to-white ratios, yet the median ratio for enlisted men's counties was nearly 40% higher than that for officers.

Because a higher proportion of officers owned slaves, the dense slave population in those home counties of enlisted men may have been an underlying force in their understanding of the need for secession and the consequences of Rebel defeat. In an unusual way, though, slave density may have been less of a factor for soldiers from the Upper South. Quite a number of those from the Deep South resided in counties that averaged more slaves than whites, and the median ratio was 88 slaves for every 100 whites. In the Upper South, the average ratio was nearly 1 slave to every 2 whites, and the median settled around 1 slave for every 3 whites. Since so many soldiers in Lee's army came from North Carolina, Virginia, Maryland, and Tennessee, their primary concern included protection of loved ones, friends, and personal property. Their homes often served as the battleground, providing them very different motives for fighting.

Only 5.7% of Lee's army resided in urban areas. Nearly 20% of all artillerymen lived in the top 100 cities, and half of all immigrant soldiers did so as well. Those urban pockets from which Lee's army drew soldiers were predominantly located in the Lower South.

With such an overwhelming percentage of soldiers from rural areas, the majority occupation for troops in Lee's army was farming. Of those tillers, only 5% were heads of households and did not own their own land. Five of every 9 infantrymen and cavalrymen cultivated the soil, while barely 3 in 10 artillerymen, with their unusual ties to cities, did so. Only 2.6% of all foreign-born and 31.0% Northern-born Confederates were agriculturists. Older soldiers and married troops (two-thirds of them) tended to work the land for a living in overwhelming proportions.

Students constituted the second largest occupational block. Two of every 9 cavalrymen were still in school in 1860. One-quarter of all soldiers from the upper economic class and one-quarter of all soldiers from slaveholding families attended school. Men from the Lower South were 60% more likely to be in school than soldiers from the Upper South. As the war dragged on and manpower pickings grew slim, the percentage of students who entered Lee's army nearly tripled. Three of 11 men who first joined the army in 1863 and 3 of 10 who signed up in 1864 were still in school in 1860.

Approximately 13%, or 1 in 8, of the men in Lee's army worked as unskilled laborers. More than half of all foreign-born troops fit into the unskilled category. Unskilled soldiers were almost twice as likely to live in the Upper South as in the Deep South. One in 5 artillerymen lacked work skills, while only 1 in 16 cavalrymen — who belonged to the wealthiest branch of service — did so. In fact, the combined personal and family wealth of 83% of all unskilled laborers in Lee's army placed them in the lower economic class.

Skilled workers comprised 10% of Lee's army. One in every 3 foreign-born and 2 in 9 Northern-born soldiers possessed work skills. Only 8% of all Southern-born troops qualified as skilled workers. The single largest block of skilled workers consisted of soldiers between 26 and 30 years of age in 1860 — 20% of that age group. Evidently, skilled workers did not necessarily accumulate much wealth. Seven of every 10 fit the guidelines for the lower economic class.

Because professional positions earned substantial income, three times as many officers, nearly 50% more men from the Lower South, and double the percentage of slaveholders to nonslaveholders, held professional positions. The only true surprise were foreign-born troops: almost 10% of them held professional jobs prior to the war.

White-collar jobs were usually a kind of apprenticeship for high-paying professional and business positions. Officers, therefore, were twice as likely to hold white-collar jobs as enlisted men. White-collar duties among soldiers from slaveholding families doubled those of nonslaveholding comrades. Men who held white-collar jobs were three times as likely to come from the upper economic class as the middle class and four times as likely to be upper-class as opposed to lower-class. With their youth and ties to wealth, virtually all soldiers who maintained prewar white-collar work enlisted in 1861 or 1862.[3]

Exactly 3 of every 8 (37.5%) soldiers in the sample were married. Not surprisingly, older troops were much more likely to be married than younger ones. For example, more than 9 of every 10 men over 40 had a wife. That figure slipped to 60% of men between 26 and 30, below which percentages declined rapidly. The infantry had the highest percentage of married soldiers at 2 of every 5, while the artillery claimed the lowest at 2 of every 9. Though Northern-born men had a median age of 29 in 1861, by far the oldest in the army, barely more than 1 in 5 were married, suggesting some bias toward them in the Southern white population. Foreign-born troops also lagged behind at a little more than 3 in 10 with wives.

Although a higher percentage of officers had taken brides, married soldiers were poorer than their single comrades. Only 30% of all married soldiers and their families owned slaves. The significant factor in that instance was that younger, single troops usually lived with their parents. Nearly half the sample lived with parents or siblings and was not the head of a household. Many of them had not struck out on their own, and they lived a richer lifestyle with their parents or other family members. Almost 42% of all single soldiers or their families owned slaves, for instance, suggesting their access to money and property.

Fewer than 2 of 7 soldiers who entered the army in 1861 were married, indicating that young, unattached single men rushed to seize arms in the *rage militaire*. The following year, almost 5 of every 9 soldiers who joined the army were married. The ratio slipped to 2 of 5 the next year, but in 1864, as the army became more desperate and took in far more older workers, marital rates jumped back to just under a majority.

Nearly a third of all Southern-born soldiers had children at home, followed closely by foreign-born troops. Like marriage rates, Northern-born Confederates lagged far behind as fathers at approximately 21%. Not only was fatherhood overrepresented in the infantry compared to the other branches of the army, but also foot soldiers had the highest average number of children at 2.7. The cavalry, the wealthiest branch, followed closely with 2.5 children per father. By and large, the frequency of fatherhood in Lee's army increased by wealth, as did the number of children they had. Yet at the same time just below one-quarter of all soldiers with personal or family slaves had children, indicating the youthful element in the army. Officers, who were generally older and had greater personal wealth than enlisted men, were 20% more likely to be fathers than enlisted men.

A breakdown of personal wealth indicates that 3 of every 4 soldiers were very poor—with total personal and property wealth below $401—and 4 of every 5 qualified for the lower economic class. One in 10 fit into the middle class, and another 1 in 10 climbed into the upper class. The infantry almost perfectly reflected the army as a whole. The cavalry had fewer poor and more rich soldiers, while the artillery accounted for the greatest proportion of poor men at 17 of 20. Officers had a higher median personal wealth at $800 than enlisted men at $0. Just below half of all officers fit into the poorest category, whereas 3 of every 4 enlisted men did so.

Southern and foreign-born troops had almost identical percentages of very poor men at just under 74%. Yet more than 1 in 10 Southern-born soldiers achieved upper-class status and no foreign-born men in the sample did. The Northern-born had the highest proportion of very poor at more than 4 of 5 and the highest ratio of men in the poor class at nearly 9 of 10. Still, almost 1 in 10 qualified for the upper class, an indicator that no real middle class existed for Northern-born Confederates.[4]

For the most part, personal wealth increased by age. For soldiers over 40, the median personal wealth was an impressive $1,700. It declined to $600 for men between 31 and 40, then to $200 for those from 26 to 30. Understandably, married troops had greater personal wealth than their single comrades, and fathers boasted greater wealth than childless troops. The median personal wealth for slaveholders was an astounding $8,000 and an average of $10,914; for nonslaveowners, it was $0 and the average eked up to $350.

The combination of family wealth with personal wealth altered the army's statistics significantly. The percentage of poor troops fell to a plurality, a true and substantial middle class emerged, and the wealthy class encompassed more than 7 of every 20 soldiers. Nearly half of all horsemen qualified for the upper class. In median wealth, cavalrymen were more than twice as wealthy as infantrymen and 3.5 times as wealthy as artillerymen. Yet the artillery proved to be an arm of economic extremes. Four of 9 men were worth less than $400, whereas 4 of 10 possessed $4,000 or more in personal and family assets. The median wealth of officers eclipsed enlisted men by 2.5 times, yet 1 in 5 officers was poor and 7 of 20 enlisted men achieved upper-class status. In fact, 96% of the poor and approximately 90% of the rich served as enlisted men in the Army of Northern Virginia. Compared to families from those states that contributed soldiers to Lee's army, his troops represented fewer poor and more affluent families.

Southern-born Confederates enjoyed triple the median personal and family wealth of Northern-born comrades, and their combined assets were 15 times greater than those of immigrant troops. Soldiers from the Lower South possessed nearly double the median wealth of those from the Upper South. Older and younger soldiers tended to be richer. The older men had had a longer time to build up assets, while younger troops still lived with their parents and benefited from their accumulated wealth over the years. Almost half of all soldiers who were born between 1844 and 1848 lived with upper-class families. Thus, married men fell far behind single soldiers in median wealth, as did fathers. And the gap between slaveholders and nonslaveholders in personal and family wealth grew huge—in median wealth, it was 15 times greater.

In household wealth, the upper class emerged as the largest bracket, followed by a 10% decline to the poor and another 10% decline to the middle category. More than 1 in 4 households amassed total assets of $10,000 or more. One in 4 enlisted men and more than 2 in 5 officers resided amid such affluence. Three of every 8 cavalrymen, 2 of every 7 artillerymen, and 1 in every 4 infantrymen resided in upper-class households. More than 3 of every 5 Northern-born troops claimed residence in upper-class households, compared to just less than 1 in 3 for Southern-born men and 1 in 9 for immigrant soldiers.

Among soldiers who were slaveholders, a disproportionate share gravitated toward the cavalry. The artillery attracted the fewest slaveowners. Officers were 3.5 times more likely to own slaves than their enlisted troops. Older soldiers, married soldiers, and soldier-parents had a much greater likelihood of owning slaves than younger, single, or childless men. With older troops who entered the army disproportionately in 1862 and 1864, it is not surprising that those years reflected a high percentage of personal ownership. In addition, with denser slave populations in the Lower South, more soldiers from that region left behind slaves than did men from the Upper South.

Once families entered the equation, statistics shifted dramatically. Four of every 9 horsemen came from slaveowning families, with the ratio of the two other branches at 3 in every 8. Nearly half of all officers and close to 3 of 8 enlisted men lived in slaveholding households. Half of all troops who were under 18 years of age in 1861 came from slaveowning families, as did 2 of every 5 men between 18 and 25. They fought at least in part to defend the slave interests of their parents and themselves. On the other end of the age spectrum, more than 4 of every 9 soldiers over 40 lived in households with slaves. No foreign-born and only 1 in 10 Northern-born men was from a slaveholding family, while 2 in every 5 Southern-born soldiers were. Nearly 4 in 9 families of troops from the Lower South held bondsmen and bondswomen, compared to less than 1 in 3 in the Upper South. Two in 9 men from middle-class families and more than 9 in 10 soldiers from upper-class families had slaves, demonstrating the powerful bonds between wealth and bondage.

Not only did a high percentage of Lee's troops come from slaveholding families, but also an unusually large proportion of them lived in planter families (20 or more slaves). One in 8 horsemen grew up in planter families, and almost 1 in 5 soldiers from upper-class families qualified as a planter. Yet there were two unusual facts about soldier-families and the planter class. Despite heavy slave concentrations in the Deep South, both sections of the Confederacy had roughly equal percentages from planter families. Moreover, the proportion of enlisted men from planter families was 76% greater than that of officers' families.

More than half of all cavalrymen and artillerymen lived in slaveholding households, and almost 4 in 9 infantrymen did so as well. Half of all troops from the Lower South resided with slaveholders, compared to 2 in 5 from the Upper South. Foreign- and Northern-born Confederates lagged far behind the Southern-born in their direct attachment to slavery. Fathers and married troops, too, resided in slaveowning homes at a rate that was nearly 70% behind childless and single soldiers.

Nearly all the soldiers who served in Lee's army entered military service in 1861 or 1862. Two of every 3 Northern-born men volunteered in that first year, and every foreign-born man in the sample had enlisted by 1862, demonstrating both their commitment to the Southern cause and, in many instances, their interest in the attractive pay and perceived opportunities offered by Confederate military service. Almost 19 of every 20 officers entered the army in 1861 or 1862, as did 17 of 20 enlisted men.

According to the sample, almost 4 of every 5 soldiers who ever served in Lee's army volunteered before the Confederacy implemented conscription. Draftees were poorer and owned fewer slaves than comrades who enlisted. Two of every 3 drafted soldiers were between 26 and 40 years of age. Even more striking, nearly 7 of every 10 conscripts were married, and every drafted, married soldier left behind children, which no doubt influenced their decision not to enlist.

Evidence of absences without leave in the Compiled Service Records is incomplete. According to that data, only 1 in 12 soldiers were absent without permission. Soldiers between the ages of 18 and 25 had twice the AWOL rate of the army as a whole. Married soldiers and those with children at home were less likely to be AWOL than single and childless troops, as were soldiers from slaveholding families.

As in the case of unauthorized absences, desertion statistics were difficult to collect during the final seven months of the war due to a breakdown in record keeping and the destruction of some records for Lee's army. From October through December 1864, evidence is spotty, but for the first four months in 1865, personal desertion records exist only if soldiers fled to the Union army.

No doubt, numerous factors affected desertion rates. Wartime hardships, casualties, and, especially late in the war, faltering morale unquestionably influenced whether and when soldiers abandoned the army. In addition to the collapsing war effort in late 1864 and early 1865, six issues—opportunity, branch of service, economic status, age, marital status, and fatherhood—proved to be the most powerful in determining who deserted. For the first two years of the conflict, almost every deserter came from the Upper South; it was too difficult for troops who came from the Lower South to desert and make it home until General Longstreet's divisions shifted to Georgia. Among the three branches, mounted men, who had the easiest means to flee the army, deserted in the highest percentages. By contrast, artillerymen deserted in the lowest percentages, despite having the highest percentage of soldiers in the lowest economic class. Artillerymen worked tightly as a team to operate their guns, and that sense of unity of purpose and lower casualty rates compared to infantrymen most likely induced these troops to persevere with their comrades. Poor troops and those from nonslaveholding families were much more prone to desertion than soldiers from well-to-do or slaveholding families, demonstrating weaker bonds to community and cause and greater wartime hardships of loved ones at home. Nondeserters had median family wealth that more than doubled that of deserters, and almost twice as many nondeserters and their immediate families owned slaves. Older soldiers, too, were more prone to desert than younger troops, as hardships wore down men in their late twenties, thirties, and forties much more quickly. Married troops were nearly a third more likely to desert. Even more powerful was the motivation to look after one's children. Fathers were 80% more likely to flee the army than childless soldiers.

Neither illness nor battlefield wounds prompted soldiers to desert in any appreciable numbers. In fact, the vast majority of troops in this category remained with the army. Approximately 20% of all deserters were wounded, but 30% of all nondeserters received at least one injury in combat. Close to 35% of all deserters endured at least one illness, while close to half of all non-deserters did so, too. Thus, the issue of desertion included numerous complicating factors, any one of which could have induced a soldier to abandon the Confederate cause. Only 1 in 6 deserters returned to the army voluntarily or involuntarily.

Among those who were killed in action, 92.4% served in the infantry. Officers were 2.25 times more likely to be killed in action than enlisted men. Two of every 3 soldiers who died in battle had enlisted in 1861, and another one-quarter entered in 1862. Those from the Lower South suffered more than double the rate of combat fatalities as troops from the Upper South, reflecting the high percentages of infantry regiments from the Lower South. Men between the ages of 21 and 25 in 1861 accounted for almost 4 of every 9 soldiers killed in combat, and soldiers between 18 and 20 totaled an additional 3 in 10. Older troops were less likely to fall in battle than younger ones. Those killed in battle had a median wealth just below that of men who survived. There was no difference in the percentage of men killed from slaveholding versus non-slaveowning families. Thus, neither wealth nor slaveholding was a discriminator when it came to death on the battlefield; branch of service, region, rank, and age were the key factors.

In most respects, age, length of service, wealth, and branch of service affected rates of death from disease. Older men succumbed to disease at much higher rates than younger troops, yet soldiers who survived for two years had comparatively little risk of dying from illness afterward.

Poorer soldiers were much more prone to die of disease. Earlier in the war, wealthier soldiers clothed themselves better and could more easily supplement the army diet through the purchase of fruits and vegetables. In addition, wealthier soldiers lived on better prewar diets, tended to be better educated, and embraced proper sanitary practices more readily. This proved true of officers compared to enlisted men: whereas no officer in the sample died of disease, 1 in 8 enlisted men did so. Infantrymen, packed densely into comparatively small campgrounds, lost 70% more per 100 men to disease than horse soldiers and more than twice as many per 100 men as artillerymen. With the preponderance of Lower South residents serving in the infantry and being unused to the climate in the Upper South, they lost 63% more per 100 men to disease than did troops from the Upper South. Five of every 9 soldiers who died of disease were married, perhaps reflecting the age factor. Three of 8 deaths due to illness fell upon soldier-parents.

Yet when we consider soldiers who were wounded at least once or killed in action, wealth and slaveholding become powerful considerations. Wealthy soldiers were 45.9% more likely to suffer at least one wound than poor soldiers and 26.9% more likely than middle-class troops. Thus, killed and wounded troops had nearly 25.0% more personal and family wealth than noncasualties, and 30.0% more of them came from slaveholding families. Among total combat casualties, the upper class suffered the heaviest losses, followed closely by the middle class, and the poor class lagged behind. The rich and the slaveholders had more at stake in the war and fought harder to preserve the Confederacy.

As noted, poor soldiers died of disease at a higher rate than soldiers from middle- and upper-class families. And while wealthy troops sustained by far the most combat wounds, a slightly higher percentage of soldiers from poor families were killed in action or subsequently died of wounds. This might suggest an unfair advantage in quality medical care for wealthier troops. There is, however, no evidence that Confederate surgeons and nurses gave greater attention and care to richer soldiers. Early in the war wealth may have been a factor in superior medical care, as richer families were better able to look after sick or injured loved ones. Providing more personal attention, caregivers at least kept their patients clean and well fed, reducing the chance of infection among the wounded and greatly enhancing the likelihood of surviving a wound or illness. By the second and third year of the war, however, that luxury vanished. Soldiers had to pull through in overcrowded and underresourced hospitals, where severity of injuries or illness and constitutional strength became vital factors in determining who recovered and who did not. Soldiers from wealthier families had an advantage, but that was largely due to superior prewar diet and health, not preferential treatment in army hospitals.

Of the three branches of military service, the infantry endured by far the greatest losses. Foot soldiers lost 86% more men killed and wounded per 100 soldiers than the artillery and 112% more than the cavalry. Three of every 4 infantrymen were killed in battle or by accident, died of disease, suffered a wound, were taken prisoner prior to Appomattox, or were discharged for age or disability. The artillery ranked second with nearly 60% fewer losses per 100 men than the infantry, and the cavalry endured the least losses, 66% behind the infantry. Only the very high percentage of horsemen who became POWs—1 in every 4—elevated the mounted branch's total losses to a level approaching the artillery's.

Officers suffered disastrously in the war. From the day Lee took command in June 1862 until midsummer 1864, the officer corps saw 1,600 men killed in action and more than 6,000 wounded. More than half of all officers who ever served in Lee's army were killed or wounded. Although enlisted men also experienced enormous casualties, they experienced 43% fewer killed or wounded in combat per 100 soldiers.

Southern-born troops lost more heavily than foreign- or Northern-born Confederates. Soldiers from the Upper South saw almost the same percentage losses as Lower South troops, but more than 1 in 5 residents of the Upper South became a POW, compared to less than 1 in 16 from the Deep South.

Troops who entered the army in 1861 and 1862 lost more than 7 of every 10 men. That percentage fell off dramatically for the 1863 and 1864 year groups. Five of 9 from the 1863 group were killed in battle, wounded, captured, died of disease, killed accidentally, or discharged for a disability; 4 of 9 from the 1864 group suffered a similar fate, indicating the ferocity of the war by that time.

There was extraordinary continuity in losses among age groups, ranging from 67.0% to 73.2%. Soldiers under 18 years of age in 1861 were the only exception. Because of the limited length of time in which they could serve, that age group lost 5 of every 9—still an extremely high ratio. Incredibly, half of all men between 21 and 25 sustained at least one wound or was killed.

In an odd split, single and childless soldiers suffered heavier combat losses than married men and fathers, yet in total losses—killed, wounded, taken prisoner, died from disease, or discharged for disability—married men's were 10% higher than those of single men. Because the infantry had by far the highest percentage of married soldiers, that statistic should not be so surprising. On the other hand, childless soldiers lost 6% more than fathers in the army, even though the infantry suffered by far the greatest losses and had the highest percentage of fathers. Yet in the infantry, the 20% discrepancy between married soldiers and fathers accounted for the difference. Fathers also deserted in the highest proportions, thereby reducing their statistics for total losses.

Of all the military forces in the Confederacy, Lee's Army of Northern Virginia implemented President Davis's strategic designs best. Davis intended to come down hard on Union invaders in the hope of convincing Federals to abandon their efforts to force the Confederacy back into the Union. Lee's army nearly accomplished that feat. For four long years, it hammered the Federal forces, inflicting approximately 45% of all Union killed and wounded in the war. Even late in the conflict, it continued to punish Union attackers. Despite tremendous wartime strain, Lee's soldiers inflicted 127,000 casualties on the Federal army in the final 12 months of the war.

At times Lee may have acted in an overly aggressive fashion, but on the whole he executed the president's strategic concept skillfully. Davis fully understood that the plan would result in high losses and extraordinary hardships both at home and in the field, but he believed the Confederate people would endure it for liberty.

Where Lee and his army could have benefited was from a different allocation of new manpower during the last two years of the war. With infantrymen doing most of the fighting and suffering the lion's share of combat losses, the Confederacy should have assigned a higher percentage of fresh soldiers to the infantry to help replace the losses and reinforce its most powerful combat arm. In 1862, 1 in every 6 recruits entered the cavalry, a decision that made sense at the time. In the Battle of First Manassas, the Confederacy's cavalry shortage inhibited its ability to pursue a defeated enemy and probably cost the Rebel army hundreds if not a couple of thousand more POWs, plus captured weapons and equipment that the Confederacy desperately needed. Yet in 1863 and 1864, one-third of all new soldiers were allocated to the artillery and cavalry. At Camp Lee, where draftees gathered before assignment, authorities designated more than 20% to cavalry units and another 11% to the artillery. Despite the low percentage of new manpower available in 1863 and 1864 — 14% of all men who ever served in Lee's army entered military service during those two years — the Army of Northern Virginia would have profited greatly from an increase in infantry troop strength. Certainly late in the war some cavalrymen were dismounted, and artillerymen without serviceable pieces picked up muskets and fought like infantrymen. The allocation of large numbers of fresh troops to the infantry would have reinforced that army even more.

Officers and enlisted men in Lee's army represented an unusually large proportion of wealthy and slaveholding families, particularly compared to the states from which Lee drew his soldiers. Why was there not more participation by poorer or nonslaveholding whites? According to the 1860 census, only 24.9% of all Southern households had slaves. Then how could 37.2% (with a margin of error of plus or minus 5.0) of soldiers or their immediate families in Lee's army own slaves, and how could 44.4% (plus or minus 5.5%) of all soldiers' households have slaves? On the surface, it seems mathematically unlikely, if not impossible. The answer, however, is simple: family size. Wealthier families had more children, and slaveholders were among the most affluent families. Statistically, moreover, there was more than a 99% chance that the wealthier a family became, pushing into the middle and upper middle or upper classes, the more likely it was to own slaves. Thus, there were more children of slaveholders to serve in the army than one would expect.[5]

This sample by no means provides us with all the answers to the study of Lee's army. But by slicing it in different ways, we are able to garner some unusual insights into the soldiers, the army, and the Confederate war effort.

NOTES

Note: Unless otherwise labeled, confidence limits are listed in the same order, left to right, as items in the relevant figure; when an extra LCI and UCI appear on the right, they are for the total.

PREFACE

1. Gary W. Gallagher, *The Confederate War: How Popular Will, Nationalism, and Military Strategy Could Not Stave Off Defeat* (Cambridge: Harvard University Press, 1997), 11; Sam P. Collier to Sister, 4 March 1864, Samuel P. Collier Papers, North Carolina Division of Archives and History, Raleigh; Beverly Wilson Palmer, ed., *The Selected Letters of Charles Sumner* (Boston: Northeastern University Press, 1990), 2:268; Emma LeConte Diary, 11 March 1865, Emma LeConte, *When the World Ended*, ed. Earl Schenck Miers (New York: Oxford University Press, 1957), 77. Also see Joseph T. Glatthaar, *General Lee's Army: From Victory to Collapse* (New York: Free Press, 2008), 464–65.
2. Some scholars have challenged the accuracy of census data. In fact, no source is perfect, and in most instances census data are quite accurate. Soldiers whose prewar wealth was listed at $0 probably did own something of value, but that property was so inconsequential that it was worth almost nothing. Others have asserted that slave numbers were incorrect. Certainly there were some mistakes, but again the records are quite accurate. Sometimes individuals owned slaves but rented them out. If the slaves lived elsewhere, the record indicated the proper owner; however, the slaves would be listed in a separate household and researchers would not find them easily. This happened to Robert E. Lee in the 1860 census. Keep in mind that it worked to Southerners' benefit for all slaves to be counted, based on the Three-Fifths Clause in the U.S. Constitution.
3. U.S. Bureau of the Census, 1860, Instructions to the Marshals, n.d., 1860, <http://usa. ipums.org/usa/voliii/inst1860.shtml#86_12, 7>.

CHAPTER 1

1. Special Orders No. 22, HQ, 1 June 1862; *The War of the Rebellion: A Compilation of the Official Records of the Union and Confederate Armies* (Washington, D.C.: Government Printing Office, 1880–1901), ser. 1, vol. 11, pt. 3:569. Hereafter the *Official Records* (OR) take the following form: volume number (part number, where applicable):page number.
2. C. W. Dabney to Brother, 24 August 1861, Charles W. Dabney Papers, Southern Historical Collection, University of North Carolina, Chapel Hill; James Langhorne to Mother, 26 June 1861, Langhorne Family Papers, Virginia Historical Society, Richmond.
3. Johnston to Sir, 5 August 1861, Gilder-Lehrman Collection, New-York Historical Society.
4. John T. Thornton to [Wife], 20 June 1862, John T. Thornton Papers, University of Vir-

ginia; J. [Nance] to Laura, 18 August 1863, James Drayton Nance Papers, University of South Carolina; H. C. Kendricks to [Father], n.d., 1863, H. C. Kendricks Papers, Southern Historical Collection, University of North Carolina, Chapel Hill.

5. Lee to Davis, 5 June 1862, Robert E. Lee Papers, U.S. Military Academy, West Point; Lee to Davis, 7 September 1862, OR 19(2):597.

6. H. J. Mitchel to Davis, 3 October 1862, M437, R62, F1035–36, and Application for Discharge of Pvt. T. W. Anderson, 8 June 1863, M437, R80, F529–32, Letters Received, Confederate Secretary of War; Charles Marshall to Capt. C. W. McCreary, 17 July 1862, and Lee to Cooper, 7 January 1863, Letters and Telegrams Sent, Army of Northern Virginia; J. A. Campbell to Lee, 17 January 1863, Letters, Telegrams, and Other Papers Received by Lee—all in Record Group 109, National Archives (hereafter cited as RG 109, NA).

7. In the chi^2 test for year of birth grouping, P=.0000.

8. Soldiers moved to another state at a rate of 26.1%. The LCI was 20.1% and the UCI was 33.1% at the 95% confidence level.

9. The records do not provide enough information for an accurate assessment of migration within states.

10. The actual statistic for urbanization was 5.69%.

11. For married soldiers, the rate was 37.5%; the LCI was 32.5% and the UCI was 42.8% For fatherhood, 31.2% had children; the LCI was 26.4% and the UCI was 36.5%. All were at the 95% confidence level.

12. In the chi^2 test for wealth and slave ownership, P=.0000, which means that in more than a 99% chance wealthy soldiers were likely to own slaves and poorer soldiers were not at the 95% confidence level.

13. I. C. Shields to Page, 1 October 1863, Monthly Progress Reports, from Before September 1862 through February 1865, Progress Reports for Conscription, chap. 1, vol. 250, RG 109, NA.

14. C. A. Hege to Father, 17 August, 15 November 1862, Lewis Leigh Collection, U.S. Army Military History Institute, Carlisle Barracks, Pa.

15. For AWOL, the LCI was 5.5% and the UCI was 11.3% at the 95% confidence level.

16. For desertion, the LCI was 11.9% and the UCI was 19.9% at the 95% confidence level.

17. In the chi^2 test for desertion and economic class, P=.0032, indicating more than a 99% chance that the wealthier a soldier was, the less likely he was to desert.

18. For killed in battle, the LCI was 9% and the UCI was 15.3%. For killed or wounded, the LCI was 32.1% and the UCI was 42.7%. For died of disease, the LCI was 8.6% and the UCI was 15.5% All were at the 95% confidence level.

CHAPTER 2

1. In the chi^2 test for the grouping of birth years by branch, P=.3507, indicating an accuracy outside the acceptable statistical limits of the U.S. Census Bureau.

2. The precise percentage was 58.5% greater than the next highest branch, the artillery, and 135% higher than the cavalry. Some 27% moved to a new state. The LCI was 19.9% and the UCI was 35.6% at the 95% confidence level.

3. In the chi^2 test for the grouping of occupations by branch, P=.0002, indicating an accuracy greater than 99%.

4. For slave-to-white density, 50.7% of all soldiers' counties were above the median for the states from which the army was drawn. The LCI was 41.7% and the UCI was 59.7% at the 95% confidence level.

5. For marital status, 39.3% of infantrymen were married. The LCI was 33.3% and the UCI was 45.8%. For fatherhood, 32.9% were fathers. The LCI was 27.1% and the UCI was 39.2%. All were at the 95% confidence level.

6. In the chi^2 test for personal wealth and branch, P=.1416, indicating an accuracy outside the acceptable statistical limits of the U.S. Census Bureau. In the chi^2 test for combined wealth and branch, P=.0898, indicating an accuracy of 91% and within the acceptable statistical limits of the U.S. Census Bureau.

7. In the chi^2 test for household wealth and branch, P=.0729, indicating an accuracy of 92.7% and within the acceptable statistical limits of the U.S. Census Bureau.

8. For 1–2 slaves, the LCI was 6.6% and the UCI was 13.4%. For 3–10 slaves, the LCI was 8.6% and the UCI was 17.5%. For 11–19 slaves, the LCI was 5.5% and the UCI was 11.6%. For 20 or more slaves, the LCI was 3.7% and the UCI was 10.3%. All were at the 95% confidence level.

9. In 1861, 62.8% infantrymen enlisted; the LCI was 54.3% and the UCI was 70.5%. In 1862, 27.0% enlisted; the LCI was 20.2% and the UCI was 35.1%. In 1863, 6.2% enlisted; the LCI was 3.2% and the UCI was 11.7%. In 1864, 4.0% enlisted; the LCI was 2.1% and the UCI was 7.4%. All were at the 95% confidence level.

10. I. C. Shields to Page, 1 October 1863, Monthly Progress Reports, from Before September 1862 through February 1865, Progress Reports for Conscription, chap. 1, vol. 250, Record Group 109, National Archives.

11. The LCI was 5.9% and the UCI was 12.3% at the 95% confidence level.

12. For desertion, the LCI was 11.2% and the UCI was 20.7% at the 95% confidence level.

13. Records on sickness were not maintained as vigilantly as historians would like.

14. One infantryman was declared missing in action. Since no subsequent records were found, I presume he was killed in action and his body was not recovered. For killed in action, the LCI was 10.0% and the UCI was 17.6%. For killed and wounded, the LCI was 34.7% and the UCI was 47.6%. For died of disease (12.7% died, and a small number were either wounded or taken prisoner), the LCI was 9.1% and the UCI was 17.4%. All were at the 95% confidence level. By factoring deserters out, I subtracted them from the denominator, rather than adding them, because it changed the number of cases in the sample.

15. Alexander to [Wife], 3 October 1864, Edward Porter Alexander Papers, Southern Historical Collection, University of North Carolina, Chapel Hill.

CHAPTER 3

1. For enlisted men, the LCI was 91.4% and the UCI was 98.2%. For officers, the LCI was 1.8% and the UCI was 8.6%. All were at the 95% confidence level.

2. In the chi^2 test for year of birth groups by branch, P=.3602, indicating an accuracy outside the acceptable statistical limits of the U.S. Census Bureau.

3. In the chi^2 test for place of birth by branch, P=.0065, indicating an accuracy of more than 99%.

4. It is unclear whether this low migratory pattern prompted Virginians, North Carolin-

ians, and South Carolinians to seek out the greater mobility of cavalry service. Some 22.6% of them moved to a new state. The LCI was 15.2% and the UCI was 32.3% at the 95% confidence level.

5. In the chi^2 test for year of occupation by branch, P=.0002, indicating an accuracy of more than 99%.

6. For slave density, 47.5% of soldiers' counties were above the median for the state in which the army drew its troops. The LCI was 36.3% and the UCI was 59% at the 95% confidence level. Technically, slave density was 48.7% greater in those counties above the median.

7. For marital status, 32.4% were married, with an LCI of 25.1% and a UCI of 40.6%. For fatherhood, 28.1% had children; the LCI was 20.7% and the UCI was 36.9%. Both categories were at the 95% confidence level.

8. In households worth between $4,000 and $10,000, the LCI was 15.1% and the UCI was 28.1%. For households worth over $10,000, the LCI was 29.6 and the UCI was 46%.

9. I. C. Shields to Page, 1 October 1863, Monthly Progress Reports, from Before September 1862 through February 1865, Progress Reports for Conscription, chap. 1, vol. 250, Record Group 109, National Archives.

10. In the chi^2 test for AWOL and branch, P=.1575, indicating an accuracy just outside the acceptable statistical limits of the U.S. Census Bureau.

11. Cavalrymen deserted at a rate of 18.7%. The LCI was 12.2 and the UCI was 27.6 at the 95% confidence level. The chi^2 test has P=.0385, which means there is a 96.2% chance that wealthy soldiers were less likely to desert. Confidence limits would have made the figure too busy to understand. Their percentages were

For Nondeserters:

UCI: 33.5, 5.8, 10.5, 15.7, 18.4, 38.0, 88.0 (total)

LCI: 17.2, 0.4, 1.7, 6.3, 7.0, 22.2, 72.0.

For Deserters:

UCI: 12.6, 0.0, 6.6, 10.5, 11., 1.0, 28.1

LCI: 3.2, 0.0, 0.7, 1.7, 2.2, 0.3, 12.0.

12. For cavalrymen killed in action, the statistic was 4.7%; the LCI was 2.3% and the UCI was 9.4%. For those killed or wounded, the statistic was 19.3%; the LCI was 12.8% and the UCI was 28.2%. Of those who died of disease, the statistic was 7.3%; the LCI was 3.8% and the UCI was 13.8%. For cavalrymen who were POWs, the statistic was 24.0%; the LCI was 17.0% and the UCI was 32.8%. All were at the 95% confidence level.

CHAPTER 4

1. In the chi^2 test for year of occupation by branch, P=.0002, indicating an accuracy of more than 99%.

2. I suspected that unskilled workers were less likely to be married because they made the least amount of money. In fact, 32 of 42 men in the artillery were single, almost exactly the same ratio as artillerymen in general. In the chi^2 test for marital status, P=.0140, indicating an accuracy of 98.6%.

3. In the chi^2 test for children, P=.0169, indicating an accuracy of 98.3%.

4. In the chi² test for slave density, P=.2001, indicating an accuracy outside the acceptable statistical limits of the U.S. Census Bureau.

5. All three components of the artillery equal 6.9% of the army; the bracketed data is the LCI and UCI: .0342 [.0283, .0413], .0107 [.0073, .0157], .0241 [.0172, .0337], .0690 [.0620, .0767].

6. In the chi² test for personal slave ownership by branch, P=.0214, indicating an accuracy of 97.9%. In the chi² test for combined (personal and family) ownership by branch, P=.0261, indicating an accuracy of 97.4%. In the chi² test for household slave ownership by branch, P=.0409, indicating an accuracy of 96.9%. In the chi² test for household wealth by branch, P=.0775, indicating an accuracy of 92.2% and well within the acceptable statistical limits of the U.S. Census Bureau.

7. In the chi² test for year of enlistment by branch, P=.0000, an accuracy above 99%.

8. In the chi² test for the percentage of officers and enlisted men by branch, P=.1154, indicating an accuracy just outside the acceptable statistical limits of the U.S. Census Bureau.

9. I. C. Shields to Page, 1 October 1863, Monthly Progress Reports, from Before September 1862 through February 1865, Progress Reports for Conscription, chap. 1, vol. 250, Record Group 109, National Archives.

10. In the chi² test for AWOL and branch, P=.1575, indicating an accuracy just outside the acceptable statistical limits of the U.S. Census Bureau.

11. In the chi² test for desertion by branch, P=.5151, indicating an accuracy well outside the acceptable statistical limits of the U.S. Census Bureau.

12. In the chi² test for killed and wounded by branch, P=.0000, indicating an accuracy greater than 99%. In the chi² test for died of disease by branch, P=.0406, indicating an accuracy of 96%. In the chi² test for POWs by branch, P=.0963, indicating an accuracy of 90.4% and within the acceptable statistical limits of the U.S. Census Bureau.

CHAPTER 5

1. *Northern-born* is defined as soldiers who were born in states that did not secede in 1861. It does not include West Virginia, which was part of Virginia when these men were born and was formed when it seceded from Virginia during the war. *Foreign-born* means all those who were born outside U.S. territory.

2. The limited variation and size of the foreign-born population prevented any confidence intervals from being tabulated. Those for the Northern- and Southern-born were as follows:

	Northern-Born		Southern-Born	
	UCI	LCI	UCI	LCI
1820 and before	.1116	.0414	.0327	.0217
1821–1830	.3002	.2460	.0380	.0317
1831–1835	.2738	.0724	.0458	.0369
1836–1840	.2035	.0963	.0479	.0447
1840 and after	.4002	.2190	.0547	.0494

3. The upper and lower confidence intervals for prewar occupations by region were:

	Northern-Born		Southern-Born	
	UCI	LCI	UCI	LCI
Farmers	16.8%	12.9%	5.5%	5.6%
Professionals	11.3	3.1	3.1	2.1
Skilled workers	25.9	13.7	3.1	2.3
Students	33.5	9.6	4.0	3.3
Unskilled workers	28.7	12.3	4.2	3.2
White-collar workers	29.8	11.4	2.5	1.5

4. The upper and lower confidence intervals for personal wealth by region were:

	Northern-Born		Southern-Born	
	UCI	LCI	UCI	LCI
$0–400	12.8%	27.6%	4.6%	5.2%
$401–799	31.3	6.5	2.7	1.8
$800–1,199	0.0	0.0	2.6	1.5
$1,200–3,999	9.7	1.2	3.0	2.2
$4,000–10,000	41.8	6.9	3.0	1.9
Over $10,000	13.6	1.8	3.1	2.1

5. For Southern-born personal slaveholding, the confidence levels in decimals were: .1410, .1095 (LCI), .1798 (UCI).

6. Dewees Ogden to Uncle Sam, 22 April 1863, Dewees Ogden Papers, Library of Virginia, Richmond; Compiled Service Record of Dewees Ogden, 1st Richmond Howitzers, Record Group 94, National Archives.

7. Lewis Leon, *Diary of a Tar Heel Confederate Soldier* (Charlotte, N.C.: Stone Publishing Co., 1913), 71.

CHAPTER 6

1. R. E. Lee to Davis, 7 June 1862, in Lynda Lasswell Crist, Mary Seaton Dix, and Kenneth H. Williams, eds., *The Papers of Jefferson Davis* (Baton Rouge: Louisiana State University Press, 1995), 8:229–30.

2. For the Lower South, the LCI was 35.8% and the UCI was 54.6%. For the Upper South, the LCI was 45.4% and the UCI was 64.3%. Both categories were at the 95% confidence level.

3. The ratio of Lower South to Upper South was 17 to 13 for the artillery and 18 to 5 for the infantry.

4. In the chi^2 test for birth state vs. resident, P=.0678, indicating a 93.2% chance that people in the Lower South were more likely than people in the Upper South to live in a state other than their birth state, an accuracy within the acceptable statistical limits of the U.S. Census Bureau.

5. For married soldiers in the Lower South, the UCI was 23.2% and the LCI was 12.5%; for those in the Upper South, the UCI was 26.0% and the LCI was 15.6%. For fatherhood in the Lower South, the UCI was 19.9% and the LCI was 10.3%; for fatherhood

in the Upper South, the UCI was 22.0% and the LCI was 12.6%. All were at the 95% confidence level.

6. File of William Vick, U.S. Census Records, 1850, Clarke County, Miss., 171; File of Aaron Sivey, U.S. Census Records, 1850, Greenbriar County, Va., 331.

7. The mean for household wealth in the Upper South was $9,606; in the Lower South, it was $14,135.

8. The upper and lower confidence intervals for personal–Upper South (P-US), personal–Lower South (P-LS), personal and family–Upper South (PF-US), personal and family–Lower South (PF-LS), household–Upper South (H-US), and household–Lower South (H-LS) were:

	UCI	LCI
P-US	.510333863	.346582
P-LS	.325926000	.468148
PF-US	.310398345	.250905
PF-LS	.302403577	.244830
H-US	.228191001	.247475
H-LS	.286219081	.238074

These are percentage differences, not ranges.

9. In the chi^2 test for slave-to-white ratios, P=.0000, indicating a 99% likelihood that men from the Lower South resided in counties with higher slave ratios.

10. J. Q. A. Nadenbousch to wife, 28 April 1862. J. Q. A. Nadenbousch Papers, Museum of the Confederacy, Richmond.

11. In the chi^2 test for officers and enlisted men, P=.4472, indicating an accuracy outside the acceptable statistical limits of the U.S. Census Bureau.

12. Year of enlistment with Lower South and Upper South (LS and US) confidence limits in decimals, based on the percentage for the army:

	1861	1862	1863	1864	Total
LS	.2569	.1382	.0307	.0241	.4499
	[.1905, .3367]	[.0965, .1942]	[.0128, .0718]	[.0131, .0439]	[.3575, .5458]
US	.3201	.1561	.0488	.0252	.5501
	[.2467, .4036]	[.1096, .2176]	[.0297, .0790]	[.0127, .0491]	[.4542, .6425]

In the chi^2 test for year of enlistment, P=.7773, indicating an accuracy outside the acceptable statistical limits of the U.S. Census Bureau.

13. The number of cases is too small for statistical accuracy.

14. These numbers do not add up because I was unable to locate some deserters in the census.

15. Children were listed in the 1860 census. Obviously, the percentage of deserters with children would have been higher, since a number of those who were childless in 1860 would have had children by the time they deserted.

16. One Lower South soldier declared missing in action most likely was killed.

17. The other mounted regiment was the 2nd Maryland Cavalry. Thanks to Gary Gallagher for this information.

18. In the Upper South, the average combined wealth was $8,228 for men killed or wounded and $6,729 for those who were not injured on the battlefield.

CHAPTER 7
1. By officers, I mean anyone who ever held a commission as second lieutenant or higher. Many officers had been at one time enlisted men.
2. Davis to Congress, 18 August 1862, OR 4(2):55.
3. Randolph to Davis, 12 August 1862, OR 4(2):42–49; An Act to Provide for the Public Defense, 16 April 1862, General Orders, No. 30, Adj. and Insp. General's Office, 28 April 1862, OR 4(1):1094–97.
4. Robert K. Krick, Lee's Colonels: A Biographical Register of the Field Officers of the Army of Northern Virginia (Dayton, Ohio: Morningside Press, 1992), 16.
5. File of Wiley P. Robertson, U.S. Census Records, Caswell County, N.C., M653, R 891, P716; File of S. F. Robertson, U.S. Slave Census, Caswell County, 355, Files of Thomas Bell [spelled Beall in U.S. Slave Census] and Jesse Hargrave, U.S. Census Records, David-son County, N.C., 775, 986; and Files of Thomas Beall and Jesse Hargrave, U.S. Slave Census, Davidson County, N.C., 26, 37–38. Statistics are based on a random sample of 17 regiments and batteries, approximately 1 in 10, that served in Virginia on 30 April 1862 and became part of the Army of Northern Virginia. The units were Chew's Battery, 1st Virginia Battalion, Wooding's (Danville) Battery, 21st North Carolina, 1st Louisiana Battalion, 3rd Virginia, 12th Alabama, Jeff Davis Legion, Fredericksburg Artillery, 16th North Carolina, Loudon Artillery, 21st Virginia, 46th Virginia, 8th Louisiana, 2nd South Carolina (2nd Palmetto), 42nd Virginia, and Armistead's Battery.
6. Lee to Beauregard, 19 June 1861, Letters Sent, Virginia Forces, R1, Record Group 109, National Archives; An Act to Amend an Act Entitled an Act to Further Provide for the Public Defense, 16 April 1862, and An Act to Further Provide for the Public Defense, 16 April 1862, OR 4(1):1081–82, 1095–96; Davis to Congress, 18 August 1862, OR 4(2):55. With citizen soldiers, there had to be some elective system. This was the least intrusive for the army.
7. The 95% confidence level for enlisted men (EM) is below. Because of the small size of the officer (O) pool, a confidence level is insufficient for a category for officers. These numbers are based on their respective percentages in the sample, 91.46% for enlisted men and 8.54% for officers:
    EM: .0561 [.0361, .0862], .1361 [.1069, .1718], .1485 [.1143, .1908], .2925 [.2495, 3396], .2813 [.2354, .3323]
    O: .0030 [0, .0212], .0296 [.0155, .0557], .0092 [.0035, .0237], .0363 [.0216, .0604], .0073 [.0023, .0231].
8. In the chi^2 test on mobility, P=.3495, indicating no acceptable statistical accuracy. In the chi^2 test on Upper vs. Lower South, P=.3476, indicating no acceptable statistical accuracy.
9. In the chi^2 test on marital status, P=.9731, indicating no acceptable statistical accuracy. In the chi^2 test on children, P=.4677, indicating no acceptable statistical accuracy.
10. Confidence levels at 95%, shown below, are based on the percentage of officers (O) and enlisted men (EM) in the sample.

EM: .0561 [.0361, .0862], .1361 [.1069, .1718], .1485 [.1143, .1908], .2925 [.2495, .3396], .2813 [.2354, .3323]

O: .0030 [0, .0212], .0296 [.0155, .0557], .0092 [.0035, .0237], .0363 [.0216, .0604], .0073 [.0023, .0231].

11. Confidence levels at 95% were:

EM: .7001 [.6472, .7482], .0504 [.032, .0787], .0277 [.0152, .0497], .0547 [.0363, .0818], .0472 [.0297, .0743], .0344 [.0199, .0589]

O: .0412 [.0246, .0683], 0 [0], .0100 [.0036, .0278], .0125 [.0049, .0312], .0038 [0, .0189], .0179 [.0086, .0370].

12. The 95% confidence levels for personal and family wealth were:

EM: .3415 [.2953, .3908], .0591 [.0367, .0939], .0562 [.0371, .0842], .1437 [.1093, .1866], .1404 [.1101, .1774], .1738 [.1370, .2179]

O: .0165 [.0064, .0417], 0 [0], .0070 [.0021, .0233], .0214 [.0106, .0428], .0089 [.0033, .0238], 0.0314 [.0182, .0538].

13. The 95% confidence levels for personal and family slaveholding were:

EM: .5847 [.5295, .6379], .0892 [.0652, .1209], .1105 [.0808, .1494], .0645 [.0444, .0929], .0656 [.0443, .0961]

O: .0431 [.0259, .0709], .0043 [.0010, .0181], .0217 [.0112, .0417], .0128 [.0051, .0316], .0035 [0.0, .0191].

14. In the chi^2 test for household slavery, P=.0201, making it 98% accurate.

15. In the chi^2 test for slave-to-white ratios in home counties, P=.9104, indicating no acceptable statistical accuracy.

16. In the chi^2 test for year of enlistment, P=.1125, indicating an accuracy just a fraction outside the acceptable statistical limits of the U.S. Census Bureau.

17. In the chi^2 test for AWOL, P=.6689, indicating no acceptable statistical accuracy. In the chi^2 test for deserters, P=.0001, indicating an accuracy greater than 99%.

18. The percentage of deserters among enlisted men with children by personal and family wealth were:

$0–399	54.8
$400–799	6.5
$800–1,199	12.2
$1,200–3,999	8.3
$4,000–10,000	3.9
Over $10,000	14.4

19. In the chi^2 test for killed and wounded, P=.0966, indicating an accuracy of 90.3% and within the acceptable statistical limits of the U.S. Census Bureau.

20. In the chi^2 test for death from disease, P=.0294, indicating an accuracy (97%) within the acceptable statistical limits.

21. Percentages of wounded vary between Figures 7.10 and 7.11 because in the latter percentages were calculated in the sequence killed in action, died of disease, wounded in action, prisoners of war, and discharged for disability. Some wounded men later died of disease and were counted under died of disease.

CHAPTER 8

1. Because of the small number of soldiers who joined in 1863 and 1864, numbers for those years distorted statistical significance in many cases.

2. At the 95% confidence level, the LCI and UCI were:

    1861: .0293 [.0153, .0553], .0813 [.0553, .1181], .0778 [.0522, .1143], .2169 [.1754, .2651], .1717 [.1310, .2216], .5769 [.5086, .6424]

    1862: .0130 [.0045, .0366], .0491 [.0313, .0761], .0653 [.0426, .0989], .0995 [.0711, .1376], .0675 [.0474, .0951], .2943 [.2362, .3601]

    1863: .0108 [.0046, .0255], .0217 [.0115, .0404], .0060 [.0015, .0236], .0103 [.0043, .0245], .0306 [.0162, .0573], .0794 [.0511, .1215]

    1864: .0060 [.0015, .0237], .0136 [.0056, .0322], .0087 [.0031, .0239], .0022 [0.0, .0068], .0189 [.0103, .0344], .0493 [.0316, .0762].

3. In the chi² test, P=.037, making it 96.3% accurate.

4. In the chi² test, P=.0036, making it 99% accurate.

5. In the chi² test, P=.0268, making it 97.3% accurate.

6. See Proclamation by President Jefferson Davis, 15 July 1863, OR 4(2):635. At the 95% confidence level, the LCI and UCI were:

    1861: .2470 [.1999, .3009], .1340 [.1002, .1768], .1960 [.1516, .2496], .5769 [.5086, .6424]

    1862: .1219 [.0923, .1594], .0654 [.0413, .1020], .1071 [.0753, .1500], .2943 [.2362, .3601]

    1863: .0320 [.0179, .0564], .0174 [.0086, .0348], .0301 [.0151, .0590], .0794 [.0511, .1215]

    1864: .0162 [.0081, .0324], .0117 [.0047, .0284], .0214 [.0101, .0446], .0493 [.0316, .0762].

7. In the chi² test, P=.006, making it more than 99% accurate.

8. In the chi² test for personal and family slavery, P=.0878, making it more than 91% accurate and within the acceptable statistical limits of the U.S. Census Bureau. In the chi² test for slaveholding households by year of enlistment, P=.8050, indicating no acceptable statistical accuracy.

9. At the 95% confidence level, the LCI and UCI for the artillery (A), cavalry (C), and infantry (I) were:

    A: .0359 [.0290, .0443], .0216 [.0152, .0307], .0051 [.0027, .0095], .0064 [.0033, .0124], .0690 [.0619, .0768]

    C: .0264 [.0185, .0375], .0512 [.0414, .0632], .0256 [.0173, .0379], .0098 [.0051, .0186], .1130 [.1121, .1139]

    I: .4990 [.4341, .5639], .2263 [.1714, .2926], .0600 [.0347, .1017], .0327 [.0175, .0604], .8180 [.8114, .8245].

10. In the chi² test, P=.1125, indicating an accuracy just outside the acceptable statistical limits of the U.S. Census Bureau.

11. In the chi² test, P=.4906, indicating no acceptable statistical accuracy.

12. In the chi² test, P=.153, indicating an accuracy just outside the acceptable statistical limits of the U.S. Census Bureau.

13. Because the sample was so small, there is no statistical accuracy.

14. Because the sample was so small, there is no statistical accuracy.

15. Because the sample was so small, there is no statistical accuracy. In 1861, the "7 times more likely to desert" may not seem to make sense, but it is true because more soldiers and their families did not own slaves.

16. Because the numbers were so small, there is no statistical accuracy.

17. At the 95% confidence level, the LCI and UCI percentages for killed (KIA) or wounded (WIA) in action were:

	KIA	LCI	UCI	WIA	LCI	UCI
1861	14.2	9.9	20.1	28.8	22.7	35.9
1862	9.5	5.7	15.5	32.6	23.9	42.8
1863	4.7	1.2	16.2	17.2	7.7	34.0
1864	11.1	2.5	38.2	11.1	2.8	35.7

18. At the 95% confidence level, the LCI and UCI for the combined percentages of killed (KIA) or wounded (WIA) at least once were:

	KIA/WIA	LCI	UCI
1861	40.0	32.8	47.6
1862	39.3	29.4	50.1
1863	21.9	11.3	38.1
1864	22.3	8.9	45.8

19. Because the numbers were so small, there is no statistical validity.

20. Because the numbers are so small, there is no statistical validity.

21. Because the numbers are so small, there is no statistical validity.

22. In the chi^2 test for personal and family slavery, P=.060, making it more than 94% accurate and within the acceptable statistical limits of the U.S. Census Bureau.

CHAPTER 9

1. In the chi^2 test for grouping of birth years and children, P=.0000, indicating that the pattern of older soldiers being more prone to have children is likely to happen more than 99% of the time. In decimals, confidence limits at a 95% accuracy were:
    1799–1820: .0141 [.0053, .0367], .0450 [.0278, .0722], .0591 [.0386, .0895]
    1821–30: .0415 [.0252, .0676], .1242 [.0945, .1617], .1657 [.1326, .2050]
    1831–35: .0715 [.0497, .1017], .0862 [.0593, .1238], .1577 [.1217, .2019]
    1836–40: .2722 [.2318, .3166], .0567 [.0373, .0853], .3289 [.2854, .3755]
    1841–48: .2887 [.2420, .3402], 0 [0], .2887 [.2420, .3402].

2. In the chi^2 test for grouping of birth years and combined personal and family wealth, P=.5438, indicating an accuracy outside the acceptable statistical limits of the U.S. Census Bureau.

3. The 95% confidence levels for wealth grouping by age were:
    1799–1820: .0168 [.0070, .0400], .0667 [.0450, .0978], .0715 [.0496, .1021],
       .1125 [.0832, .1503], .0905 [.0631, .1282]
    1821–30: .0030 [0.0, .0213], .0133 [.0045, .0388], .0141 [.0061, .0322], .0133
       [.0045, .0388], .0155 [.0067, .0352]

1831–35: .0038 [0.0, .0189], .0149 [.0067, .033], .0095 [.0033, .0274], .0163 [.0063, .0416], .0187 [.0092, .0376]

1836–40: .0073 [.0023, .0232], .0325 [.0192, .0546], .0206 [.0107, .0392], .0580 [.0384, .0868], .0466 [.0291, .0739]

1841–48: .0103 [.0038, .0277], .0201 [.0103, .0388], .0152 [.0069, .0329], .0594 [.0406, .0861], .0444 [.0267, .0730]

Total: .0179 [.0086, .0369], .0182 [.0092, .0357], .0268 [.0150, .0475], .0694 [.0456, .1042], .0729 [.0511, .1029]

4. For personal slave ownership and grouping of birth years, the 95% confidence levels were:

1799–1820: .0347 [.0198, .0601], .0244 [.0130, .0452], .0591 [.0386, .0895]
1821–30: .1285 [.0963, .1695], .0371 [.0231, .0592], .1657 [.1326, .2050]
1831–35: .1336 [.1028, .1719], .0241 [.0131, .0440], .1577 [.1217, .2019]
1836–40: .2884 [.2465, .3344], .0404 [.0250, .0647], .3289 [.2854, .3755]
1841–48: .2843 [.2380, .3357], .0043 [.0010, .0179], .2887 [.2420, .3402]
Total: .8696 [.8331, .8991], .1304 [.1009, .1669]

5. In the grouping of birth years and combined personal and family slaveholding, confidence levels at 95% were:

	No Slaves	Slaves	Total
1799–1820	.0317	.0274	.0591
	[.0176, .0566]	[.0141, .0527]	[.0386, .0895]
1821–30	.1242	.0415	.1657
	[.0922, .1652]	[.0265, .0643]	[.1326, .2050]
1831–35	.1097	.0480	.1577
	[.0809, .1473]	[.0315, .0725]	[.1217, .2019]
1836–40	.2003	.1285	.3289
	[.1626, .2443]	[.0982, .1664]	[.2854, .3755]
1841–48	.1619	.1268	.2887
	[.1222, .2113]	[.0958, .1660]	[.2420, .3402]
Total	.6278	.3722	1
	[.5725, .6800]	[.3299, .4275]	

For those under age 18, 53.3% lived in slaveowning households.

6. In the grouping of birth years and region, confidence levels at 95% were:

1799–1820: .0255 [.0125, .0513], .0336 [.0191, .0586], .0591 [.0386, .0895]
1821–30: .0784 [.0519, .1167], .0873 [.0627, .1203], .1657 [.1326, .2050]
1831–35: .0849 [.0550, .1288], .0728 [.0501, .1048], .1577 [.1217, .2019]
1836–40: .1391 [.1024, .1863], .1897 [.1456, .2434], .3289 [.2854, .3755]
1841–48: .1220 [.0891, .1648], .1667 [.1232, .2216], .2887 [.2420, .3402]

In groupings of birth years and slave-to-white ratios, confidence levels at 95% were:

1799–1820: .0255 [.0125, .0513], .0336 [.0191, .0586], .0591 [.0386, .0895]
1821–30: .0784 [.0519, .1167], .0873 [.0627, .1203], .1657 [.1326, .2050]
1831–35: .0849 [.0550, .1288], .0728 [.0501, .1048], .1577 [.1217, .2019]
1836–40: .1391 [.1024, .1863], .1897 [.1456, .2434], .3289 [.2854, .3755]

1841–48: .1220 [.0891, .1648], .1667 [.1232, .2216], .2887 [.2420, .3402]

Total: .4499 [.3575, .5458], .5501 [.4542, .6425], 1

7. In the chi^2 test for grouping of birth years and year of enlistment, P=.0000, in-dicating more than a 99% chance that there was a relationship between age and time of enter-ing the army:

1799–1820: .0591 [.0386, .0895]

1821–30: .1657 [.1326, .2050]

1831–35: .1577 [.1217, .2019]

1836–40: .3289 [.2854, .3755]

1841–48: .2887 [.2420, .3402]

8. Men over 40 in 1861 were not subject to conscription until 1863, which reflects their low numbers in the sample.

9. In the grouping of birth years and branch of service, confidence levels at 95% were:

	Artillery	Cavalry	Infantry	Total
1799–1820	.0032	.0081	.0478	.0591
	[.0013, .0078]	[.0043, .0152]	[.0286, .0786]	[.0386, .0895]
1821–30	.0080	.0203	.1373	.1657
	[.0047, .0136]	[.0147, .0281]	[.1057, .1766]	[.1326, .2050]
1831–35	.0144	.0179	.1254	.1577
	[.0099, .0211]	[.0121, .0263]	[.0912, .1700]	[.1217, .2019]
1836–40	.0214	.0268	.2806	.3289
	[.0150, .0305]	[.0198, .0363]	[.2389, .3265]	[.2854, .3755]
1841–48	.0219	.0398	.2269	.2887
	[.0164, .0292]	[.0317, .0500]	[.1823, .2786]	[.2420, .3402]
Total	.0690	.1130	.8180	1
	[.0620, .0767]	[.1078, .1184]	[.8090, .8267]	

10. In the grouping of birth years of officers and enlisted men, confidence levels at 95% were:

	Enlisted Men	Officers	Total
1799–1820	.0561	.0030	.0591
	[.0361, .0862]	[0.0, .0212]	[.0386, .0895]
1821–30	.1361	.0296	.1657
	[.1069, .1718]	[.0155, .0557]	[.1326, .2050]
1831–35	.1485	.0092	.1577
	[.1143, .1908]	[.0035, .0237]	[.1217, .2019]
1836–40	.2925	.0363	.3289
	[.2495, .3396]	[.0216, .0604]	[.2854, .3755]
1841–48	.2813	.0073	.2887
	[.2354, .3323]	[.0023, .0231]	[.2420, .3402]
Total	.9146	.0854	1
	[.8839, .9378]	[.0622, .1161]	

11. In the grouping of birth years of nondeserters and deserters, confidence levels at 95% were:

	Nondeserters	Deserters	Total
1799–1820	.0485	.0106	.0591
	[.0297, .0785]	[.0044, .0254]	[.0386, .0895]
1821–30	.1375	.0282	.1657
	[.1072, .1746]	[.0158, .0498]	[.1326, .2050]
1831–35	.1320	.0258	.1577
	[.0989, .1740]	[.0141, .0466]	[.1217, .2019]
1836–40	.2844	.0445	.3289
	[.2422, .3306]	[.0264, .0741]	[.2854, .3755]
1841–48	.2531	.0355	.2887
	[.2111, .3004]	[.0195, .0639]	[.2420, .3402]
Total	.8555	.1445	1
	[.8097, .8917]	[.1083, .1903]	

12. In the chi² test for calculating the percentage of casualties, P=.0038, indicating more than a 99% chance that older soldiers were less likely to be killed (KIA) or wounded (WIA) in combat. Confidence levels at 95% were:

	Noncasualties	KIA/WIA	Total
1799–1820	.0553	.0038	.0591
	[.0354, .0854]	[0.0, .0189]	[.0386, .0895]
1821–30	.1144	.0513	.1657
	[.0887, .1463]	[.0317, .0819]	[.1326, .2050]
1831–35	.0964	.0613	.1577
	[.0702, .1310]	[.0415, .0897]	[.1217, .2019]
1836–40	.1694	.1595	.3289
	[.1348, .2106]	[.1233, .2038]	[.2854, .3755]
1841–48	.1791	.1096	.2887
	[.1399, .2264]	[.0813, .1461]	[.2420, .3402]
Total	.6146	.3854	1
	[.5581, .6682]	[.3318, .4419]	

13. In the chi² test for grouping birth years and died of disease, P=.0923, indicating a relationship between age and death by disease and an accuracy within the acceptable statistical limits of the U.S. Census Bureau. Confidence levels at 95% were:

	Survived	Died	Total
1799–1820	.0437	.0155	.0591
	[.0267, .0707]	[.0071, .0333]	[.0386, .0895]
1821–30	.1470	.0187	.1657
	[.1164, .1838]	[.0088, .0394]	[.1326, .2050]
1831–35	.1360	.0217	.1577
	[.1074, .1708]	[.0098, .0473]	[.1217, .2019]
1836–40	.2887	.0401	.3289
	[.2447, .3371]	[.0248, .0645]	[.2854, .3755]
1841–48	.2691	.0195	.2887
	[.2247, .3188]	[.0095, .0398]	[.2420, .3402]
Total	.8845	.1155	1
	[.8431, .9160]	[.0840, .1569]	

1. Josiah B. Patterson to Wife, 4 December 1861, Josiah Blair Patterson Papers, Georgia Department of Archives and History, Atlanta. Note that the statistics for marital status and parenthood are not equal. I was able to ascertain the marital status of 560 men but could find only 542 soldiers in the census, which provides information on parenthood. Thus, my calculations based on information from military records may show slightly higher numbers in the marital status category.

2. At the 95% confidence level, the LCI and UCI for married (M), single (S), childless (C), and father (F) were:

   M: .0557 [.0355, .0862], .1335 [.1031, .1712], .0980 [.0693, .1368], .0874 [.0626, .1207], 0.0 [0.0, .0039]

   S: .0038 [.0013, .0109], .0333 [.0189, .0578], .0608 [.0413, .0885], .2431 [.2041, .2869], .2840 [.2382, .3359]

   C: .0141 [.0053, .0367], .0415 [.0252, .0676], .0715 [.0497, .1017], .2722 [.2318, .3166], .2887 [.2420, .3402]

   F: .0450 [.0278, .0722], .1242 [.0945, .1617], .0862 [.0593, .1238], .0567 [.0373, .0853], 0 [0].

3. In the chi^2 test for marital status and mobility, P=.7187. In the chi^2 test for parenthood and mobility, P=.5436. In the chi^2 test for marital status and Upper vs. Lower South, P=.8679. In the chi^2 test for parenthood and Upper vs. Lower South, P=.7766. In the chi^2 test for marital status and slave-to-white ratio groupings, P=.5332. And in the chi^2 test for parenthood and slave-to-white ratio groupings, P=.6928. All test results indicated an accuracy that was well outside the acceptable limits of the U.S. Census Bureau.

4. The 95% confidence limits for upper confidence–married UCM), lower confidence–married (LCM), upper confidence–single (UCS), lower confidence–single (LCS), upper confidence–childless (UCC), lower confidence–childless (LCC), upper confidence–father (UCF), and lower confidence–father (LCF) were:

UCM	LCM	UCS	LCS	UCC	LCC	UCF	LCF
4.5%	3.8%	5.3%	5.4%	5.1%	5.3	3.8%	3.2%
2.7	1.6	2.0	0.9	2.0	1.0	2.7	1.5
47.8	1.3	1.8	0.6	2.0	0.9	2.0	1.1
2.7	1.8	1.1	1.0	1.9	1.1	2.7	1.7
2.7	1.6	1.6	0.7	2.0	1.0	2.5	1.4
2.9	1.7	1.6	0.8	1.6	0.8	2.9	1.6

5. The 95% confidence levels for married/single and father/childless in personal and family wealth were:

UCM	LCM	UCS	LCS	UCC	LCC	UCF	LCF
4.2%	3.6%	4.9%	4.3%	5.2%	4.6%	3.9%	3.3%
3.1	2.3	4.6	3.7	4.6	3.8	3.1	2.2
4.2	3.1	5.2	4.5	5.4	4.8	3.7	2.6

6. The 95% confidence limits in decimals for household wealth by married (M), single (S), childless (C), and father (F) were:

M: [.1193, .1952], [.0152, .0554], [.0163, .0510], [.0326, .0734], [.0234, .0663], [.0496, .1113]

S: [.0837, .143], [.0173, .0664], [.0214, .0675], [.0843, .1625], [.1048, .1755], [.1522, .2310]

C: [.1052, .1755], [.0169, .0657], [.0259, .0736], [.0885, .1680], [.1119, .1824], [.1702, .2500]

F: [.1010, .1682], [.0153, .0553], [.0120, .0430], [.0275, .0670], [.0172, .0559], [.0348, .0854].

7. The 95% confidence levels in decimals for personal–married (PM), personal–single (PS), personal and family–married (PFM), personal and family–single (PFS), household–married (HM), household–single (HS), personal–childless (PC), personal–father (PF), personal and family–childless (PFC), personal and family–father (PFF), household–childless (HC), and household–father (HF) were:

PM: [.2370, .3329], [.0672, .1262], [.3248, .4281]

PS: [.5323, .6381], [.0245, .0608], [.5719, .6752]

PFM: [.2189, .3109], [.0827, .1519], [.3248, .4281]

PFS: [.3113, .4183], [.2169, .3125], [.5719, .6752]

HM: [.2107, .3025], [.0907, .1602], [.3248, .4281]

HS: [.2497, .3548], [.2753, .3798], [.5719, .6752]

PC: [.5903, .6892], [.0297, .0725], [.6352, .7360]

PF: [.1872, .2754], [.0593, .1173], [.2640, .3648]

PFC: [.3506, .4594], [.2368, .3365], [.6352, .7360]

PFF: [.1836, .2703], [.0632, .1217], [.2640, .3648]

HC: [.2878, .3940], [.2976, .4041], [.6352, .7360]

HF: [.1763, .2640], [.0696, .1289], [.2640, .3648].

8. Stuart to Wife, 4 March 1862, J. E. B. Stuart Papers, Virginia Historical Society, Richmond. In the chi^2 test for marital status and year of enlistment, P=.0000, indicating an accuracy of over 99%.

9. The 95% confidence levels in decimals for entry into military service by marital status (married/single — M/S) and parenthood (childless/father — C/F) were:

	1861	1862	1863	1864
M	[.1236, .2078]	[.1175, .2092]	[.0174, .0568]	[.0126, .0455]
S	[.3597, .4754]	[.1037, .1731]	[.0286, .0805]	[.0148, .0438]
C	[.3800, .5013]	[.1302, .2179]	[.0296, .0811]	[.0175, .0484]
F	[.1032, .1802]	[.0879, .1741]	[.0163, .0551]	[.0098, .0405]

10. The 95% confidence levels in decimals for branch of service were:

	Artillery	Cavalry	Infantry
M	[.0126, .0221]	[.0288, .0470]	[.2727, .3746]
S	[.0453, .0601]	[.0684, .0864]	[.4453, .5465]
C	[.0496, .0659]	[.0722, .0915]	[.4992, .5985]
F	[.0083, .0167]	[.0236, .0424]	[.2221, .3210]

In the chi^2 test for marital status and branch, P=.0140, indicating an accuracy of 98.6%. In the chi^2 test for parenthood and household wealth, P=.0169, an accuracy of over 98.0%.

11. In the chi^2 test for marital status and officers vs. enlisted men, P=.9731, indicating an accuracy well outside the acceptable statistical limits of the U.S. Census Bureau. In the chi^2 test for parenthood and officers vs. enlisted men, P=.4677, also well outside the acceptable limits for accuracy.

12. In the chi^2 test both for marital status and parenthood and for entry into the service, P=.5261 indicating an accuracy well outside the acceptable statistical limits of the U.S. Census Bureau.

13. In the chi^2 test for marital status and AWOL, P=.1817, indicating an accuracy outside the acceptable statistical limits of the U.S. Census Bureau. In the chi^2 test for parenthood and AWOL, P=.0251, indicating an accuracy of about 97.5%. In the chi^2 test for marital status and desertion, P=.2928, well outside the acceptable limits for accuracy. In the chi^2 test for parenthood and desertion, P=.0357, indicating an accuracy of almost 96.5%.

14. Of husbands, 16% deserted; of fathers, 20% deserted.

15. In the chi^2 test for marital status and killed and wounded, P=.3919. In the chi^2 test for parenthood and killed and wounded, P=.5171, well outside the acceptable limits for accuracy. In the chi^2 test for marital status and POWs, P=.6493, well outside the acceptable limits for accuracy. In the chi^2 test for parenthood and POWs, P=.6513. All test results indicated an accuracy well outside the acceptable statistical limits of the U.S. Census Bureau.

16. In the chi^2 test for marital status and death from disease, P=.0067, indicating an accuracy of over 99%. In the chi^2 test for parenthood and death from disease, P=.3124, indicating an accuracy well outside the acceptable statistical limits of the U.S. Census Bureau.

17. In the chi^2 test for marital status and left the service, P=.2094, indicating an accuracy well outside the acceptable statistical limits of the U.S. Census Bureau.

18. In the chi^2 test for parenthood and left the service, P=.5115, indicating an accuracy well outside the acceptable statistical limits of the U.S. Census Bureau.

CHAPTER 11

1. Before the war, soldiers in my sample variously resided in Alabama, Arkansas, Florida, Georgia, Kentucky, Louisiana, Maryland, Mississippi, North Carolina, South Carolina, Tennessee, Texas, and Virginia. Thanks to Dr. Karl Eschbach, Texas State Demographer, for help with the IPUMS, a 1% sample of the 1860 census.

2. At the 95% confidence level, LCI and UCI were:
    Lower: [.0089, .0435], [.0559, .1133], [.0612, .1186], [.0950, .1646], [.0737, .1501]
    Middle: [.0043, .0282], [.0300, .0744], [.0163, .0550], [.0516, .1059], [.0440, .0961]
    Upper: [.0147, .0534], [.0240, .0604], [.0268, .0654], [.0976, .1681], [.0872, .1561].

3. At the 95% confidence level, LCI and UCI were:
    Lower: [.1031, .1862]
    Middle: [.0447, .1084]
    Upper: [.0304, .0854].

4. At the 95% confidence level, the decimal number and LCI and UCI were:
    Lower: .1881 [.1522, .2301], .2252 [.1826, .2745], .4133 [.3627, .4658]
    Middle: .0805 [.0573, .1119], .1493 [.1126, .1953], .2298 [.1842, .2829]
    Upper: .1065 [.0752, .1487], .2504 [.2050, .3021], .3569 [.3007, .4173].

5. In the chi² test for children at home and the average number of children of soldier-fathers by class, P=.0083, indicating an accuracy of over 99%.
6. The poor made up 6.6% of the 9.2% skilled workers and 11.01% of the 13.2% unskilled workers.
7. At the 95% confidence level, the LCI and UCI were:

    Lower: [.1580, .2383], [.0038, .0246], [.0452, .0951], [.0118, .0504], [.0810, .1491], [.0029, .0238]

    Middle: [.1125, .1973], [.0055, .0325], [.0045, .0249], [.0150, .0486], [.0069, .0430], [.0035, .0284]

    Upper: [.1507, .2404], [.0218, .0644], [.0078, .0322], [.0613, .1194], [0, .0196], [.0106, .0477].

8. At the 95% confidence levels for personal–lower (PL), personal–middle (PM), personal–upper (PU), personal and family–lower (PFL), personal and family–middle (PFM), personal and family–upper (PFU), household–lower (HL), household–middle (HM), and household–upper (HU), the LCI and UCI were:

	Nonslaveholding	Slaveholding
PL	.4171	0
	[.3672, .4688]	0
PM	.2093	.0190
	[.1675, .2584]	[.0090, .0395]
PU	.2431	.1114
	[.1988, .2937]	[.0830, .1481]
PFL	.4166	0
	[.3666, .4683]	0
PFM	.1776	.0507
	[.1399, .2228]	[.0324, .0786]
PFU	.0336	.3209
	[.0199, .0562]	[.2669, .3802]
HL	.3630	.0541
	[.3136, .4154]	[.0372, .0780]
HM	.1613	.0670
	[.1253, .2053]	[.0442, .1003]
HU	.0315	.3231
	[.0182, .0540]	[.2690, .3823]

9. In the chi² test for household slaveowning by economic class, P=.0000, indicating an accuracy of over 99%.
10. At the 95% confidence level, the LCI and UCI in decimals were:

	Artillery	Cavalry	Infantry
Lower	[.0283, .0413]	[.0277, .0481]	[.2982, .3978]
Middle	[.0073, .0157]	[.0165, .0335]	[.1503, .2469]
Upper	[.0172, .0337]	[.0434, .0642]	[.2248, .3375]

11. At the 95% confidence level, the LCI and UCI in decimals were:

	Enlisted Men	Officers
Lower	[.3511, .4522]	[.0064, .0417]
Middle	[.1607, .2457]	[.0156, .0513]
Upper	[.2624, .3710]	[.0253, .0640]

12. The number of cases was so small that there is no statistical accuracy.

13. At the 95% confidence level, numbers and the LCI and UCI in decimals were:

	Nondeserters	Deserters	Total
Lower	.3418	.0754	.4171
	[.2920, .3953]	[.0516, .1087]	[.3672, .4688]
Middle	.1846	.0437	.2283
	[.1456, .2313]	[.0259, .0728]	[.1829, .2812]
Upper	.3291	.0255	.3546
	[.2764, .3864]	[.0142, .0455]	[.2991, .4142]

14. At the 95% confidence level, numbers and the LCI and UCI in decimals were:

	Uninjured	Killed/Wounded	Total
Lower	.2680	.1491	.4171
	[.2240, .3170]	[.1119, .1961]	[.3672, .4688]
Middle	.1496	.0787	.2283
	[.1150, .1925]	[.0537, .1139]	[.1829, .2812]
Upper	.1970	.1576	.3546
	[.1567, .2446]	[.1215, .2019]	[.2991, .4142]

15. These statistics were derived from IPUMS. In the chi^2 test for family size and wealth, P=.0000, indicating there was more than a 99% chance that larger families in general enjoyed greater wealth. In the chi^2 test for wealth and slaveholding, P=.0000, indicating there was more than a 99% chance that the greater a family's wealth, the more likely it was to own slaves.

CHAPTER 12

1. For combined personal and family slaveholding at 37.22% and at the 95% confidence level, the range was 32.00% and 42.75%. Slaves could be found in 44.42% of all households of soldiers in Lee's army; at the 95% confidence, the range was 38.90% and 50.10%. Because IPUMS does not match slaveowners from the U.S. Slave Census to names in the census, we could not run data comparing families in Lee's army to their states.

2. At the 95% confidence level, numbers and the LCI and UCI in decimals for nonslaveowners (NS) and slaveowners (S) were:

NS: .0317 [.0176, .0566], .1242 [.0922, .1652], .1097 [.0809, .1473], .2003 [.1626, .2443]

S: .0274 [.0141, .0527], .0415 [.0265, .0643], .0480 [.0315, .0725], .1285 [.0982, .1664].

3. At the 95% confidence level, numbers and the LCI and UCI in decimals for nonmobility versus mobility were:

	Nonmobility	Mobility
Nonslaveowners	.4168	.2105
	[.3574, .4786]	[.1637, .2663]
Slaveowners	.3222	.0505
	[.2690, .3805]	[.0296, .0851]

4. At the 95% confidence level, numbers and the LCI and UCI in decimals for occupations—farmers (F), professionals (P), skilled workers (SW), students (S), unskilled workers (UW), and white-collar workers (WC) among nonslaveowners and slaveowners at a personal and family level—were:

	Nonslaveowners	Slaveowners
F	.3305	.2061
	[.2850, .3795]	[.1663, .2526]
P	.0273	.0335
	[.0152, .0486]	[.0186, .0598]
SW	.0764	.0159
	[.0546, .1061]	[.0078, .0322]
S	.0464	.0913
	[.0276, .0769]	[.0658, .1253]
UW	.1248	.0067
	[.0936, .1644]	[.0019, .0239]
WC	.0184	.0226
	[.0088, .0381]	[.0117, .0431]

5. In the chi^2 test for slaveholders and nonslaveholders and marriage, P=.0273, indicating an accuracy of 97.3%. In the chi^2 test for marital rates among slaveholders, P=.0727, indicating an accuracy of more than 92.7% and within the acceptable statistical limits of the U.S. Census Bureau.

6. In the chi^2 test for slaveholding and children, P=.0131, indicating more than a 98.7% chance that slaveholders had more children. By slave groups, P=.0361, indicating a 96.4% chance that as the number of slaves increased, so did the number of children in the home.

7. In the chi^2 test for slaveholders and nonslaveholders and wealth, P=.0000, indicating more than a 99% chance that slaveholders were more affluent. In the chi^2 test for wealth categories and combined personal and family slaveholding categories, P=.0000, indicating more than a 99% chance that slaveholders and their families had more wealth. The average assets were exactly $10,914.

8. In the chi^2 test for slaveholders, P=.0000, indicating an accuracy of more than 99%.

9. In the chi^2 test for slaveholders and slave density, P=.0009, indicating an accuracy of more than 99%.

10. In the chi^2 test for personal and family slaveholding by branch, P=.0000, indicating an accuracy of more than 99%.

11. At the 95% confidence level, numbers and the LCI and UCI in decimals were:

	1861	1862	1863	1864
Nonslaveowners	.3734	.1705	.0548	.0292
	[.3172, .4331]	[.1316, .2179]	[.0333, .0887]	[.0168, .0504]
Slaveowners	.2036	.1239	.0246	.0200
	[.1588, .2571]	[.0900, .1681]	[.0111, .0539]	[.0107, .0371]

12. In the chi² test for officers and enlisted men, P=.1573, indicating an accuracy of 84.3% and outside the acceptable statistical limits of the U.S. Census Bureau.

13. The AWOL figures are not statistically accurate.

14. In the chi² test for desertion, P=.0145, indicating an accuracy of 98.6%. At the 95% confidence level, numbers and the LCI and UCI in decimals were:

	Nondeserter	Deserter	Total
Nonslaveowners	.5145	.1133	.6278
	[.4596, .5690]	[.0815, .1554]	[.5725, .6800]
Slaveowners	.3410	.0312	.3722
	[.2913, .3945]	[.0169, .0570]	[.3200, .4275]

15. No test for statistical accuracy was available.

16. In the chi² test for killed and wounded, P=.0546, indicating an accuracy of more than 94.5% and within the acceptable statistical limits of the U.S. Census Bureau.

17. Casualty figures cover only that 91% of the soldiers I found in census records.

18. At the 95% confidence level, numbers and the LCI and UCI for soldiers who died of disease were:

	LCI	UCI
Nonslaveowners	3.9%	6.4%
Slaveowners	4.1%	5.6%

Losses also included three instances of accidental death.

CONCLUSION

1. Wife [Elizabeth Phoebe Key Howard] to [Husband], September [1862], Elizabeth Phoebe Key Howard Papers, Maryland Historical Society, Baltimore.

2. S. M. B. to Children, 10 April 1863, Bemiss Family Papers, Virginia Historical Society, Richmond; William Pitt Ballinger Diary, 18 May 1863, R10, William Pitt Ballinger Papers, Briscoe Center for American History, University of Texas at Austin.

3. See Peter Carmichael, *The Last Generation: Young Virginians in Peace, War, and Reunion* (Chapel Hill: University of North Carolina Press, 2005), for an excellent portrait of young, well-educated, aspiring professionals and their level of commitment to the Confederacy.

4. Poverty among Northern-born troops may have influenced their low marriage rate, too.

5. These statistics were derived from IPUMS. In the chi² test for family size and wealth, P=.0000, indicating there was more than a 99% chance that larger families in general had more wealth. In the chi² test for wealth and slaveholding, P=.0000, indicating there was more than a 99% chance that the more wealth a family enjoyed, the more likely it was to own slaves.

SOURCES

For individuals who are interested in a detailed bibliography on the Army of Northern Virginia, please see my *General Lee's Army: From Victory to Defeat* (New York: Free Press, 2008).

The statistics presented in this volume are a product of numerous sources. The central elements are the Compiled Service Records (CSRs) located in the National Archives. These are carded records gathered from muster rolls and placed in a packet for each soldier. Frequently, a CSR will contain documents such as enlistment papers, POW documents, medical information, and parole data. Confederate CSRs are available on microfilm and, more recently, online.

The other principal source of this work is the U.S. Census Bureau. Census records are online through Ancestry.com, but due to the spelling of handwritten documents and search engines, serious researchers will also have to refer to the microfilmed census records in the National Archives and various other repositories.

I also consulted Confederate pension files, which are located in state archives. Confederate veterans applied for pensions in the state in which they resided at the time of application, not the state in which they resided during the war. States usually have published or online indexes of pension applications submitted by soldiers or their widows. Other useful sources were obituaries in newspapers, county histories, family genealogical books, burial records, and other materials.

The data was recorded in notebooks, which I loaded into the software program ACCESS. Much of the original computation was done in Excel. Later, I transferred the ACCESS files to the software program STATA. All the data has been computed in STATA and examined for accuracy by Dr. Karl Eschbach, former state demographer of Texas.

INDEX

Absent without leave (AWOL), 12–13, 27, 39, 51–52, 64, 77, 107, 122–23, 149, 161, 173

Age, 3-4, 16, 58, 65, 70–71, 85, 93–94, 98–99, 115, 142, 166–67
artillery, 44–45, 121–22
AWOL, 122–23
birthplace, 115
cavalry, 34, 121–22
conscription, 121
desertion, 123, 124, 173–74
enlistment by year, 120–21
fatherhood, 116, 121, 127–29
infantry, 21–22, 121–22
losses, 123–26, 174, 176
Lower South, 120
marital status, 116, 121, 127–29
occupations, 115–16, 122
rank, 122
slaveholding, 119–20, 155–57
Upper South, 120
wealth, 116–19, 142, 170

Alabama, 5, 22
military units
3rd Battalion Infantry, 5
14th Infantry, 73
44th Infantry, 29–30
50th Infantry, 5

Alexander, Edward Porter, Brig. Gen., 32

Allen, John, Pvt., 3

Allison, John H., 23–24

Anderson, T. W., Pvt., 3

Antietam, Battle of, 2

Appomattox Court House, Va., 30, 80, 81

Arkansas, 5, 69
military units
3rd Infantry, 69

Army of Northern Virginia
combat effectiveness, 1–3, 31–32, 42–43, 44, 56, 166, 173, 176–77
families, 6–7, 11, 177–78
motivation, 1–3, 74–75, 154, 164–65, 166
strength, 1, 97–98
urban vs. rural, 5, 22–23, 34–35, 46, 58, 168

Army of the Potomac (C.S.A.), 1

Artillery, 44–56, 166–67, 177
age, 44–45, 121–22
AWOL, 51–52
birthplace, 45, 46
comparison with cavalry, 45–55, 69
comparison with infantry, 45–55, 69
conscription, 51
deserters, 52–53, 173
enlisted men, 50
enlistment by year, 50, 52, 104–5, 106
fatherhood, 47–48, 134–35
losses, 54–56
marital status, 47–48, 134–35
occupations, 46–47
officers, 50
reforms, 44
slaveholding, 49–51, 160, 171–72
state of residence, 45–46
urban vs. rural, 46
wealth, 48–49, 50, 147–49, 171–72

Bean, Elwood M., 2nd Lt., 63
Beauregard, P. G. T., Gen., 1, 68, 69
Bevil, John C., Pvt., 86
Big Bethel, Battle of, 67
Birthplace, 4, 22, 34, 57–67, 86, 142–44,
    167
  age, 58, 115, 129
  AWOL, 64
  conscription, 64
  desertion, 64–65
  entry by year, 58, 99, 172
  fatherhood, 58
  foreign, 4, 22, 45, 46, 57–67, 167, 169,
    170, 171, 172, 176
  losses, 65–67, 176
  Lower South, 57
  marital status, 58
  Northern, 4, 22, 45, 46, 57–67, 167, 169,
    170, 171, 172, 176
  occupation, 58–59
  slaveholding, 155–56, 172
  Upper South, 57
  urban vs. rural, 58
  wealth, 167, 170–71
Bishop, John C., Pvt., 3, 21
Bivins, John T., Pvt., 115
Brady, Philip, Pvt., 51, 63, 106
Bratton, Joseph, Pvt., 78

Camp Lee, 26–27, 38, 51
Cavalry, 33–43, 166, 177
  age, 34, 34, 121–22
  AWOL, 39, 52
  birthplace, 34
  comparison with artillery, 45–55, 69
  comparison with infantry, 34, 36, 37,
    41–42, 45–55, 69
  conscription, 38–39, 51
  deserters, 39–41, 52–53, 173
  enlisted men, 33–34
  enlistment by year, 33, 52, 104–5, 106
  fatherhood, 36, 134–35, 170
  losses, 40–43, 54–55
  marital status, 36, 134–35

  occupations, 34–35
  officers, 33–34
  slaveholding, 37–38, 40, 160, 171–72
  state of residence, 34
  urban vs. rural, 34–35
  wealth, 36–39, 41–42, 147–49, 171–72
Charlotte, N.C., 67
Chitwood, Thomas J., Pvt., 24
Clute, James E., 2nd Lt., 63
Coleman, Wiley, Capt., 50
Combat, 16–20, 30–32, 40–41, 54–55, 65–
    67, 79–81, 94–96, 109–14, 123–26,
    136–39, 162–65, 174–77
Compton, Samuel W., 21, 23
Conscription, 10–11, 26–27, 38–39, 51,
    63–64, 77, 83–84, 91–92, 98, 106–7,
    121, 149, 173
Conscription Act of 1862, 12, 83, 97–98
Cooley, Henry S., 79–80

Dabney, Charles W., Capt., 1
Daingerfield, Foxhall A., Capt., 33
Davis, Jefferson, President, 32, 68, 83,
    97–98, 115, 176
Deahl, David Henry, Pvt., 73–74
Deep South. *See* Lower South
Desertion, 13–16, 77–79, 106, 174
  age, 16, 64–65, 93–94, 123, 124, 173–74
  artillery, 52–53, 173
  birthplace, 64–65
  cavalry, 39–41, 53
  economic class, 14, 16–17, 39–40, 78–79
  enlistment by year, 107–9
  fatherhood, 16, 40, 53, 79, 93, 107–8,
    123, 150–51, 173–74
  impact of battles, 13–14, 174
  infantry, 27–30, 53
  injuries, 28, 29–30
  marital status, 16, 40, 53, 79, 108, 123,
    150–51, 173–74
  month and year, 13, 15
  occupations, 14
  proximity to home, 13–14
  rank, 92–94

slaveholding, 14, 28, 40, 53, 78–79, 93, 108–9, 161–62, 173
wealth, 14–16, 28–30, 31, 39–40, 53, 78, 92–93, 108–9, 149–51, 161–62, 173
Dickerson, James W., Capt., 50
Dickert, A.P., Pvt., 73, 74
Disability, 18, 30–32, 41–42, 55–56, 80–81, 95–96, 113–14, 125–26, 152–53, 175–76
Disease, 17–20, 23, 30–32, 42, 55–56, 65–67, 80, 82, 94–96, 112–14, 124–26, 137–39, 151–53, 163–65, 174–76

Economic class, 8–9, 36–38, 50, 102, 104, 140–53, 170–72, 178
age, 142
AWOL, 149
birthplace, 142–44, 170
branches of service, 147–49
compared with families and households from states of army, 140–41, 142
conscription, 149
desertion, 14, 16–77, 39–40, 53, 92–93, 109, 149–51, 173
entry by year, 148
fatherhood, 143–44, 150–51
guidelines, 140
losses, 30–31, 41–42, 54–55, 150–53
marital status, 143, 150–51
occupations, 144–46
rank, 148–49
slaveholding, 145–47, 158–59
wealth, 141
Elmira Prison Camp, 67
Enlisted men, 21, 32, 33–34, 62–63, 75–76, 83–96
age, 85, 122
AWOL, 92
birthplace, 86
conscription, 91–92
desertion, 92–94
entry year, 91, 92, 105, 172
fatherhood, 86, 135, 170
losses, 94–96, 174–77

marital status, 86, 135
occupation, 86
rank, 94
slaveholding, 88–90, 160–61, 171
slave density, 167–68
wealth, 76, 87–89, 148–50, 171
Enlistment, 10, 26, 58
Entry by state, 4–5, 22, 34, 45–46, 57–58, 69, 99, 167
Entry by year, 26, 30, 33, 62, 76–77, 92, 93, 94–114, 177
age, 98–99, 120–21
AWOL, 107
birthplace, 99, 172
conscription, 106–7, 135
desertion, 107–9
fatherhood, 100–101, 114, 133–34
losses, 109–14, 176
Lower South, 99
marital status, 100, 114, 133–34
occupation, 100, 101
rank, 105, 134, 172
slaveholding, 102–5, 160–61, 171–72
Upper South, 99
wealth, 101–2, 148
Evans, William A., 70

Farrar, Cicero, Pvt., 70
Farrar, Thomas, 71
Fatherhood, 6–7, 23–24, 36, 47–48, 58, 70, 100–101, 114, 116, 121, 127–39, 170, 177–78
age, 127–29
AWOL, 135–36, 173
birthplace, 129
branch of service, 134–36
conscription, 135, 173
desertion, 16, 28–30, 53, 79, 93, 136–37, 150–51, 173–74
entry by year, 133–35
losses, 136–39, 176
marital status, 127–39
occupation, 128, 130
slaveholding, 133–34, 157–58, 171

urban vs. rural, 129
    wealth, 130–33, 143–44, 150–51
First Manassas, Battle of, 33, 44, 97, 177
Fisher's Hill, Battle of, 82
Florida, 5
Foreign-born soldiers, 4, 22, 45, 46, 57–67,
    106, 167, 168–69, 170, 172, 176
Forner, William, 46

Gallagher, Gary W., 140
Georgia, 4, 5, 22, 34, 45, 51, 57, 77, 167
    military units
        Macon Light, 45, 51
        Sumter Artillery, 5
        19th Infantry, 82
        21st Infantry, 21, 23, 79
Gettysburg, Battle of, 21, 66, 67, 78
Gibson, James Obey, Pvt., 82
Gilliam, James D., Pvt., 115
Gillman, Peter E., Corp., 57
Grant, Ulysses S., Lt. Gen., 80
Groshen, John F., Capt., 63

Hampton, Wade, Maj. Gen., 43
Hege, Christian, Pvt., 12
Hite, John S., Pvt., 36
Hope, William, Pvt., 51
Howard, Elizabeth Phoebe Key, 166
Hunt, Samuel J., 38

Infantry, 21–32, 177
    age, 21–22, 34, 121–22
    AWOL, 27, 52
    birthplace, 22
    comparison with artillery, 45–55, 69
    comparison with cavalry, 34, 36, 37, 41,
        45–55, 69
    conscription, 27
    deserters, 27–30
    enlisted men, 21
    enlistment by year, 26, 52, 104–5, 106
    fatherhood, 23–24, 28–30, 134–35
    losses, 21, 29–32, 54–55, 80–81, 174,
        175–76

marital status, 23, 28–30, 134–35
occupations, 23
officers, 21
slaveholding, 25–27, 31, 160, 171–72
state of residence, 22
urban vs. rural, 5, 22–23
wealth, 24–25, 30–31, 147–49, 171–72
Irvin, Howlit, 8

John Brown's raid, 97
Johnston, Joseph E., Gen., 1–2, 33, 68
Jones, William B., Capt., 50

Kennon, William D., 48
Kentucky, 5
Kerns, Cyrus McLean, Lt., 86
Killed in action, 17–18, 20, 30–32,
    54–55, 65–67, 79–80, 81, 86, 109,
    123–26, 136–39, 150–53, 162–64,
    174–76
Krick, Robert K., 84

Lamb, Miles, 5
Langhorne, James, Lt., 1
Lee, Robert E., Gen., 1, 2–3, 44, 68–69
Leech, Elbert, Capt., 5
Leon, Lewis, 67
Lincoln, Abraham, 4, 14
Linticum, William, Pvt., 71
Longstreet, James, Lt. Gen., 13, 173
Losses
    captured, 18, 30–32, 41–42, 55–56,
        65–66, 95–96, 110–14, 125–26,
        137–39, 162–65, 175–76
    combat, 16–18, 20, 30–32, 54–55,
        65–67, 79–81, 94–96, 109–14,
        123–26, 136–39, 162–65, 174–77
    disability, 18, 30–32, 41–42, 55–56,
        80–81, 95–96, 113–14, 163–65,
        175–76
    disease, 17–20, 23, 30–32, 55, 80, 94–96,
        112–14, 124–26, 137–39, 151–53,
        163–65, 174–75
    killed, 16–18, 30–32, 54–55, 65–67,

79–80, 81, 94–96, 109–14, 123–26,
136–39, 150–53, 162–64, 174–77
slaveholding, 20, 30–31, 41–42, 55, 82,
96, 111–12, 162–65
wealth, 20, 30–31, 41–42, 55, 66, 95, 111,
150–53, 175
wounded, 17–18, 20, 29–32, 54–55,
65–66, 82, 94–96, 109–14, 124–
26, 136–39, 150–53, 162–64,
174–77
Louisiana, 5, 45, 46
military units
1st Infantry, 51, 63, 106
3rd Battalion Infantry, 64
Lovvorn, John, Pvt., 29–30
Lower South (Deep South), 4–5, 13–14, 22,
34, 57, 68–82, 167–68
age, 70–71
AWOL, 77
composition, 69
conscripts, 77
desertion, 77–79
enlisted men, 75–76, 86
enlistment by year, 76–77, 99
fatherhood, 70, 79
losses, 79–82, 174, 176
marital status, 70, 79
occupations, 70–72
officers, 75–76, 86
slave density, 74, 172
slaveholding, 73–74, 75, 76, 78–79, 159,
172
urban vs. rural, 69
wealth, 71–73, 74, 75, 77, 78–79, 82,
147–48, 171

Marital Status, 6–7, 23–24, 36, 47–48,
57, 70, 100, 114, 116, 121, 127–39,
169–70, 177–78
age, 127–29
AWOL, 135–36, 173
birthplace, 129
branch of service, 134–36
conscription, 135, 173

desertion, 16, 28–30, 53, 79, 108, 136–37,
150–51, 173–74
entry by year, 133–35
losses, 135–39, 176
occupation, 128, 130
rank, 135
slaveholding, 133–34, 157, 171
urban vs. rural, 129
wealth, 130–33, 143, 150–51
Maryland, 6, 63, 168
military units
2nd Artillery, 46
1st Infantry, 63
McCaskill, Daniel, Pvt., 66
McGlown, Pat, Pvt., 45, 46
McPherson, James, 140
McVicker, James A., Pvt., 82
Miller, John L., Col., 3, 21
Mississippi, 5, 22, 57, 66, 70
military units
Bradford's Confederate Guards, 57
2nd Infantry, 78
21st Infantry, 21
42nd Infantry, 70
Mitchel, Hiram J., 2nd Lt., 3
Mulqueen, John, 64

Nance, James T., 2
New Orleans, La., 64
New York, 66, 67
North Carolina, 4, 5, 10, 22, 23–24, 34,
46, 51, 57, 82, 167, 168
military units
16th Battalion Cavalry, 38, 77
1st Infantry, 67
26th Infantry, 66
48th Infantry, 12
50th Infantry, 3
53rd Infantry, 67
54th Infantry, 39
Northern-born soldiers, 4, 22, 45,
46, 57–67, 167, 168–69, 170, 172,
176

Occupations, 5–6, 23, 34–35, 46–47, 58–59, 70–72, 86, 100, 101, 115–16, 128, 130, 144–46, 156–58, 168–69
Officers, 21, 32, 33–34, 46–47, 62–63, 75–76
  age, 85, 122
  AWOL, 92
  birthplace, 86
  conscription, 91–92
  desertion, 92–94
  enlistment by year, 91, 105, 172
  fatherhood, 86, 170
  marital status, 86
  losses, 94–96, 174–76
  occupation, 86
  rank, 94
  selection, 83–85
  slave density, 167
  slaveholding, 88–91, 160–61, 171
  wealth, 75–76, 86–89, 91–92, 148–50, 171
Ogden, Dewees, Pvt., 66–67

Paris, David, Pvt., 82
Parker, Hersey B., Pvt., 38–39, 77
Pendleton, William Nelson, Brig. Gen., 44
Pennal, Robert E., Pvt., 71
Point Lookout Prison Camp, 67
Prisoners of war, 17–18, 20, 30–32, 41, 42, 54–55, 65–66, 67, 80–81, 95–96, 106, 125–26, 137–39, 152–53, 163–65

Rank, 122
Remly, Conrad, 64
"Rich man's war, poor man's fight" argument, 9–10, 20, 153
Richmond, Va., 2, 64
Rothwell, James O., Pvt., 113
Ruffin, Edmund, 115

Seavey, William H., Pvt., 70
Second Manassas, Battle of, 82
Seven Days' Battles, 86
Sherman, William T., Maj. Gen., 14

Simmons, Henry H., 21
Slaveholding
  age, 155–56
  AWOL, 161
  birthplace, 155–56
  branches of service, 160
  compared to nonslaveholders, 154–65
  conscription, 11, 107, 161–62
  desertion, 14, 28, 40, 53, 78–79, 108–9
  entry by year, 160–61, 171–72
  fatherhood, 157–58, 171
  infantry, 25–26
  household, 9–10, 26–27, 37–38, 40, 61, 63, 74, 90–91, 104, 105, 119–20, 133–34, 146–47, 154, 172
  losses, 20, 41, 162–65
  marital status, 157, 171
  occupation, 156–58
  overrepresentation in Lee's Army, 154
  personal, 8–10, 24, 27, 37, 40, 61, 63, 73, 88, 102–3, 105, 119, 133–34, 145–47, 171
  personal and family, 8, 24–27, 37–38, 40, 61, 63, 73–74, 88–90, 103, 105, 119–20, 134–34, 146–47, 154–65, 172
  planters, 9, 38, 74, 88, 90, 103–4, 146, 154, 156, 158, 172
  wealth, 158–59, 162
Slave population density, 5–6, 23, 35, 48, 74, 90–91, 92, 104, 120, 147, 159, 167–68
Slingluff, John L., 64
Small, Robert F., 9
South Carolina, 4, 5, 34, 45, 57, 70, 72
  military units
    4th Battalion Reserves, 3
    12th Infantry, 12
    20th Infantry, 3, 21
    27th Infantry, 107
Stuart, James Ewell Brown, Maj. Gen., 43, 105, 134
Substitution, 10, 106

Talley, Crawford, Pvt., 106
Tennessee, 5, 70, 168
Texas, 5
  military units
    5th Infantry, 63
Texas Brigade, 69
Thompson, John R., Pvt., 39
Thompson, Robert C., Pvt., 49
Thornton, John T., Lt. Col., 2
Twenty Negro Law, 104

Upper South, 4–5, 13–14, 22, 34, 57,
    68–82, 167–68
  age, 70–71
  AWOL, 77
  composition, 69
  conscripts, 77
  desertion, 77–79
  enlisted men, 75–76, 86
  enlistment by year, 76–77, 99
  fatherhood, 70, 79
  losses, 79–82, 174, 176
  marital status, 70, 79
  occupations, 70–72
  officers, 75–76, 86
  slave density, 74, 172
  slaveholding, 73–74, 75, 76, 78–79, 159,
    172
  urban vs. rural, 69
  wealth, 71–73, 74, 75, 77, 78–79, 82,
    147–48, 171

Vick, Julius A., 70
Virginia, 4, 5, 22, 34, 45, 51, 57, 70, 77, 167,
  168
  military units
    Albemarle Everette, 113
    Bryan Artillery, 3
    Chew's Battery, 74
    Kirkpatrick's Artillery, 48
    Lynchburg Artillery, 50, 51, 115
    Neblett's Heavy Artillery, 50
    Peninsula Artillery, 50
    Richmond Howitzers (1st Co.), 66

Richmond Howitzers (2nd Co.), 51, 57,
  64, 106
Surry Light, 49
1st Cavalry, 39
3rd Cavalry, 38
4th Cavalry, 39
8th Cavalry, 35, 39
11th Cavalry, 33
12th Cavalry, 39
13th Cavalry, 39
14th Cavalry, 36
25th Cavalry, 82
1st Battalion Infantry, 27
42nd Infantry, 24
48th Infantry, 71

Watson, Opie N., 35, 39
Wealth, 11–12, 71, 92, 106–7, 170–71
  artillery, 48–49
  birthplace, 59–62
  cavalry, 36–39, 41–42
  combat, 20, 30–31, 41–42, 54–55
  desertion, 14–16, 28–30, 39–41, 53,
    64–65, 78–79, 92–93, 108–9, 173
  disease, 20, 31, 42, 55, 175
  household, 8–9, 25–26, 37, 48–49, 61,
    72–73, 87, 118–19, 131–33, 171–72
  infantry, 24–25, 30–31
  personal, 7–8, 24, 36, 48–49, 59–61, 71,
    73, 86, 88, 101, 103, 116–17, 130–31,
    170
  personal and family, 7–8, 24–25, 36–37,
    48–49, 60–62, 72, 74, 87, 89, 101–2,
    103, 117–18, 130–32, 170–71
West, Charles H., 71, 107
Wiley, Ferdinand, Pvt., 27
Winchester, Battle of (1864), 79–80
Woody, William H., Pvt., 48
Wounded in action, 17–18, 20, 30–32, 41,
  42, 54–55, 65–66, 71, 78, 79–81,
  94–96, 109–14, 124–26, 136–39,
  150–53, 162–64, 175–76
Wrenn, Flavious J., Pvt., 39
Wright, Daniel Girand, 1st Lt., 63

CPSIA information can be obtained at www.ICGtesting.com
Printed in the USA
BVOW02s0337060115

382050BV00003B/45/P